Erika Kovács | Martin Winner (eds.)

Stakeholder Protection in Restructuring

Selected Company and Labour Law Issues

Nomos

The Deutsche Nationalbibliothek lists this publication in the Deutsche Nationalbibliografie; detailed bibliographic data are available on the Internet at http://dnb.d-nb.de

ISBN 978-3-8487-5044-3 (Print)
978-3-8452-9216-8 (ePDF)

British Library Cataloguing-in-Publication Data
A catalogue record for this book is available from the British Library.

ISBN 978-3-8487-5044-3 (Print)
978-3-8452-9216-8 (ePDF)

Library of Congress Cataloging-in-Publication Data
Kovács, Erika / Winner, Martin
Stakeholder Protection in Restructuring
Selected Company and Labour Law Issues
Erika Kovács / Martin Winner (eds.)
ca. 280 p.
Includes bibliographic references and index.

ISBN 978-3-8487-5044-3 (Print)
978-3-8452-9216-8 (ePDF)

1st Edition 2019

Foreword

Corporate restructurings such as national and cross-border mergers and divisions, as well as cross-border conversions, enable companies to grow and adapt to a changing environment. At the same time, they can have a significant impact on companies' stakeholders, in particular creditors, shareholders, and employees. Corporate restructurings entail even additional risks for these groups if they occur across borders.

The current regulation of cross-border corporate mobility within the European Union provides a very fragmented picture and consists of a mixture of harmonized EU regulation, case law of the Court of Justice of the EU, and national rules. In the development of the Common Market, it is crucial for the EU to facilitate freedom of establishment. The Commission's proposal on corporate cross-border mobility from April 2018[1] intends to foster the cross-border mobility of companies between the Member States by the creation of a predictable and harmonised legal framework across the EU. The contributions were drafted in 2018 and partly updated in February 2019. Developments since that time could not be taken into account.

The contributions in this book address the challenges company law and labour law face in both national and cross-border corporate restructurings. Both the company and the labour law angles are crucial for an adequate treatment of the topic as, in the face of the ever-growing internationalisation of the corporate world, our legal systems have to pursue some delicate balances – on the one hand, between flexibility and security and, on the other hand, between the conflicting aims of economic growth and employment protection.

This collection contains the results of a conference we organised on 12-13 February, 2018, at the Vienna University of Economics and Business with the title 'Stakeholder Protection in Restructuring – Selected Company and Labour Law Issues', where company and labour lawyers discussed the implications and pitfalls of corporate reorganisations and the possible legal answers. The conference was the closing event of the IMPULSE project, in which company and labour lawyers from the Vienna University

1 Proposal of the European Commission for a Directive amending Directive (EU) 2017/1132 as regards cross-border conversions, mergers and divisions.

of Economics and Business, Austria, the Faculty of Law of the University of Belgrade, Serbia, and the Ss. Cyril und Methodius University, Macedonia, cooperated and conducted a comprehensive research on restructuring of companies from the perspective of the EU requirements. The cooperation was financed by the Austrian Agency for International Cooperation in Education and Research (OeAD, Österreichischer Austauschdienst) for the term 1st April 2016 – 31st March 2018.

The book includes four essays on company law challenges. Fuentes analyses the European legal framework regarding cross-border conversions, while Winner covers creditor protection in domestic and cross-border mergers in European law. Mirjana Radović and Vuk Radović focus on creditor and shareholder protection in various forms of restructurings in Serbian law. The six papers on labour law address two major issues related to company restructuring, namely transfers of undertakings and employee participation in the boards. The cross-border corporate restructuring of the company creates a challenge for employee participation in the boards. The contributions of Seifert and Kovács provide a critical analysis of the existing and planned European legal framework on this issue. Ales reveals the controversial issues of the Transfer of Undertakings Directive, while Niksova deals with the cross-border transfer of undertakings. Finally, the papers of Kovačević and Kalamatiev/Ristovski highlight the national pitfalls of the implementation of the European rules on transfer of undertakings.

We do hope you will enjoy reading the contributions.

Vienna, March 2019 — Erika Kovács and Martin Winner

Table of contents

Authors

Edoardo Ales is a senior, level I expert in EU, comparative, foreign and national Labour and Social Security Law as well as in EU Employment and Social Inclusion policies. He has teaching and research experiences all around Europe. He has coordinated, participated and evaluated various EU and national level research projects for the EU Commission, for the European Parliament and for national research authorities. Since 2006, he is member of the Scientific Committee and National Expert for Italy of the European Labour Law Network (ELLN now ECE). He his author of various book and articles as well as member of boards of directors of international journals. He has been keynote speaker at many international conferences and he has organized several of them. As co-editor he has recently published with Y. Curzi, T. Fabbri, O. Rymkevich, I. Senatori, G. Solinas, *Working in Digital and Smart Organizations. Legal, Economic and Organizational Perspectives on the Digitalization of Labour Relations*, London – New York – Shanghai: Palgrave Mcmillan, 2018 and with M. Bell, O. Deinert, S. Robin-Olivier, *International and European Labour Law. A Commentary*, Baden – Baden: Nomos Verlag, 2018.

Todor Kalamatiev is Full Professor and Head of the Department of Labour and Social security law at the 'Ss. Cyril and Methodius' University in Skopje (Faculty of Law 'Iustinianus Primus' - Skopje). From 2008 to 2012, Professor Kalamatiev was a Vice Dean for Education at the Faculty of Law 'Iustinianus Primus' – Skopje. He teaches labour law and other similar subjects at the undergraduate, postgraduate and doctoral studies within the Faculty of Law 'Iustinianus Primus.' Professor Kalamatiev also is a Member of the Study Group on a Restatement of Labour Law in Europe and a National Expert for the Republic of Macedonia in the European Labour Law Network.

Ljubinka Kovačević, Dr. iur., is Associate Professor at the University of Belgrade Faculty of Law in Serbia. Prior to joining this Faculty in 2005, she was a researcher at the Institute of Comparative Law in Belgrade. She is the author of two monographs ("Legal subordination in employment relationship and its limitations" /2013/ and "Valid reasons for dismissal" /2016/) and many papers on Serbian, international, European and comparative labour law and social security law.

Erika Kovács, Dr. iur., is Assistant Professor at the Vienna University of Economics and Business (WU) in Austria. She read law in Hungary and Germany and worked for the IAAEU at the University of Trier, where she completed her doctoral thesis. Prior to joining the WU in 2012, she was a researcher at the University of Pécs, Hungary. She is specialized in European and Austrian labour and social security law.

Mónica Fuentes Naharro, Dr. Iur., is (tenured) Associate Professor at the Law Faculty of the Universidad Complutense de Madrid, in Spain. She is also of Counsel at Estudio Jurídico Sánchez Calero. She lectures business law (company law, financial markets, contracts and insolvency law), and is specialized in company law. She is a member of several international company law groups' experts: the EMCA (European Model Company Act), the ICLEG (Informal Company Law Experts Group) and the European Business Code.

Diana Niksova, Dr. iur., is a 'post-doc' Research and Teaching Associate at the Department of Labour Law and Social Security Law at the University of Vienna. Her main research interests lie in the field of Austrian and European labour and social security law, with a strong focus on cross-border situations. Currently (in 2018/19), she is an academic visitor at the Institute of European and Comparative Law (IECL) at the University of Oxford.

Mirjana Radović, Dr. iur., LL.M. (Humboldt), is an Associate Professor at the Faculty of Law University of Belgrade. After obtaining her magister degree at the Faculty of Law in Belgrade (in 2006), she finished her LL.M. studies at the Faculty of Law, Humboldt University in Berlin (Germany), where her master's thesis "*Möglichkeiten und Grenzen des Depotstimmrechts*" was awarded as the best master's thesis in 2006/2007. She obtained her PhD at the Belgrade Faculty of Law in 2011. Mirjana Radović specialises in Capital Markets Law, Company Law, Commercial Law, Banking Law and Law on Electronic Communications. Her most important monographs include: 1. *The Law on Payment Services* (2016); 2. *Safeguarding and Administering Securities* (2014); and 3. *Contract on Interconnection of Public Telecommunication Networks* (2008).

Vuk Radović, Dr. iur., is a Full-time Professor at the Faculty of Law University of Belgrade, where he is currently teaching the following courses: Company law, Commercial law, Bankruptcy law and EC Company law. Apart from the Faculty of Law in Belgrade, he has been teaching courses at other faculties as well, such as the Faculty of Law in Graz, the Faculty of Geography in Belgrade, the Faculty of Law in East Sarajevo and the Faculty of Law (UDG) in Podgorica. Most important books: 1. *Bankruptcy Law – Part I (introduction to bankruptcy law, basic notions of bankruptcy law, bankruptcy proceeding, legal consequences of opening bankruptcy proceeding)*, 2018, 2. *Bankruptcy Law – Part II (avoidance powers, reorganization, international bankruptcy, bankruptcy of corporate groups)*, 2018, 3. *Company Law of the EU*, 2011, 4. *Executive Compensation*, 2011, 5. *Target Company Defensive Tactics Against Takeovers*, 2008.

Aleksandar Ristovski is Assistant Professor at the 'Ss. Cyril and Methodius' University in Skopje (Faculty of Law 'Iustinianus Primus'). He teaches labour law and other similar subjects at the undergraduate and postgraduate studies within the Faculty of Law 'Iustinianus Primus' – Skopje. Dr. Ristovski is a Member of the Study Group on a Restatement of Labour Law in Europe and a National Expert for the Republic of Macedonia in the European Labour Law Network. He also is a member of the CEElex network of national legal experts on labour and industrial relations in Central and Eastern Europe.

ACHIM SEIFERT is Professor in Private Law, German and European Labour Law and Comparative Law at the Friedrich-Schiller-University Jena/Germany. He previously taught European and International Labour Law at the University of Luxembourg. His main fields of interest are European and International Labour Law as well as Comparative Labour Law, Employee Participation, the Horizontal Effect of Fundamental Rights and Employee Data Protection. Achim Seifert serves as Member of the Editorial Board of the European Labour Law Journal (ELLJ), the Comparative Labor Law & Policy Journal (CLLPJ) and of the Revue de droit comparé du travail et de la sécurité sociale.

MARTIN WINNER, Dr. iur. and Mag. rer. soc. oec., is full professor of business law at the Vienna University of Economics and Business (WU) in Austria. He is also Chairman of the Austrian Takeover Commission, the regulator for public takeovers in Austria. As member of the Informal Expert Group on Company Law (ICLEG), he has advised the European Commission *inter alia* in the course of the preparation of the recent corporate mobility package. Martin Winner areas of experise lie in company law, capital markets law, intellectual property law and comparative law with a special focus on CEE.

Cross-Border Conversions and the Company Law Package

Mónica Fuentes Naharro[*]

Summary

A. *The Need for a European Legal Framework Regarding Cross-Border Conversions*

By means of a cross-border transfer of seat, a legal entity governed by the Member State of origin is converted into a legal entity governed by the law of the chosen Member State, retaining its legal identity but changing its *lex societatis*. Hence, it is correct to say that the company is converted (or "reincorporated") into another one: the legal type chosen at the new Member State.

Currently, the term "conversion" has replaced that of the "transfer of seat" traditionally used by scientific doctrine and by the Draft Fourteenth Directive, which is associated, as widely known, with the problem of defining what "seat" means as a connecting factor and the policy issues associat-

* Associate Professor at the Law Faculty of the Universidad Complutense de Madrid.

ed with it ("incorporation theory" *versus* "real seat theory"). Besides, the fairly widespread use of the term "conversion" reveals a policy approach focused — more correctly — on the legal nature of the transaction (that of a "structural change").[1]

I. Lack of Legal European Harmonization and Difficulties of Converting Cross-Border

The "right to convert cross-border" is protected by European primary law under the principle of freedom of establishment (Arts. 49 and 54 of the Treaty — TFEU) and by the European Court of Justice (ECJ) jurisprudence (*Sevic*,[2] *Cartesio*,[3] *Vale*[4] and, more recently, *Polbud*).[5] However, there is no secondary law in the European Union ("EU") for implementing cross-border conversions. In regards to cross-border mobility, the European law provides a specific legal framework only for (1) cross-border mergers through the Directive 2005/56/CE (current Chapter 2 of the consolidated company law Directive 2017/1132);[6] and (2) for the cross-border transfer of seat of the *Societas Europaea* (SE) (Art. 8 SE Regulation)[7] and the *Societas Cooperativa Europaea* (SCE) (Art. 7 SCE Regulation).[8] Thus, there is no harmonization on this issue at the European level.

Although the absence of rules in European secondary law is not a precondition for the implementation of the freedom of establishment, it is likely to deter companies that have their seat in another Member State from exercising the freedom of establishment laid down by the Treaty; thus, a harmonization of European law would be desirable to facilitate

1 Many national laws consider that this transaction has a legal nature relating to the structural change of a company, as in the case of Spanish law: see Art. 92 et seq. of Ley 3/2009 on *Modificaciones Estructurales* (hereafter, "LME").
2 C-411/03 *Sevic*, EU:C:2005:762.
3 Case C-210/06 *Cartesio*, EU:C:2008:723.
4 C-378/10 *VALE*, EU:C:2012:440.
5 C-106/16 *Polbud*, EU:C:2017:80.
6 Directive 2017/1132 of the European Parliament and of the Council of 14 June 2017 relating to certain aspects of company law (codification) [2017] OJ L 169/46.
7 Council Regulation (EC) No. 2157/2001 of 8 October 2001 on the Statute for a European Company.
8 Council Regulation (EC) No. 1435/2003 of 22 July 2003 on the Statute for a European Cooperative Society.

cross-border conversions.[9] The lack of harmonization leads to several problems. Some Member States do provide a legal framework (or permit these operations through the analogous application of the cross-border merger rules or SE rules), but the differences and inconsistencies among them – among those different legal frameworks- make cross-border conversions much more difficult to carry out and, in any case, increase legal advisory costs due to the technical difficulties associated with them. Some other Member States do not provide any legal framework at all (neither accepting the analogical application of cross-border merger rules or SE rules) and require a prior liquidation and subsequent reincorporation.

Recently published studies on the initiative of both the European Commission and Parliament, the *Study on the Law Applicable to Companies* (2016)[10] and the *Cross-Border Mergers and Divisions, Transfers of Seat: Is There A Need to Legislate?* (2016),[11] respectively, as well as the Commision's *Inception Impact Assessment*, have supported the need to adopt a cross-border conversion directive on these same grounds.[12]

II. The Company Law Package

The problem already outlined is currently in the spotlight. However, it is not a new problem. The project of a directive on cross-border transfer of seat has been on and off the European Commission's agenda for the past 20 years, ever since a first pre-proposal in 1997,[13] and again when it was

9 Case C-378/10 Vale Építési kft, paras 36-38. Carsten Gerner-Beuerle, Federico M. Mucciarelli, Edmund-Philipp Schuster, Mathias Siems, "Cross-Border Reincorporations in the European Union: The Case for Comprehensive Harmonization", *Journal of Corporate Law Studies*, vol. 18, 1 (2018), 1-42; Vanessa Knapp, "Cross-Border Mobility: What Do We Need in Practice?", *ERA Forum* (https://link.springer.com/article/10.1007/s12027-018-0495-6) (2018).

10 https://publications.europa.eu/en/publication-detail/-/publication/259a1dae-1a8c-11e7-808e-01aa75ed71a1/language-en.

11 http://www.europarl.europa.eu/thinktank/en/document.html?reference=IPOL_STU(2016)556960.

12 Final Report (2017) *Inception Impact Assessment* https://ec.europa.eu/info/law/better-regulation/initiatives/ares-2017-2377472_en.

13 Proposal for a Fourteenth European Parliament and Council Directive on the transfer of the registered office of a company from one Member State to another with a change of applicable law, YV/D2/6002/97-EN REV. 2.

"revived" in the 2012 Action Plan.[14] Within the context of this Action Plan, the Commission launched a call for experts in company law to provide ideas and technical support on cross-border mobility in general (i.e., to regulate cross-border conversions, improve directives on cross-border mergers and, in certain cases, to regulate cross-border divisions), as well as to develop a study on the recognition of the so-called "interest of the group" and the transparency of the corporate group's structure. This group of experts is known as the Informal Company Law Expert Group (ICLEG) and has worked for the European Commission since 2014,[15] discussing how to improve cross-border transactions of EU companies, as it may be inferred from the minutes of the group's meetings.[16]

The collaboration of the ICLEG with the European Commission has led to the drafting and recent publication by the Commission of the so-called Company Law Package, on April 25th of this year (2018).[17] This package aims at establishing "*simpler and less burdensome rules for companies*" regarding incorporations and cross-border transactions and consists of two Proposals.

The Commission's Proposal 2018/0114[18] on cross-border mobility addresses cross-border conversions, mergers and divisions by amending and incorporating several provisions into the current (codified) company law Directive 2017/1132. As already known, this directive already includes rules for internal mergers, divisions and cross-border mergers. The proposal introduces some changes in the existing regulation of cross-border mergers. However, the most novel addition is the introduction of common procedures for cross-border divisions and conversions. These procedures closely follow the existing one for cross-border mergers, in particular the drawing

---

14 The Commission, in its Action Plan on European Company law and corporate governance – a modern legal framework for more engaged shareholders and sustainable companies, of 12 December 2012, COM(2012) 740 final, announced that it would continue to study the need and viability of a directive on the cross-border transfer of company seats.

15 Its members are: John Armour, Gintautas Bartakus, Blanaid Clarke, Pierre-Henri Conac, Harm-Jam de Kluiver, Holger Fleischer, Mónica Fuentes, Jesper L. Hansen, Vanessa Knapp, Marco Lamandini, Arkadiusz Radwan, Christoph Teichmann, Robbert van Het Kaar, Martin Winner: http://ec.europa.eu/transparency/regexpert/index.cfm?do=groupDetail.groupDetail&groupID=3036.

16 http://ec.europa.eu/transparency/regexpert/index.cfm?do=groupDetail.groupDetail&groupID=303.

17 https://ec.europa.eu/info/publications/company-law-package_en.

18 https://eur-lex.europa.eu/legal-content/EN/TXT/HTML/?uri=COM:2018:241:FIN&from=EN.

up of the draft terms and the director's and expert's reports, disclosure of these documents, shareholders' approval, and finally, assessment and issuance of a certificate by the competent authority of the Member State of origin (or home MS) and registration in the Member State of destination (or host MS).

The Commission's Proposal 2018/0113 intends to promote the use of digital tools and procedures in company law.[19] Member States will need to allow a fully online procedure for the registration of new companies and branches of other companies, permitting incorporation without the physical presence of any member before any public authority (except when a fraud or abuse might concur). Proposal 2018/0113 "*sets safeguards against fraud and abuse such as mandatory identification control, rules on disqualified directors and a possibility for Member States to require the involvement of a person or body in the process, such as notaries or lawyers*". The proposal also establishes the need to offer free access to companies' most relevant information in the registers. This Proposal will require important changes in national legislation and its implementation will be a technological challenge for the Member States that want to preserve the current level of control in the incorporation of companies. The question of online identification will undoubtedly be of special interest and complexity, especially in countries (such as Spain) that use a Latin notarial system (or Roman system).

Though the Proposal on digitalization certainly deserves more detailed examination, this paper is focused on Proposal 2018/0114 regarding cross-border conversions, mergers and divisions (hereinafter also referred as "Cross-border Mobility Proposal" or just "Proposal"), and, more specifically, on the cross-border conversions regime and the main policy issues addressed by it, especially regarding the protection of stakeholders. To that end, we will refer to (1) the technical work and debates within the ICLEG — as to the extent, only, of the contents published in the minutes;[20] (2) the several studies published on this specific issue (mainly, the 2016 studies drawn up at the request of the Commission and Parliament on cross-border transfer of seat and applicable law to companies); and (3) those solutions contained in other European legal instruments (mainly, current cross-border mergers and European Company rules) and compared law (mainly, Spanish law).

---

19 https://eur-lex.europa.eu/legal-content/EN/TXT/?uri=COM%3A2018%3A239%3AFIN.

20 https://ec.europa.eu/transparency/regexpert/index.cfm?do=groupDetail.groupDetail&groupID=3036.

B. The Cross-Border Mobility Proposal. Main Policy Issues on Cross-Border Conversions

I. Scope of the Proposal

One of the first policy issues to be addressed when facing the regulation of cross-border conversions was on whether the subjective scope should be extended to include all forms of establishments (as envisioned in Art. 54 TFEU),[21] to all limited liability companies (public and private), or to public limited liability companies only.[22]

The Proposal has opted for a restricted subjective scope around all limited liability companies listed in Annex II of the Directive 2017/1132 [Art. 86.a)1º], giving Member States the ability to exclude cooperatives and collective investment entities [Art. 86.a) 3º, 4º]. Besides this, the Proposal has excluded the possibility to convert for companies in situations such as winding up, liquidation or a severe financial crisis[23] [Art. 86.c) 2º] as well as to those conversions implying an abuse of law [Art. 86.c) 3º] under the wide concept of "*artificial arrangement aimed at obtaining undue tax advantages or at unduly prejudicing the legal or contractual rights of employees, creditors or minority members*" (see *infra* B.II and III).

II. The Real Seat Theory Issue: To Set Aside?

1. The Controversial

The most delicate policy issue on cross-border conversions refers to the selection of the connecting factor for the *lex societatis* to be applied: either a

---

21 *Cross-Border Mergers and Divisions, Transfers of Seat: Is There A Need to Legislate?* (2016) (9, 33); see the debates in the ICLEG Minutes from July 10th and 11th, 2017.

22 See the debates in the ICLEG Minutes from May 15th, 2017.

23 Art. 86.c establishes: "A company shall not be entitled to carry out a cross-border conversion in any of the following circumstances: (a) proceedings have been instituted for the winding up, liquidation, or insolvency of that company; (b) the company is subject to preventive restructuring proceedings initiated because of the likelihood of insolvency; (c) the suspension of payments is on-going; (d) the company is subject to resolution tools, powers and mechanisms provided for in Title IV of Directive 2014/59/EU of the European Parliament and of the Council; (e) preventive measures have been taken by the national authorities to avoid the initiation of proceedings referred to in points (a), (b) or (d)."

formal one like the registered office, as in the case of those countries aligned with the so-called "incorporation theory", or a material one (head office or central administration), as with those countries following the so-called "real seat theory". The question of whether or not to impose the real seat theory through secondary law (and then require that the central administration or head office move together with the registered office), has turned out to be a type of "classic" controversy whenever any cross-border operation related to the freedom of establishment enters into discussion. In fact, this issue "obstructed" and, finally, prevented a clear move forward with the adoption of the Draft Fourteenth Directive.[24]

This controversy was raised as a prominent issue during the most recent meetings of the ICLEG in 2017, probably due to the influence of the *Polbud* case.[25] These debates were triggered by Advocate General Kokott's position, under discussion at the time, on whether or not to impose — and to what extent — some sort of so-called "soft" real seat theory: the requirement of an "effective economic link" (not the central administration or head office, which would be required to follow a "hard" or "pure" real seat theory) in order to avoid the creation of letterbox companies through a cross-border conversion. While some experts considered that Member States should have — or, rather, keep — the option to decide whether or not they wish to impose restrictions on outgoing companies (be it a genuine economic link or head office),[26] others expressed the view that restrictions should be mandatory.[27]

24 While some recent studies support the adoption of the incorporation theory: *Cross-Border Mergers and Divisions, Transfers of Seat: Is There A Need to Legislate?* (2016), (34), for some others the requirement of unity of seats or, at least, a genuine link at the European level is a "must" for any cross-border conversion draft directive: see the 4th Congress of Notaries of Europe: https://www.notariesofeurope-congress2017.eu/wp-content/uploads/2017/10/TEMA-2_es_def.pdf.

25 Case C-106/16 *Polbud*, EU:C:2017:804.

26 Currently, our ECJ accepts (within Arts. 49 and 54 TFEU) that a Member State can voluntarily impose restrictions for those companies that pretend to be incorporated into its territory (i.e., companies that want to transfer their registered seat to its territory). See infra footnote 30.

27 See ICLEG Minutes from 26th February, 2016, 27th June, 2016 and, specially, 14 and 15th of June, 2017 and 10 and 11th of July, 2017.

2. *After Polbud: The Proposal's Anti-Abuse Clause on "Artificial Arrangements"*

a. The Polbud Judgment

After the last meeting of the ICLEG with the Commission (October 4th 2017), the judgment on *Polbud* was delivered (October 25th 2017) and, as it is known, the ECJ endorsed the grounds of the "incorporation theory" (allowing any company to freely chose a company law more suitable for itself). The discussion on whether or not to include the "effective economic link" in any draft directive on cross-border conversions was clearly over after this judgment. As the Explanatory Memorandum of the Proposal notes out, the ECJ has stated very clearly that no effective economic link or activity can be required for the cross-border conversion to be effective:

> *"The ECJ held that the freedom of establishment is applicable when the registered office alone, without the real head office, is transferred from one Member State to another if the Member State of new incorporation accepts the registration of a company even without the exercise of an economic activity there: in that case Article 49 TFEU does not require such an economic activity as a precondition for its applicability* ".[28]

However, the *Polbud* judgment is not so different from its precedents. Its doctrine "gets back to the basics" in regards to the limits for each Member State for imposing rules or restrictions for cross-border conversion.[29] The ECJ confirmed its previous jurisprudence in *Polbud* allowing restrictions to the extent that: (1) they were permitted by the Treaty derogations (in particular: Arts. 51 and 52 TFEU); (2) they were justified by overriding requirements in the public interests according to the so-called "*Gebhard* test"[30] (any restriction must be appropriate to protect those interests and must not go beyond what is needed to achieve that objective); or (3) in the

28 Proposal's Explanatory Memorandum (2).

29 As the *Polbud* case recalls, in the absence of harmonization, Member States are competent to decide the connecting factor of a company to its national order and thus apply their own incorporation requirements to incoming companies (*Polbud – Wykonawstwo*, Case C-106/16, ECLI:EU:C:2017:804, para 40; *Daily Mail and General Trust*, 81/87, EU:C:1988:456, paras 19 to 21; *Cartesio*, C-210/06, EU:C:2008:723, paras 109 to 112; *VALE*, C-378/10, EU:C:2012:440, para 32).

30 Named in this way after the ECJ judgment of 30.11.1995, *Gebhard* case C-55/94, ECLI:EU:C:1995:411, para 37.

case of abuse of the freedom of establishment ("wholly artificial arrangements" within the meaning of the *Cadbury Schweppes* judgment).[31]

This context explains why the Proposal, abandoning any effective economic link requirement with the Member State of destination, has introduced a general anti-abuse clause well known in the tax law field and ECJ jurisprudence: the so-called artificial arrangements. As we will see below, this general clause, which aims to prohibit the abusive use of cross-border conversion procedures, is not so far away from the postulates of what it has been previously called a "soft" real seat theory in relation to Advocate General Kokott's position.

b. The ECJ's Tax Doctrine Behind the "Artificial Arrangement" Anti-Abuse Clause

In the judgment on *Cadbury Schweppes*[32] (following the previous case *Lankhorst*),[33] the ECJ expressed its position regarding the adequacy of the rules on "controlled foreign companies" with the freedom of establishment enacted by the Treaty.[34] In its judgment, the court stated that "*the fact that the company was established in a Member State for the purpose of benefiting from more favourable legislation does not in itself suffice to constitute abuse of that freedom*" (para 37). However, the court made an assertion more significant for the purpose of this paper in para 51:

> "*On the other hand, a national measure restricting freedom of establishment may be justified where it specifically relates to wholly artificial arrangements aimed at circumventing the application of the legislation of the Member State concerned*[35]".

The analysis of this concept (a "wholly artificial arrangement"), incorporated previously by the ECJ in *Lankhorst* case, is deliberately indeterminate and has raised many doubts among both Spanish and international

31 ECJ judgment of 12.9.2006, *Cadbury Schweppes*, Case C-196/04, ECLI:EU:C:2006:544, paras 51ff, 68, 72, 75.

32 CJEU, 12.9.2006, *Cadbury Schweppes*, Case C-196/04.

33 CJCE, 12.12.2002, *Lankhorst-Hohorst*, C-324/2000.

34 Jose M. Almudí, "El régimen antielusivo de transparencia fiscal internacional", en (dir. F. Serrano) *Fiscalidad internacional*, www.cef.es, (2015), 1037 (1195 et seq.).

35 The judgment referred to previous decisions: Case C-324/00 *Lankhorst-Hohorst* [2002] ECR I-11779, para 37; *De Lasteyrie du Saillant*, para 50; and *Marks & Spencer*, para 57.

tax doctrine. Thus, perhaps, the greatest merit of the *Cadbury* judgment is to specify a little more of its content when clarifying the advent of a wholly artificial arrangement dependent on the fact that the company obtaining a tax advantage actually pursues "*an economic activity through a fixed establishment*" in that country. As the Court states:

> "(…) *the concept of establishment within the meaning of the Treaty provisions on freedom of establishment involves the actual pursuit of an economic activity through a fixed establishment in that State for an indefinite period (see Case C-221/89 Factortame and Others [1991] ECR I-3905, para 20, and Case C-246/89 Commission v. United Kingdom [1991] ECR I-4585, para 21). Consequently, it presupposes actual establishment of the company concerned in the host Member State and the pursuit of genuine economic activity there*".[36]

Despite the difficulties of defining such a broad concept as "actual pursuit of an economic activity", in order to assess whether a particular operation (in the present case, a cross-border conversion) is an artificial arrangement, it seems clear that the introduction of this anti-abuse clause means that the Commission has not "left aside" the real seat issue. The application of the *Cadbury*'s doctrine leads to a requirement that is not so far away from Advocate General Kokott's position in *Polbud:* while in *Polbud* an "effective economic link" of the converted company with the Member State of destination was required, in *Cadbury*, an "actual pursuit of an economic activity" was necessary.

The difficulty of defining the concept — again, deliberately broad — of the *Cadbury* judgement's doctrine underlies determining when an "actual pursuit of an economic activity" (*implantación real*)[37] exists or not. This is likely why the Proposal intends to facilitate the authority's assessment task (see below III.2) to determine whether an artificial arrangement exists, by providing a list of elements (*numerus apertus*) to take into account when

36 Paras 54 and 66 of CJEU, 12.9.2006, *Cadbury Schweppes*, Case C-196/04.

37 Jose M. Almudí, (2015), 1037 (1225), points out that some of our neighboring countries such as France, Germany, Sweden or the United Kingdom have already begun to modify their controlled foreign companies regulations to adapt them to the *Cadbury* case. Most of them have chosen to incorporate a series of objective criteria related to proportionality into the aforementioned regulation of the material and human resources used by the entity that has participated in the development of its activity. This author ask the Spanish legislator to follow the example of those Member States, nevertheless taking into account that some activities (such as finance, intermediation, etc.) may be developed by the subsidiary with a small volume of employees and a reduced physical presence (1226).

the procedure (a so-called "in-depth assessment") is opened due to the fact that the national authority has a well-founded suspicion that the cross-border conversion might constitute an abuse (Art. 86.n). These elements, which, as the norm indicates, are only

> "*considered as indicative factors in the overall assessment and therefore shall not be considered in isolation*", are the following: "*the characteristics of the establishment in the destination Member State, including the intent, the sector, the investment, the net turnover and profit or loss, number of employees, the composition of the balance sheet, the tax residence, the assets and their location, the habitual place of work of the employees and of specific groups of employees, the place where social contributions are due and the commercial risks assumed by the converted company in the destination Member State and the departure Member State*".

Therefore, the "actual pursuit of an economic activity" required by *Cadbury* and the "effective economic link" required by General Advocate Kokott are not so different from each other; both of them point to some sort of economical bond with the Member State of destination for the reincorporated or converted company. The main difference underlying both doctrines is that this economical or material bond for a cross-border conversion expressly requires some sort of "subjective element" of abuse (or fraud) — the aim to "*obtaining undue tax advantages or unduly prejudicing the legal or contractual rights of employees, creditors or minority shareholders*" — to be applied.

However, from a legal policy approach (these technical issues will be addressed further, see III.2), the general anti-abuse clause represented by the artificial arrangements is controversial. Since the Proposal already protects the legal or contractual rights of employees, creditors or minority shareholders from any undue prejudice, in practice, it seems that the only field where this anti-abuse clause could be applied would be that of "*obtaining undue tax advantages*". Hence, it seems more appropriate that these tax law problems continue to be addressed — as they currently are — by tax law and jurisprudence, not by corporate law (especially taking into account that, from the tax law perspective, the artificial arrangement doctrine works *ex post* and "does not affect the validity of the transaction as such but combats artificial arrangements by ignoring them for tax law purposes only").[38]

38 Being — as it has been pointed out "this targeted approach probably superior": See the accurate critical approach by ECLE, "The Commission's 2018 Proposal on

III. Harmonised Procedure and Anti-Abuse Assessment

The elaboration of a harmonised proceeding in the EU is a key tool for cross-border conversions to be (technically) possible and to offer legal certitude for the various stakeholders involved in the operation. Common procedural elements are therefore needed, not only for the conversion to be made ("enabling law perspective"), but also to provide common grounds for the protection of those stakeholders to be exercised or invoked along the lines of the conversion procedure ("protective law"). The Proposal assumes this reasoning and, as expressly indicated in the Explanatory Memorandum, aims to combine these two perspectives of legal policy:

> *"In light of the foregoing considerations, the main objectives of the harmonised rules for cross-border conversions are twofold:*
> *- enabling companies, particularly micro and small, to convert cross-border in an orderly, efficient and effective manner;*
> *- protecting the most affected stakeholders such as employees, creditors and shareholders in a suitable and proportionate manner".*[39]

To this end, the Proposal parts from the procedural framework of the so-called "European model for structural changes",[40] which was set out for the first time in the merger Directive, subsequently adopted in the divisions Directive and by the cross-border mergers Directive (the three of them now consolidated in Directive 2017/1132) and it is also present in the procedural rules on cross-border transfer of seat in Art. 8 SE Regulation and Art. 7 SCE Regulation.

1. The Phases of the Cross-Border Conversion Procedure

The Proposal provides for a conversion procedure structured in several phases, which will culminate in a double control (scrutiny) of its legality, firstly, by the authority of the Member State of origin and, secondly, by the Member State of destination's authority. Basically, as already stated, the system already existing in the current regulation of cross-border mergers is

---

Cross-Border Mobility – An Assessment", September, 2018 (https://europeancompanylawexperts.wordpress.com/publications/the-commissions-2018-proposal-on-cross-border-mobility-an-assessment-september-2019/#_ftnref36).

39 Proposal's Explanatory Memorandum (3).

40 Suggested, among many others, by Jessica Schmidt in *Cross-Border Mergers and Divisions, Transfers of Seat: Is There A Need to Legislate?* (2016) (9).

followed by and — with the necessary adjustments and improvements — is transferred to both the procedural model of conversions and divisions drafted by the Proposal. This model involves articulating the operation in three phases.

a. Preliminary Phase: Conversion Draft and Reports

In the first phase, the management body will prepare the draft terms on the cross-border conversion. This draft will be joined by two reports, also prepared by the same organ, to be delivered to the shareholders (Art. 86.e) and to the employees (Art. 86.f), dealing with the implications that the conversion will have for them as well as remedies for their protection. The report for the shareholders may be waived if all of them agree.

The conversion draft terms, which must be made public at least one month before the general meeting (Art. 86.h), must contain some minimum information (Art. 86.d) regarding the change of the company's legal form as well as the protection offered to shareholders, creditors and employees. The Proposal (Art. 86.d) also offers companies the possibility to provide the draft terms in the official languages of the Member States concerned, as well as in the language most commonly used in business transactions (presumably English). In this sense, Member States will be able to determine which language is preferable in case of discrepancies.

In this first phase, it is worth noting that the preparation of a report by an independent expert (Art. 86.g) is also mandatory — though only for medium and large companies[41] — and its appointment will have to be requested by the company from the competent authority (in Spain, this will be the mercantile register). The independent expert's report must examine the accuracy of the draft terms and reports prepared by the management body. This requirement, logically, will increase the cost of the operation, but it plays a central role in the procedure defined by the Proposal since this independent expert will provide the factual basis for the assessment to be carried out by the authority on the risk that the operation could be abusive (that is, on the risk that it constitutes an artificial arrangement, see below 2).

---

41 As Art. 86.g para 6 states: "Member States shall exempt 'micro' and 'small enterprises' as defined in Commission Recommendation 2003/361/EC (**) from the provisions of this Article.".

The conversion draft, the management reports and, if the case requires, the independent expert report, will be made available to the public for free [Art. 86.h)6º][42] and completely online [Art. 86.h)4º]. Besides, shareholders, creditors and employees may submit any comments on them, before the date of the general meeting, to the company and to the competent authority [Art. 86.h)1º, 4º].

b. The Resolution on Conversion and Protection Remedies

From that moment on, the second phase of the operation opens up. This is built, on the one hand, around the adoption of a resolution by the general meeting on the approval of the draft terms (Art. 86.i) and, on the other hand, around the eventual exercise of the rights that the Proposal recognises in terms of those stakeholders who might be adversely affected by the cross-border conversion: minority shareholders dissatisfied with the conversion (Art. 86.j), creditors (Art. 86.k) and employees (Art. 86.l) (as for those rights, see in detail below IV).

The Proposal requires the resolution of the general meeting to be adopted by a qualified majority ("*Member States shall ensure that the approval of any amendment to the draft terms of the cross-border conversion requires a majority of not less than two-thirds*"), expressly imposing a maximum threshold [Art. 86.i)3º] of 90% of the voting rights ("*but not more than 90% of the votes attached either to the shares or to the subscribed capital represented*"), oriented to prevent unanimity from being demanded by any Member State (as occurs under French law). The provision also requires that "*In any event the voting threshold shall not be higher than that provided for in national law for the approval of cross-border mergers*." A few comments can be drawn out from the current wording of the provision.

42 The European Commission aims to reduce publicity costs associated with these kind of cross-border transactions. Thus, para 6 of Art. 86.h states: "*Member States shall ensure that the documentation referred in paragraph 1 is accessible by the public free of charge*." However, the MMSS may "*require, in addition to the disclosure referred to in paragraphs 1, 2 and 3, that the draft terms of the cross-border conversion, or the information referred to in paragraph 3 is published in their national gazette (…)*", and, if such is the case, "*Member States shall further ensure that any fees charged to the company carrying out the cross-border conversion by the registers for the disclosure referred to in paragraphs 1 and 3 and, where applicable, for the publication referred to in paragraph 5 shall not exceed the administrative costs of providing the service*.".

Firstly, the mention of "*the approval of any amendment to the draft terms*" might be the result of a "typo", since the provision is aimed to regulate the approval of the transaction by the general meeting (and, if it is the case, its amendments).[43] Thus, "of" should be replaced with "or", in order to establish that "*Member States shall ensure that the approval* or *any amendment to the draft terms…*".

Secondly, from the perspective of Spanish law — in regards to its future implementation — the current drafting of Art. 86.i)3º could raise some technical difficulties when confronting the rule on the minimum qualified majority (not less than two-thirds) with the rule (in the same provision) that requires the voting threshold to not be higher than the one provided for in national legislation for the approval of cross-border mergers. Although this provision apparently follows the current Directive 2017/1132 (Art. 93.1), an important statement — at least from the Spanish law perspective — is missing in the current Proposal: the one that allows that, under certain conditions, a simple majority may suffice (see Art. 93.1 subpara 2º).[44] Indeed, the simple majority is the voting threshold (under certain conditions for public limited companies in Spain, Art. 201.2º LSC) for these kind of transactions under Spanish law (see Arts. 40 and 97 LME for national mergers and transfer of seat, both referring to Art. 201 LSC).

c. The Two-Pronged Scrutiny

Finally, as part of the third phase of the cross-border conversion, the resolution of the general meeting, together with the relevant information and documents, will be submitted to the national authority of the Member State of origin, which will decide whether to issue a certificate of "pre-conversion". This phase is built upon a two-pronged scrutiny or double control of the legality of the transaction. While Arts. 86.m (pre-conversion certificate) and 86.n (in-depth assessment) refer to the control task in the Mem-

---

43 This possibility (the "amendment" of the draft terms is not permitted under current Spanish law neither for (national or cross-border) mergers nor cross-border transfer of seat (see Art. 40.1 LME, for mergers and applicable for cross-border mergers and transfer of seat).

44 This subparagraph says: "The laws of a Member State may, however, provide that a simple majority of the votes specified in the first subparagraph shall be sufficient when at least half of the subscribed capital is represented. Moreover, where appropriate, the rules governing alterations to the memorandum and articles of association shall apply".

ber State of origin, Art. 86.p (scrutiny of the legality of the cross-border conversion) regulates the revision by the authority of the Member State of destination. These are rules that, in short, reproduce the scheme and the principles already foreseen in the SE Regulation and in the rules regarding cross-border mergers (Arts. 117 and 128 Directive 2017/1132).

With regard to this first control (the one made by the Member State of origin's authority), the aforementioned provisions require two tasks: (1) to assess whether or not the formal procedure of the cross-border conversion has been made in accordance with the provisions of its national legislation; and (2) whether or not the operation constitutes an artificial arrangement. To carry out these tasks, the national authority counts with a maximum period of one month that might be extended, if there are well-founded suspicions that the conversion is abusive, i.e. "artificial" (see below 2), to another two more months.

If the national authority issues the pre-conversion certificate after such analysis, this will then be sent to the authority of the Member State of destination (Art. 86.p), who will then carry out an examination of the part of the procedure governed by its legislation, ensuring that the converted company adheres to its national regime on incorporations (minimum capital, contributions, requirement — if it is the case — that the company has its real seat in its territory, etc.) and, where appropriate, that the arrangements for employee participation have been determined in accordance with Art. 86.l).

Once the double control of the legality has finished, the company will be registered in the Member State of destination and its registration in the Member State of origin will be cancelled (Art. 86.q). The cross-border conversion will then have legal effects (Art. 86.s) and it cannot be declared void (Art. 86.u). The ground supporting this latter provision — already known in the field of cross-border mergers — is to guarantee the legal certainty of these kind of complex transactions in which several Member States are involved. It is presumed that the *ex ante* control to which the conversion is submitted should offer a total guarantee that it complies with the legal requirements and is not fraudulent and, therefore, cannot be challenged.[45]

---

45 Segismundo Álvarez, "The Commission's Company Law Package: Overview and Critical View of the Proposal for Cross-Border Transactions" (2018) (https://europeanlawblog.eu/2018/06/07/the-commissions-company-law-package-overview-and-critical-view-of-the-proposal-for-cross-border-transactions) criticises this provision saying it supposes a kind of "blessing" of the operation, even if the company had

2. *The Control of the "Artificial Arrangements"*

As already mentioned (see above II), a fundamental element of the procedure is built around the notion of artificial arrangement to prevent the execution of certain cross-border operations (specifically, conversions and divisions). This new requirement is the most important and controversial difference with the cross-border merger drafted procedure (which, surprisingly, does not include this general anti-abuse clause). However, despite being such a central element, when analyzing the "gestation" of the Proposal, the artificial arrangement concept (and the assessment procedure associated with it) cannot be traced. The minutes of the ICLEG's meetings with the Commission, especially the last three sessions of 2017[46] held just before the judgment on *Polbud*, prove that the technical debate was focused on whether or not to impose the requisite of keeping an effective economic link with the Member State of destination on the converted company. There was no debate on this opportunity and on the model of supervision of the abusiveness of the operation based on the jurisprudential construction of artificial arrangements. Hence, its incorporation by the Commission is — presumably — linked to the ECJ judgment on *Polbud* (see above II).

The assessment of the eventual abusive character of a cross-border conversion (or, if it is the case, of a cross-border division) is supported by the scrutiny made by two different entities: firstly, by the independent expert; secondly, by the authority of the Member State of origin. As from Art. 86.g, an independent expert must express an opinion on "*the accuracy of the reports and information submitted by the company*". The purpose of this opinion is to facilitate the authority for checking out not only the formalities of the conversion — as it does in mergers — but also whether or not the cross-border conversion is "*an artificial arrangement aimed at obtaining undue tax advantages or at unduly prejudicing the legal or contractual rights of employees, creditors or minority members*". Thus, the independent expert report (when required)[47] is an essential tool designed to help the authority to

---

been able to hide the fraudulent purpose of the operation of both the independent expert and the competent authority of the Member State of origin.

46 http://ec.europa.eu/transparency/regexpert/index.cfm?do=groupDetail.groupDetail&groupID=3036.

47 See supra footnote 41 where small and micro companies are exempted from this report.

carry out his assessment on the eventual abusiveness of the conversion.[48] As Art. 86.m)7º establishes, this authority has a one month period to issue a pre-conversion certificate. Should the authority have serious doubts that the cross-border conversion could constitute an artifice, it will proceed to carry out a comprehensive evaluation (or, as Art. 86.n says, an "in-depth assessment") of the conversion. That examination and the corresponding decision must be completed within two months.

This in-depth assessment is probably the most sensitive issue of the Proposal from a purely technical perspective[49] and its transposition into the Spanish legal system will cause some difficulties, as briefly explained herein. The design of this special procedure broadens the competences that mercantile registrars — the authority that, under Spanish law, would *a priori* be in charge of this task — currently play under Spanish company law in general and also under Spanish rules on cross-border transfer of seat. The scrutinizing role that the Spanish registrars have been expressly asked to play, however, only examines whether the formal legal procedure of the cross-border transaction complies with the provisions of the domestic legislation (see Arts. 101 to 103 LME). However, if the Proposal is finally approved as it is, this authority will also have to assess whether the conversion is abusive or artificial, which seems to not be an assessment of a formal nature, but rather a substantive one.[50]

Indeed, some Spanish authors have already called into question whether this *ex ante* control stands as an efficient way of preventing the abuse of these kinds of cross-border transactions. Firstly, because the expert report's content is complex, it will accordingly take time and money to complete it.

48 Because of the importance that the independent expert attaches to this and other cross-border mobility operations, Art. 86.t requires the Member States to include in their respective national regulations some rules governing the civil liability of independent experts in charge of elaborating the reports referred to here.

49 See a critical approach from the ECLE, "The Commission's 2018 Proposal on Cross-Border Mobility – An Assessment", September, 2018 (https://europeancompanylawexperts.wordpress.com/publications/the-commissions-2018-proposal-on-cross-border-mobility-an-assessment-september-2019/#_ftnref36).

50 In a different manner — though it is not the same problem envisaged here — Spanish notaries have been assessing (in the *ex ante* control of the operation for the public deed to be granted) on some issues relating to abusive behaviors, like the control of the beneficial owner in relation with the anti-money laundering directive. Then, though the cross-border conversion Proposal seems to designate the authority that issues the pre-conversion certificate to the one who must assess whether the conversion is abusive or not (i.e., the mercantile registers in Spain), it is not sure which "authority" will be in charge — should the Proposal be approved in these terms — of this assessment.

Once it has been obtained, the competent authority has to determine, based on the report, if the operation constitutes an artificial arrangement that unduly avoids taxes or harms stakeholders. This implies further delays of up to three months: the first month to issue the certificate — Art. 86.m)7º — and, in case of serious doubts — Art. 86.n) — an in-depth investigation can take two additional months. In addition, if the authority is not a judge, as is the case in Spain, there is a right to judicial review of the authority's decision (Art. 86.o). All of that means, as previously stated, that the timeline of the operation becomes absolutely unpredictable and potentially very long. It is also questionable whether or not this system can fulfill its objective because the concept of artificial arrangement is far from clear, and additionally because it is extremely difficult for the competent authority, as well as for the expert, to determine the intention to defraud tax or other stakeholders before the transaction is effective (*ex ante*). Besides this, the complexity of this assessment task for the authority of the Member State of origin is increased when facing a cross-border conversion of small and micro companies, in which the independent expert's report is not required [Art. 86.g)6º]. Finally, a further concern is that this procedure might lead to arbitrary decisions, as *ex ante* judging the intentions of the company is very difficult and some States might therefore be tempted to pressure the national authority to be very strict to prevent the departure of companies to other Member States.[51]

In view of the above, it seems quite appropriate that, during the negotiation of the Proposal, these issues be the subject of careful debate and improvement at the technical level, in order either to eliminate the entire complex procedure (in line with what the critics also posed above, II.2), or in the case it remains, to facilitate the assessment by the corresponding national authority. Perhaps, if this anti-abuse clause and the procedure for its assessment remains, a list of presumptions *iuris tantum* of what is to be considered a potentially artificial operation (in coherence with the doctrine already marked by the ECJ referred above) could be a fruitful first step for a technical review of the Proposal.

51 Segismundo Álvarez (2018); in the same line, pointed out that it is difficult to determine *ex ante* if an arrangement is artificial in this sense; see Jaime Sánchez, "Cross-Border Conversions and Ex-Ante Control of Artificial Arrangements: Is This An Adequate Reaction to Polbud?" (Oxford Business Law Blog, 20 September 2018, https://www.law.ox.ac.uk/business-law-blog/blog/2018/09/cross-border-conversions-and-ex-ante-control-artificial-arrangements).

IV. The Need to Protect Stakeholders

1. General Overview

There are obvious differences between a cross-border conversion and a cross-border merger or division. Conversions do not entail a substantial change in the patrimonial structure of the company. However, this does not mean that the shareholders, the creditors and the employees' rights cannot be negatively affected by the conversion due to the change of *lex societatis* that this entails.[52] The Proposal has addressed these concerns by introducing several specific remedies that will provide harmonised protection rules for these stakeholders to be applied, not only in the context of conversions, but in mergers and divisions as well (since the grounds for their protection are similar in any cross-border transaction).

As for the protection of minority shareholders, the Proposal has incorporated a legal instrument already used by several Member States on cross-border transactions: an exit right granted (in a very broad sense, as commented below) to those "*members holding shares with voting rights and who did not vote for the approval of the draft terms of the cross-border conversion*", as well as to those "*members holding shares without voting rights*" (Art. 86.j). As for the protection of creditors, the Proposal (Art. 86.k) addresses both a solvency test (facultative for the national laws) and the right to ask for adequate safeguards from the administrative or judicial authority of the Member State of origin, and a list of presumptions of no prejudice for creditors linked to an expert report.

The Proposal also addresses the delicate issue of the employees' protection in relation to their co-determination rights. This was a topic thoroughly debated and worked at within the ICLEG, whose members proposed several innovative approaches. However, the Proposal finally opted (Art. 86.l) for a — so to say — "conservative" policy option that follows, basically, the European Company's well-known rules on employee protection. Under this provision, a company will have to follow the rules of the Member State of destination unless its national legislation does not pro-

---

52 This same issue, with regards to the European Company, has been addressed by Luis Fernández del Pozo, "Domicilio y nacionalidad de la SE: traslado internacional de domicilio de la SE. La publicidad registral de la SE", en (dirs. G. Esteban/L. Fernández del Pozo) *La sociedad anónima europea: régimen jurídico, societario, laboral y fiscal*, Marcial Pons, Madrid-Barcelona (2004) (121 et seq.); Guillermo Palao Moreno, *El traslado de domicilio social de la sociedad anónima europea*, Thomson-Aranzadi, Cizur Menor (2006).

vide for the same level of the employees' participation in the company's management or supervisory organs, as in the case of Spain. This provision shall also apply where the number of employees exceeds four-fifths of the threshold established in the national legislation of the Member State of origin, triggering the employees' participation right pursuant to Art. 2 of Directive 2001/86/EC or, irrespective of the number of the employees, the rules of employees' participation if the Member State of destination does not provide for the same level of the participation. If this is the case, the company will have to enter into negotiations with the employees. This negotiation is mandatory and must result either in a bespoke arrangement regulating the involvement of employees or, in case no agreement is reached within 6 months, the standard rules of employees' participation as laid down in the Annex -in particular point (a) of Part 3]- of Directive 2001/86/EC will apply. In accordance with this Directive, the negotiations have to start as soon as possible after the draft terms of the conversion are made publicly available. The company will have to preserve the employees' participation rights for at least three years in substance in case of subsequent operations like mergers, divisions or conversions.

This paper will focus hereafter on those remedies observed by the Proposal for protection of minority shareholders and creditors.[53]

2. *Minority Shareholders' Protection*

a. General Considerations: Grounds and Techniques to Protect Minority Shareholders

The most obvious stakeholder interests to be protected in a cross-border conversion are those of the shareholders (i.e., minority shareholders). The change of the *lex societatis* implies something more than a mere modification of the articles of association that can substantially affect the shareholders' legal position (rights and obligations) to the company.

Selecting the appropriate minority protection technique is not a simple matter. It seems that "handing over" the defense of their rights to share-

53 Protection of employees' co-determination rights have been studied with regard to the European Company from the Spanish perspective by Gaudencio Esteban, "La implicación de los trabajadores de la sociedad anónima europea en la Ley 31/2006 de transposición de la Directiva", *Revista de Derecho Bancario y Bursátil*, 105 (2007), 180 et seq.

holders, who should be in the position to better evaluate their own interests, would be the most correct solution. However, when choosing from amongst the different mechanisms, one has to avoid two equally undesirable extremes: that of the risk of expropriation and that of extortion. When there is insufficient or no protection, the majority shareholders can unfairly expropriate the position — patrimonial and political — of the minority shareholder. When there is overprotection, the minority can abuse their position (minority abuse).[54] One way to avoid the "expropriation risks" could be to demand the individual consent of the affected shareholders, since the change of *lex societatis* could attack their legal position as such shareholders. This rule has been accepted by the French law (L-223-30 Ccom). However, this "maximum" solution implies a right of *veto* in favour of the individual shareholder and leads to overprotection: it offers the shareholder extortion possibilities and presents serious obstacles for the execution of a cross-border conversion. Therefore, from a policy perspective, it seems more correct to search for a sufficiently powerful protection remedy without compromising the collegial nature of the organs that have to operate, as such, pursuant to the majority rule. This can be achieved by strengthening the quorum and voting majority for the adoption of the resolution by the general meeting on the one hand, and the recognition of a legal right to withdraw the company on the other hand.

The debate on protection rules regarding cross-border transactions is something of a standard topic of interest among European scholars. Several Member States have already included these kinds of protective provisions in their national laws when regulating cross-border transactions. Some of these remedies are likewise present in European secondary law (cross-border mergers rules and cross-border transfer of seat rules of the European Company). This (brief) comparative approach will be useful so as to better understand the remedies incorporated by the Proposal.

b. Protection Techniques for Cross-Border Mobility in European Secondary Law and National Laws

Regarding cross-border mergers, the European secondary law does not provide for any specific protection rights for minority shareholders. Art. 121.2º of the consolidated Directive 2017/1132 empowers each Member State to "*adopt provisions designed to ensure appropriate protection for mi-*

54 Luis Fernández del Pozo (2004) 121 (188).

nority members who have opposed the cross-border merger". The result has been a wide-ranging spectrum of very different protection regimes, ranging from no special rules (i.e., in UK) to rather elaborate protection systems (v.gr. in Germany, where minority shareholders have an exit right against with cash compensation and a right to additional cash compensation if the share exchange *ratio* is not adequate). This lack of harmonization, which the Proposal intends to solve, has blocked some cross-border mergers.[55]

As for the transfer of seat of the European Company, the SE Regulation has adopted a *de minimis* solution, as in the cross-border merger rules. That is to say that it does not predispose a specific technique but leaves the decision for Member States to adopt "*provisions aimed at guaranteeing adequate protection for minority shareholders*" (Art. 8.5º SE Regulation). The only remedy observed by SE Regulation is the requirement of a qualified majority of the general meeting to adopt the resolution when transferring the registered seat cross-border (Art. 8.6º and Art. 59 SE Regulation).

As for the Member States national rules, as mentioned before, Spain is one of the few countries in Europe with an *ad hoc* regulation of cross-border conversions (or, rather, cross-border transfer of seat, since Spanish law follows the "traditional" terminology in this regard). These rules (Arts. 92 to 103 LME) recognise an exit right for those shareholders who voted "against" the resolution to transfer the registered seat (Art. 99 LME). The enforcement of this exit right is remitted to the general rules on this institution in Spanish company law (Art. 347 et seq. *Ley de Sociedades de Capital*, "LSC").[56] This exit right is also granted in other "structural changes transactions" under Spanish law, including cross-border mergers (Art. 62 LME) or domestic conversions (Art. 15 LME). However, under Spanish law, the exit right was conceived within a narrower scope than in the cross-border conversion Proposal, as it will be explored further. This is in line with the cross-border merger rules currently in place, which force Member States to adopt protective provisions "*for minority members who have opposed the cross-border merger*" (Art. 121.2º Directive 2017/1132).

55 See an overview with doctrinal references in "Cross-Border Mergers and Divisions: Is There A Need to Legislate?" (2016) (19-20).

56 The regime for the reimbursement of the shares under Spanish Law is contained in Arts. 353 to 357 LSC.

c. Protection techniques under the Proposal

The Proposal recognised an exit right for those members "*who did not vote for the approval of the draft terms of the cross-border conversion*", as well as for those "*members holding shares without voting rights*" (Art. 86.j). Either the company, the remaining shareholders, or the third parties, upon the request of the shareholders concerned, should acquire their shares in exchange for an "*adequate cash compensation*". This issue (the adequacy of the compensation) can trigger conflicts. This is why the provision observes that in case the shareholders consider that the cash compensation offered has been inadequately set, they are entitled to challenge its amount before the courts of the Member State of origin.

Several issues, at least from the perspective of Spanish law, arise from the drafting of this provision. On the one hand, the subjective scope of the provision raises some questions regarding those shareholders entitled to the exit right and, specially, regarding those subjects who are entitled to acquire the shares of the exiting shareholder. On the other side, the enforcement of the exit right also deserves reconsideration. Due to the nature of this paper, we cannot venture deeper into these issues, but simply take a general approach to the most relevant issues.

c.1. Subjective Scope

In regards to the subjective scope of Art. 86.j (i.e., who are the shareholders entitled to the exit right pursuant para 1), *a priori*, it is correct to state that the provision opts for a broad protective approach, recognizing that right not only in favour of those who expressly "*opposed*" (i.e., voted against the resolution to convert as inferred from Art. 121.2º Directive 2017/1132),[57] but also in favour of those who did not have voting rights and those who abstained from voting or did not attend the meeting. This is a very wide range of subjects. However, the wording of the draft proposal raises some doubts that probably arise from the current wording of the referenced Art. 121.2º Directive 2017/1132 and the protection to those shareholders who expressly "*opposed*" the transaction. On the one hand, Art. 86.d)1(i),

57 This provision gave Member States the possibility "in the case of companies participating in a cross-border merger and governed by its law" to "adopt provisions designed to ensure appropriate protection for minority members who have opposed the cross-border merger".

when providing for the minimum content of the conversion's draft, refers to those members "opposing" the cross-conversion ("*details of the offer of cash compensation for the members opposing the cross-border conversion in accordance with Art. 86.j*"). In the same line, Art. 86.e)2(c), when establishing the content of the report drafted by the management to the shareholders, refers again to those members "opposing" the transaction ("*the rights and remedies available to members opposing the conversion in accordance with Art. 86.j*"). Notwithstanding, the wording issue is not a great problem, since the reference to Art. 86.j is made in both provisions. On the other hand, the real problem lying behind the option for a wider subjective scope ("*did not vote for*") instead of a narrower one ("*members opposing*") is a traditional issue when addressing the exit right correctly. The risk of decapitalization is clear, and recognizing this exit right in a broad sense increases that risk. Hence, it may turn out that the company cannot finally execute the cross-border transaction because it does not fulfil the minimum capital requirements of the Member State of destination (unless the remaining shareholders face an increase of capital). Due to this risk, after several instances a narrower approach has been proposed,[58] while from others this risk is minimised.[59] In our opinion, should a narrower solution finally be accepted, it should respect in any case the exit right given by the Proposal to those shareholders without voting rights (and, as such, shareholders illegitimately deprived of the right to vote should be included as well).

The second issue regarding the subjective scope affects para 2 of Art. 86.j, which refers to those subjects entitled to acquire the shares of the exiting shareholder. The provision encompasses, again, a very wide range of subjects: (i) the "*company carrying out the cross-border conversion*"; (ii) the "*remaining shareholders of that company*"; or even (iii) by "*third parties in agreement with the company carrying out the conversion*". As for the first subject, the company will have to observe the rules governing the acquisition of its own shares [Art. 86.j)3]. As for the second and third subjects, acquir-

58 Juana Pulgar, "El traslado de domicilio social: protección de socios y acreedores", Revista de Derecho Mercantil, 309, 2018, 2 et seq.; Reaction of the Association of German Attorneys to the Company Law Package, *Neue Zeitschrift für Gesellshaftsrecht*, 2018, (857) 860.

59 The ECLE Report, *The Commission's 2018 Proposal on Cross-Border Mobility – An Assessment*, September 2018, (8) says that the narrower approach "would incentivise shareholders to vote against and might actually block the transaction" and that, in practice this is not such a big problem since companies "can usually find was to make a transaction conditional upon sufficient shareholders not making use of or even waiving their exit right in order to avoid an excessive outflow of cash".

ing the shares of the exiting shareholder, it should be noted that these last two possibilities are observed neither by the Spanish statutory regime on exit right (Art. 346 et seq. LSC), nor by Art. 114 of Directive 2017/1132.[60] In fact, traditional Spanish doctrine has argued that this should not be an exit right in the strict sense because it is said there is an exit right not when the shares' ownership changes, but only when the company acquires them for their further redemption by means of a reduction of capital.[61] Hence, in case the Proposal is approved as it is currently drafted, Spanish law will have to incorporate a "new", wider conception of the exit right.[62]

---

60 Art. 114 (a) of Directive 2017/1132 establishes "Member States shall not impose the requirements set out in Articles 95, 96 and 97 in the case of a merger within the meaning of Article 113 if the following conditions are fulfilled: (a) the minority shareholders of the company being acquired are entitled to have their shares acquired by the acquiring company". This provision does not observe the acquisition by "other shareholders" or by "third parties", but only by the "acquiring company".

61 A similar debate, albeit one of less subjective scope (referring only to the acquisition by the company and not by other members or third parties), was related to the configuration of the "right to acquire shares" that was recognised by the partners in the Third Directive (Art. 28), current Art. 114 of the codified Directive. About this issue and the position of the traditional doctrine: *In extenso*, Adoración Pérez Troya, *La tutela del accionista en la fusión de sociedades*, Citivas, Madrid (1998), (526 et seq.). See also: Fernando Martínez/Achim Puetz, "El derecho de separación de los socios en las modificaciones estructurales", (coord. A. Rojo et al.), *Las modificaciones estructurales de las sociedades mercantiles*, Aranzadi, Cizur Menor (2015), 309, (345-348).

62 Recently, however, some authors, as well as the registers' criteria, seem to have changed. According to this recent interpretation, the wording of Art. 86.j (as regards "other members" or "third parties") should not be so difficult to fit into Spanish law. In practice, if provided by the articles of association, this possibility is admitted by the Mercantile Registry: Alberto Emparanza, "Art. 356", (dirs. Rojo/Beltrán) *Comentario a la Ley de Sociedades de Capital*, Thomson-Reuters, Cizur Menor (2011), 2515 (2526). In the same line, Ricardo Cabanas, "Las fusiones y escisiones transfronterizas", (coord. A. Rojo et al.), *Las modificaciones estructurales de las sociedades mercantiles*, Aranzadi, Cizur Menor (2015), (403) (477). Hence, following this interpretation, the implementation of the Proposal in Spanish law, as regards this specific point, would endorse an admitted practice and, once in force, this practice would no longer require a specific statutory provision.

c.2. Enforcement of the Exit Right

The time period for the shareholder to exercise the exit right (or, as the provision says, "*to exercise their right to dispose of their shareholdings*") should be stated by national law. However, the Proposal implicitly limits the time period in Art. 86.j)3º: "*Member States shall also establish the period for the acceptance of the offer, which shall not in any event exceed one month after the general meeting* (…)." Besides this, in line with the digitalization proposal, Art. 86.j)3º imposes on Member States the obligation to ensure that the converting company is able to accept an offer communicated electronically to an address provided by the company for that purpose.

As for the reimbursement of shareholdings, the Proposal establishes that this can only be executed with cash. Additionally, the acquisition should be made in exchange for an "*adequate compensation*" already contained and published in the conversion draft terms (Art. 86.j.3º). This provision, or, more specifically, the mandatory cash consideration for the shares, could trigger some discussion from the Spanish law perspective where, though reimbursement of shares must be made in cash (pursuant to Art. 356 LSC), it is accepted that it can be also made *in natura* if the articles of association allow for this possibility.[63]

As the Proposal says, the cash compensation must be "*adequate*"; however, it holds that the shareholders cannot challenge the resolution of the general meeting approving the conversion on the *sole* ground that the compensation offered is not adequate [Art. 86.i)5º]. Rather, the Proposal entitles any shareholder who has accepted the offer to challenge the amount ("*to demand recalculation*") before the courts of the Member State of origin within one month of the acceptance of the offer [Art. 86.j)5º, 6º]. This is a solution aimed to, simultaneously, guarantee the adequacy of the compensation for the shareholder and to disallow him to challenge (and block) the whole transaction on the basis of a disagreement over the compensation amount. It has been pointed out that it is difficult to understand why the independent expert does not have the role to review the adequacy of the cash compensation, especially given the fact that — with the exception of transactions concerning micro and small enterprises — in every cross-border conversion an expert has to be appointed in any case to provide the national authority with information on the factual basis for its assessment of "artificial arrangements".[64]

---

63 Alberto Emparanza, (2011), 2515 (2518).

64 ECLE (2018), 9.

Finally, another issue regarding this cash compensation deserves a second thought, at least from the perspective of Spanish law. The Proposal, attempting to strike a balance between the protection of shareholders and the proper functioning of cross-border transactions, has observed (Art. 86.j.4º) that, on the one hand, Member States shall ensure that the "*offer of cash compensation is conditional upon the cross-border conversion taking effect*" in accordance with Art. 86.r, and, on the other hand, that Member States "*shall further establish the period for the cash compensation to be paid, which shall not in any event exceed one month after the cross-border conversion takes effect*". This wording should lead to an understanding that the cash compensation is a condition for the conversion to take effect; however, the time period for it to be paid to the shareholder could take up until (but "*shall not in any event exceed*") a whole month after the cross-border conversion took place (and, therefore, the company by this time is "reincorporated" in the Member State of destiny). This could force shareholders, if the compensation was not finally paid and since the cross-border conversion has already taken effect, to litigate abroad against the converted company to claim the payment.

This is not the policy option assumed by Spanish law under the current regime of cross-border conversions. According to LME, the actual payment of the compensation (and not only its "offer") is conditional for the conversion (the transfer of seat, in Spanish terminology) to take effect; i.e., compensations must be made effective (by means of capital reduction or the acquisition of the shares by the company) for the transaction to be notarised and then incorporated at the Business Register (Arts. 358, 359 LSC, Arts. 208, 219.2, 222.1 RRM).[65]The Spanish approach is more accurate and protective for shareholders and the Proposal should consider reviewing this issue. Notwithstanding, should the text remain the same, the exposed problem can be avoided by national laws (since the time period for payment is a maximum limit that Member States can restrict) and, therefore, Spain could keep its more protective system. However, this would result in less harmonization of the cross-border conversion procedure, with the difficulties associated with it already exposed.

---

65 Ricardo Cabanas, (2015), 403 (478); Fernando Martínez/Achim Puetz, (2015) 309, (343).

3. *Creditors' Protection*

a. General Considerations: Grounds and Techniques for the Protection of Creditors

Any cross-border conversion entails potential risks for creditors that justify their specific protection. The main reason to protect creditors is that — just as it happened to be with shareholders — their debtor company will be governed by a different company law that might offer less protection for creditors after the conversion. The different remedies in Member States to protect creditors in company law are based upon rules on capital formation, capital maintenance and minimum capital requirements in public companies. However, the intensity of creditor protection varies from one Member State to another. Therefore, the change of *lex societatis* may entail a reduction of the rights that were granted by the Member State of origin.[66]

Indeed, by means of a cross-border conversion, more can change (for worse) than just the mere protection of capital rules and creditors' rights recognised by corporate law. When it comes to protecting the interests of creditors (shareholders as well), one cannot forget to also take into consideration some issues relating to the law of groups of companies. If a subsidiary has its registered seat in a country with a group law that provides some protection to minority shareholders and creditors, the transfer of the seat (i.e. the cross-border conversion) may impair the rights of both. It is possible for the parent company to use its power to influence on the general meeting of the subsidiary to "flee" from a country with a substantive regime of groups that is excessively "unfriendly" (e.g., German, Portuguese or Italian law) to another state that is more "attractive" with no "group law regime" (for instance, Spain).[67]

Besides this, when the company is cross-converted and relocates its registered office abroad, while such a change has no effect on the applicable law for contracts,[68] it may affect the appropriate jurisdiction for their enforcement, i.e., there might be a shift (as a general rule subject to exceptions) of the competent *forum*/jurisdiction for creditors to claim their credits (or, if

66 As the *Study on the Law Applicable to Companies* (2016) (222).

67 Luis Fernández del Pozo (2004) 121 (191).

68 To the extent that one party's "habitual residence" is relevant to determining the proper law of a contract, this is fixed as at the time of conclusion of the contract: Regulation (EC) No. 593/2008 on the law applicable to contractual relations (Rome I) OJ [2008] L 177/6, Art. 19(3).

it is the case, to enforce their guarantees).[69] This shift of the international jurisdiction will likely happen.[70] Thus, a creditor, in principle, will have to sue his debtor — a company — before the courts of a foreign country, the Member State of destination.[71]

There are two basic models for harmonization of creditors' protection: commencement of the protection period before (*ex ante*), or after the conversion has taken effect (*ex post*). *Ex ante* protection has the advantage of allowing creditors to exercise their rights against the "converting" company, whereas *ex post* protection means that they have to exercise their rights against the "converted" company, i.e. potentially abroad. A third model could be added: the European Company model, which provides for a special conflict of law rule that permits creditors to sue in the jurisdiction of the Member State of origin.

b. Protection Techniques for Cross-Border Mobility in European Secondary Law and National Laws

Directive 2017/1132 does not provide for any specific remedy in regards to the protection of creditors by cross-border merger rules. Just as it happened with the minority shareholders protection, the directive only points out the need to protect them (Art. 121.2º).[72]

As for the European Company rules, the SE Regulation focuses on the disadvantages that could bring a shift of the competent forum for creditors. Therefore, it provides that, if a company decides to relocate its regis-

69 Unless, of course, the contract contains a forum clause. The forum shifting depends on the applicable provisions of the Brussels I Regulation [1215/2012 of December 12th, 2012, on jurisdiction and the recognition and enforcement of judgments in civil and commercial matters (recast)] and any contractual provisions. As for tortious or delictual obligations, the place where the harmful event occurred or may occur will continue both to govern choice of law and take (special) jurisdiction, regardless of the defendant's registered office or seat: Regulation (EC) No. 864/2007 on the law applicable to non-contractual obligations (Rome II), [2007] OJ L199/40, Art. 4(1); Brussels I bis Regulation, Art .7(2).

70 "Likely" because not every cross-border conversion implies a forum shifting, as referred to in footnote 68. *In extenso*, Guillermo Palao (2006) (185 et seq.).

71 Luis Fernández del Pozo (2004) 121 (190).

72 "The provisions and formalities referred to in point (b) of paragraph 1 shall, in particular, include those concerning the decision-making process relating to the merger and, taking into account the cross-border nature of the merger, the protection of creditors of the merging companies (…)".

tered office to another Member State, it shall be deemed, in respect of any cause of action arising prior to the transfer, to continue to have its registered office in the Member State of origin (SE Regulation, Art. 8, 16º and SCE Regulation, Art. 7, 16º). This policy option has been considered advisable, though this general principle of "jurisdictional continuity" should not apply to insolvency proceedings included in the scope of the Insolvency Regulation Recast.[73]

Member States' national laws basically observe two types of *ex ante* remedies for creditors in the context of cross-border transactions: (a) a right to object or block the merger or the seat transfer/conversion,[74] or (b) a right to claim a safeguard/security of their credits (the option most adopted by the Member States).

Spanish law provides creditors with a right to claim an adequate safeguard pursuant to Art. 44 LME (for mergers), which is applicable to cross-border conversions (through the remission made by Art. 100 LME). Although the wording of the provision says that creditors whose credits were born before the publication date of the conversion's draft terms have the right to "oppose/object" the transaction until their credits are guaranteed (Art. 44.1º LME), this is not a "pure" right to block (*"derecho de oposición"*) the conversion any more,[75] but simply a right to ask the mercantile register to inscribe that this creditor exercised his right timely in order to, if the case, claim before the court (of the Member State of origin) that guarantee.[76]

c. Protection Techniques under the Proposal

The first remedy that the Proposal provides to protect creditors is determined by narrowing the subjective scope of the companies to convert cross-border. In order to avoid opportunistic conversions to be adopted in

---

73 *Study on the Law Applicable to Companies* (2016) (344).

74 This was the case with Spanish law before the last reform and it is the case with Cyprus and the Czech Republic: *Study on the Law Applicable to Companies* (343).

75 Since the reform of the LME introduced by Ley 1/2012 on simplification of information and documentation duties of mergers and divisions of limited liability companies.

76 According to Art. 44.4 LME, the court will further decide if the creditor really "deserved" a guarantee. Likely, by then, the cross-border conversion will have taken effect and converted into another MS company because the transaction will not be paralyzed by the creditor.

insolvency or in the vicinity of insolvency, the Proposal prohibits companies against which proceedings for liquidation, insolvency or suspension of payments have been brought from reincorporating abroad (Art. 86.b).[77] With this provision, which has already been criticised for excluding the possibility to be used for restructurings in crisis situations, the Proposal is said to aim to protect creditors — indirectly — in situations of economic "vulnerability" from the company's choice of a less favourable jurisdiction for them (jurisdiction that, in any case, is determined within the insolvency context, as known, by the so-called COMI coincident with the real seat).[78] A second protective provision for creditors is granted through the mandatory information that the draft terms of the cross-border conversion must contain the "*details of the safeguards offered to the creditors*" [Art. 86.d)1(f)]. This information is an essential tool for creditors to exercise the right to request an adequate safeguard from the competent authorities when they are not satisfied with the safeguards offered by the company, as seen below.

Apart from this, the Proposal contains a whole single provision (Art. 86.k) exclusively dedicated to the "protection of creditors". The policy approach of this rule is that of an *ex ante* protection, i.e., before the conversion is effective. Before addressing its content, it must be pointed out that, finally, despite all the debates within the ICLEG, the proposal has not delimitated the subjective scope of the provision; i.e., which creditors are protected by the norm.[79]

Art. 86.k provides in its first paragraph a facultative, protective remedy when establishing that Member States "may" require that the management organ of the company carrying out the cross-border conversion issues a "declaration" stating that the transaction will not affect its ability to fulfil its obligations and that the creditors will not be harmed (i.e., a solvency

---

77 See this suggestion already in *Study on the Law Applicable to Companies* (2016) (344).

78 Juana Pulgar (2018), 2 et seq.

79 See the minutes of the ICLEG meetings: http://ec.europa.eu/transparency/regexpert/index.cfm?do=groupDetail.groupDetail&groupID=3036. There was a clear consensus within the group in favor of incorporating those "contingent"; it was controversial whether to include creditors who had this status before the publication of the conversion draft terms (or merger or division terms), just as the consolidated Directive 2017/1132 observes for mergers (Art. 99.1 "*whose claims antedate the publication of the draft terms of merger and have not fallen at the time of such publication*"), or extend it to all those who had this condition until the deadline where the creditor could demand from the authority the mechanism of protection of their credit.

statement). The solvency statement, when adopted by the national law, will be part of the content of the conversion draft [referred in Art. 86.d.1(f) when requiring that the draft term shall include at least "*details of the safeguards offered to the creditors*"]. The solvency statement shall declare that,

> "*on the basis of the information available to the management or administrative organ of the company at the date of the declaration, and after having made reasonable enquiries, they are unaware of any reason why the company should, after the conversion takes effect, be unable to meet the liabilities when those liabilities fall due*".

This declaration shall be made no earlier than one month before the draft terms of the cross-border conversion are disclosed (in accordance with Art. 86.h). Finally, the Proposal's Explanatory Memorandum (Recital 17) establishes that each Member State will be free to rule on the director's liability with regard to the accuracy of those solvency declarations and their eventual consequences:

> "*As legal traditions vary amongst Member States with regard to the use of solvency declarations and their possible consequences, it should be up to Member States to draw appropriate consequences for providing inaccurate or misleading declarations, including effective and proportionate sanctions and liabilities in compliance with Union law*".

The declaration of solvency is a recurring topic on the European Commission's agenda that has already been raised in the context of the Directive Proposal "*Societas Unius Personae*",[80] connected to pending controversial policy issues such as the revision of the adequacy of the principles of capital as a mechanism for the protection of creditors, which was already raised with the Winter Report and, now, has come up once again in connection with cross-border conversions.

The second paragraph of Art. 86.k provides another remedy for creditors (cumulatively, with a solvency statement if the Member State had incorporated this requirement into its national law): those creditors dissatisfied with the protection provided in the draft terms of the transaction as required by Art. 86.d.1(f), on "*the safeguards offered to the creditors*" shall be entitled with the right to request from the competent authorities of the

80 Mónica Fuentes, "Una primera aproximación al test de solvencia recogido en la Propuesta de Directiva sobre la *Societas Unius Personae (SUP)*", Working Paper, Eprints Complutense, 2015/97, (https://eprints.ucm.es/33715/1/Una%20primera%20aproximaci%C3%B3n%20al%20test%20de%20solvencia.pdf).

Member State of origin adequate safeguards within one month of the disclosure of the draft terms [Art. 86.k)2º]. This means that the petition has to be made, at the latest, on the day of the general meeting on the merger.[81] This creditor's right is not intended to give or recognise a right to "oppose" (i.e., to block) the conversion, but rather as a right to "*apply to the appropriate administrative or judicial authority for adequate safeguards*".[82]

For the competent administrative or judicial authority to evaluate whether they deserve "*adequate protection*", the Proposal provides these authorities with several rebuttable presumptions (*iuris tantum*) that the creditors are not harmed by the cross-border conversion when: (i) the company discloses, together with the draft terms of the conversion,[83] an independent expert report "*that has concluded that there was no reasonable likelihood that the rights of creditors would be prejudiced (the independent expert should be appointed or confirmed by the authority and must fulfil with the requisites of Art. 86.g.2º*"; or (ii) if the company offered creditors a right to payment,

> "*either against a third-party guarantor, or against the company resulting from the cross-border conversion of at least equivalent value to their original claim, which may be brought in the same jurisdiction as their original claim, and which is of a credit quality at least commensurate with the creditor's original claim immediately after the completion of the conversion*" [Art. 86.k)3º].

As for the first paragraph of Art. 86.k)3º, it has been noted out that the Proposal follows a gatekeeper approach:[84] this report would reduce the uncertainty of whether or not such creditors' claims will be made, since the independent expert report will assess –if the case- that no reasonable likelihood exists that the creditors' rights will be unduly prejudiced and, therefore, that they would not be entitled to claim additional safeguards (it seems that this could be the case when there is no change of jurisdiction

81 As pointed out by ECLE (2018), asking for clarification on the consequences of including in the draft terms "*details of the safeguards offered to the creditors*".

82 However, some Spanish author consider that this does not prevent the national legislator to condition or submit the cross-border conversion to a "pure" creditor's right to oppose the transaction: Segismundo Álvarez, "La propuesta de la Comisión sobre fusiones, escisiones y transformaciones transfronterizas: un paso adelante y otro atrás", *Diario La Ley*, 9223, (2018), 2.

83 In this regard, the reference to the draft terms is relevant, since that draft [Art. 86.d.1(f)] shall include "*details of the safeguards offered to the creditors*".

84 ECLE (2018).

and the claim remains of the same credit quality). It would therefore be a major incentive for companies to get such a report (despite the costs).

Regarding the quite complex wording of Art. 86.k)3º (probably subject to revision), in its second paragraph, creditors are deemed not to be prejudiced if they have a claim against a third party or the company resulting from the cross-border conversion of at least the same value as the original claim "*and which is of a credit quality at least commensurate with the creditor's original claim immediately after completion of the conversion*"; additionally, the creditor has to be able to bring the claim "*in the same jurisdiction as the original*". The *ratio* is quite clear: if the company offers a right to payment that (i) can be brought within the same jurisdiction as the original claim; and (ii) with the same "quality", there is no justification to order additional safeguards for creditors.[85]

Bibliography

Almudí, Jose M., "El régimen antielusivo de transparencia fiscal internacional", en (dir. F. Serrano) *Fiscalidad internacional*, www.cef.es, (2015), 1037 et seq.

Álvarez, Segismundo, "The Commission's Company Law Package: Overview and Critical View of the Proposal for Cross-Border Transactions" (2018) (https://europeanlawblog.eu/2018/06/07/the-commissions-company-law-package-overview-and-critical-view-of-the-proposal-for-cross-border-transactions).

Cabanas, Ricardo, "Las fusiones y escisiones transfronterizas", (coord. A. Rojo et al.), *Las modificaciones estructurales de las sociedades mercantiles*, Aranzadi, Cizur Menor (2015), 403 et seq.

Gerner-Beuerle, Carsten/Mucciarelli, Federico M./Schuster, Edmund-Philipp/Siems, Mathias "Cross-Border Reincorporations in the European Union: The Case for Comprehensive Harmonization", *Journal of Corporate Law Studies*, 18, (2018), 1 et seq.

Emparanza, Alberto, "Art. 356", (dirs. Rojo/Beltrán) *Comentario a la Ley de Sociedades de Capital*, Thomson-Reuters, Cizur Menor (2011), 2515 et seq.

---

85 In this regard, it has been pointed out that while the first condition makes full sense in the context of conversions, the second one seems to refer to the context of cross-border mergers in which the quality of the credit might be impaired and not to conversions (where neither the asset base nor the circle of creditors change but only the applicable company law and, sometimes, a *forum* shifting). The ECLE also said that it is unclear who decides upon the credit quality; since the independent expert is not mentioned, it remains open if this decision would be assumed by a credit rating agency, or if these are just circumstances to be taken into account by the independent expert when making his assessment on whether or not the rights of creditors are unduly prejudiced: see ECLE (2018).

Esteban, Gaudencio, "La implicación de los trabajadores de la sociedad anónima europea en la Ley 31/2006 de transposición de la Directiva", *Revista de Derecho Bancario y Bursátil*, 105 (2007), 180 et seq.

Fernández del Pozo, Luis, "Domicilio y nacionalidad de la SE: traslado internacional de domicilio de la SE. La publicidad registral de la SE", en (dirs. G. Esteban/L. Fernández del Pozo) *La sociedad anónima europea: régimen jurídico, societario, laboral y fiscal*, Marcial Pons, Madrid-Barcelona (2004) 121 et seq.

Fuentes, Mónica, "Una primera aproximación al test de solvencia recogido en la Propuesta de Directiva sobre la *Societas Unius Personae*", Working Paper, Eprints Complutense, 2015/97, (https://eprints.ucm.es/33715/1/Una%20primera%20aproximaci%C3%B3n%20al%20test%20de%20solvencia.pdf).

Knapp, Vanessa, "Cross-Border Mobility: What Do We Need in Practice?", *ERA Forum* https://link.springer.com/article/10.1007/s12027-018-0495-6 (2018).

Martínez, Fernando/Puetz, Achim, "El derecho de separación de los socios en las modificaciones estructurales", (coord. A. Rojo et al.), *Las modificaciones estructurales de las sociedades mercantiles*, Aranzadi, Cizur Menor (2015) (309).

Palao, Guillermo, El traslado de domicilio social de la sociedad anónima europea, Thomson-Aranzadi, Cizur Menor (2006).

Pérez, Adoración, La tutela del accionista en la fusión de sociedades, Civitas, Madrid (1998).

Pulgar, Juana, "El traslado de domicilio social: protección de socios y acreedores", *Revista de Derecho Mercantil*, 309 (2018), 2 et seq.

Sánchez, Jaime, "Cross-Border Conversions and Ex-Ante Control of Artificial Arrangements: Is This An Adequate Reaction to Polbud?" (Oxford Business Law Blog, 20 September 2018, https://www.law.ox.ac.uk/business-law-blog/blog/2018/09/cross-border-conversions-and-ex-ante-control-artificial-arrangements).

--- "La propuesta de la Comisión sobre fusiones, escisiones y transformaciones transfronterizas: un paso adelante y otro atrás", *Diario La Ley*, 9223, (20188).

Documents and Studies

ECLE, "The Commission's 2018 Proposal on Cross-Border Mobility – An Assessment", September, 2018 (https://europeancompanylawexperts.wordpress.com/publications/the-commissions-2018-proposal-on-cross-border-mobility-an-assessment-september-2019/#_ftnref36).

European Parliament (Schmidt, Jessica), "Cross-Border Mergers and Divisions, Transfers of Seat: Is There A Need to Legislate?" (2016)

European Commission, (Gerner-Beuerle, Carsten/Mucciarelli, Federico M./Schuster, Edmund-Philipp/Siems, Mathias), *Study on the Law Applicable to Companies* (2016).

Creditor Protection in Mergers in Europe

Martin Winner[*]

Summary

A. Introduction

European Union law on mergers and divisions (Art. 87 et seq. Council Directive 2017/1132/EU)[1] is characterized by enabling law. It is designed to facilitate necessary restructuring, either in the form of independent businesses merging together or by de-merging one business into new separate enti-

* Professor at the Vienna University of Economics and Business (WU).

1 Council Directive (EU) 2017/1132 of 14 June 2017 relating to certain aspects of company law, OJ L 169 of 30 June 2017, 46.

ties. Additionally, another issue has been brought to the fore over the last two decades, primarily through case law of the European Court of Justice,[2] but also via legislative measures[3] and that is that European law facilitates cross-border restructurings. This is the case even when there is little "restructuring" involved, but the issue is rather the choice of the applicable law.[4]

Under this reading, creditor (or albeit shareholder) protection is not the primary purpose of European Union law, but rather a necessary constraint for companies in the process of such restructuring. The following analysis will assume at a normative level, that any legal rule in the field of creditor protection aims at making it impossible for shareholders to use a merger or division as a means for transferring value from creditors to themselves.

On this basis, the following article will deal with issues of creditor protection in domestic and cross-border mergers. We will first analyse the risks to creditors and then the European approach at mitigating these risks before giving an overview of some national solutions.[5] We then conclude by making some remarks de lege ferenda, including brief mention of the changes suggested by the Commission's recent proposal on cross-border mobility.[6]

However, due to lack of space, we will not address divisions, either domestic or cross-border, since a European legislative framework for the cross-border transactions currently remains lacking.[7] For the sake of brevity, the analysis will be limited to "typical" creditors and thus exclude hybrid positions which pose additional difficulty due to their similarities with equity (see Art. 101 Council Directive 2017/1132/EU). Similarly, we will not deal with the position of bondholders, for whom some Member

2 Case 411/03 13.12.2005 *Sevic Systems AG* ECLI:EU:C:2005:762; Case 210/06 16.12.2008 *Cartesio Oktató és Szolgáltató bt* ECR I-9641; Case 378/10 12.7.2012 *VALE Építési kft* ECLI:EU:C:2012:440; Case 106/16 25.10.2017 *Polbud - Wykonawstwo sp. z o.o.* ECLI:EU:C:2017:804.

3 Cf. Council Regulation (EC) 2001/2157 of 8 October 2001 on the Statute for a European Company, OJ L 294 of 10 November 2001, 1; Art. 95 et seq. Council Directive (EU) 2017/1132 (on cross-border mergers).

4 As has been amply demonstrated in Case 106/16 25.10.2017 *Polbud - Wykonawstwo sp. z o.o.* ECLI:EU:C:2017:804.

5 Of course, this endeavour can only provide the roughest sketch and will almost certainly become victim to the usual pitfalls of any such analysis.

6 Proposal for a Directive amending Directive (EU) 2017/1132 as regards cross-border conversions, mergers and divisions, 2018/0114 (COD).

7 Which, of course, does not make such transactions impossible, but calls for a two-step approach: a national division followed by a cross-border merger.

States provide some type of collective decision-making regarding certain transactions, as foreseen by Art. 100 and Art. 146 para 5 Council Directive 2017/1132/EU. We will also leave aside the issue of contingent creditors, which was raised in the wake of the ECJ's *Hipermercados* judgment.[8]

B. Domestic Mergers

I. Introduction

As a scenario for our analysis, we will use the merger by acquisition between two companies from the same Member State as regulated by Art. 91 et seq. Council Directive 2017/1132/EU. This type of merger is, to my knowledge, more common than the merger by formation of a new company. Under such a transaction, both the assets and the liabilities of one company, the transferring company or the company being acquired, are transferred to another company, the acquiring company; the company being acquired then ceases to exist and the shareholders of that company become shareholders of the acquiring company (see Art. 105 para 1 Council Directive 2017/1132/EU). There is thus a merger taking place at both levels in that case: assets and members.

II. Risks for Creditors

The creditors of the company to be acquired face a change of debtor, as the liabilities become those of the acquiring company.[9] This is of course exceptional, as under general rules, a change of debtor is only possible with creditor consent. The shareholders nevertheless take the decision on the merger transaction and as a result of universal succession, the transferring company's debts are ultimately transferred to the acquiring company. Protection for the transferring company's creditors was thus on the legislative agenda very early on. Suffice it to say that originally, under Austrian and German

8 Case 343/13 5.3.2015 *Modelo Continente Hipermercados SA* ECLI:EU:C:2015:146.
9 See Matthias Habersack and Dirk Verse, *Europäisches Gesellschaftsrecht* (2011), 249.

law, only the creditors of the transferring company were offered protection.[10] The situation in many Member States was similar.[11]

This does not constitute the modern understanding of the issue, however, which has evolved towards an approach looking at the substantial effects of the merger. Today we recognise that for the creditors of the acquiring company, a merger may be detrimental even though their debtor does not change at all. They are nevertheless no less worthy of protection than creditors of the transferring company.[12] Additionally, the change of debtor as such is neutral, as it can have positive or negative effects on creditors. Rather, two distinct and partially offsetting effects have to be taken into account.

First, as a result of the merger, the asset base changes. In extreme cases, this may lead to a smaller asset base after the merger. This happens if an over-indebted company is merged with a sound entity; such transactions are only partially covered by Art. 87 para 3 Council Directive 2017/1132/EU, according to which Member States need not apply the European merger rules if the company being acquired is the subject of bankruptcy proceedings. However, apart from such exceptional circumstances, the asset base is enlarged as a result of the merger.

Second, this would be favourable to the creditors if it were not for the fact that the number of creditors likewise increases.[13] Whereas before the merger, two separate groups of creditors (those of the transferring and those of the acquiring company) enjoyed access to separate sets of assets, after the merger, these groups share a single asset base. It is easy to demonstrate that this will normally be to the benefit of one creditor group and to the detriment of the other. Let us just imagine a merger of a highly leveraged company with a conservatively financed one. For the creditors of the highly leveraged company, the merger ends up bringing a windfall profit,[14] while the claim quality of the sounder company's creditors turns out, however, to be impaired.

---

10 See Art. 241 German (and since 1938) Austrian Stock Corporation Act 1937 (in Austria in substance in force until 1996).

11 Vanessa Edwards, *European Company Law* (1999) 109 et seq.

12 See, however, below III and IV for further discussion of the legal bases; Marcus Lutter, Walter Bayer and Jessica Schmidt, *Europäisches Unternehmens- und Kapitalmarktrecht* (2017), 668.

13 See Susanne Kalss and Christoph Klampfl, *Europäisches Gesellschaftsrecht* (2015) 64.

14 Especially if they are credit institutions advancing loans, as banks usually will have taken the higher risk into account when determining the applicable interest rate.

This central topic of creditor protection in mergers is coupled with some technical issues resulting from merger regulation itself. A merger may, for example, result in cash payments being made to shareholders, either as part of the consideration to be paid[15] or as a result of shareholders making use of exit rights under national law; in both instances, from the creditors point of view the effects will be similar to those of a distribution to shareholders. Additionally, accounting effects may result in balance sheet profits arising out of the merger without any change in the profits made by the underlying business. Such profits may then be distributed to the shareholders and will diminish the asset base available for the creditors' claims.

Of course, a well-known line of thought holds that creditors are in the best position to protect themselves by private ordering, e.g. by negotiating protection through covenants in credit agreements ("acceleration clauses").[16] If this were true, legal measures would probably be of little importance to creditors, as tailor-made solutions generally seem to be superior. While the argument has strengths for certain types of creditors with experience and bargaining power, like e.g. banks, it is less convincing for (smaller) trade creditors or customers, who lack the requisite knowledge, sophistication or bargaining power.[17] Finally, involuntary creditors, especially creditors in tort, do not even have the opportunity to negotiate prior to the company's obligation entering into play.

As a result, creditor protection rules in mergers are not trivial, especially for less professional creditors or creditors in tort. However, one has to bear in mind that any system that heavily relies on creditor initiative before, during or after the merger, will probably only be partially efficient, as it is based on active and knowledgeable creditors who are willing and able to make use of the instruments provided by law. Such creditors, however, are more likely to have made use of private ordering in the first place. For

15 See Art. 89 para 1 Council Directive 2017/1132/EU (providing for a cash payment of up to 10% of the nominal value of the shares to be issued).

16 See the discussion in John Armour, "Share Capital and Creditor Protection: Efficient Rules for A Modern Company Law" (2000) 63 Modern Law Review, 355; Luca Enriques and Jonathan R. Macey, "Creditors Versus Capital Formation: The Case Against the European Legal Capital Rules" (2001) 86 Cornell Law Review, 1165.

17 See e.g. Paul Davies; *Introduction to Company Law* (2002) 70 et seq., 78 et seq.; from the German point of view Peter Mankowski, "Does Contract Suffice to Protect the Creditors of A Company and Their Interests?" in Marcus Lutter (ed), *Legal Capital in Europe* (2006), 394; Wolfgang Schön, "The Future of Legal Capital" (2004) 5 EBOR, 429, 438.

small and passive[18] creditors, a system stepping in automatically may be more adequate.

III. European Solution

Arts. 99-101 Council Directive 2017/1132/EU contain rules on creditor protection for domestic mergers. The provisions cover claims that antedate the publication of the draft terms of the merger and that have not become due at that moment. Member States may nevertheless introduce a broader definition of creditors. Generally, Art. 99 para 1 empowers Member States to provide for an adequate system of protection of creditors' interests; it does not prescribe certain methods of protection or block others. Specifically, it does not hold that creditors must be able to block a merger or at least a detrimental one,[19] but it does empower Member States to introduce such provisions. Additionally, Member States may choose different protection mechanisms for creditors of the acquiring company and those of the transferring company (Art. 99 para 3 Council Directive 2017/1132/EU), which is due to the (erroneous; above B. II.) assumption that creditors of the transferring company have less need for protection.

However, Art. 99 para 1 Council Directive 2017/1132/EU goes further[20] by also setting a minimum level of protection: creditors shall be entitled to apply to the company and to the appropriate administrative or judicial authority for adequate safeguards, where the financial situation of the merging companies makes such protection necessary and where they do not have such safeguards already. For that purpose, creditors have to credibly demonstrate that due to the merger, the satisfaction of their claims is at stake.

On that note, two brief remarks are in order: first, the impairment of the claim has to be due to the merger. The creditor thus has to demon-

18 It is a well-known tenet of economic analysis that holders of small claims are less likely to make use of protective instruments, as the costs of enforcement are often not covered by the expected benefits ("rational apathy").

19 However, creditors obviously may have a factual blocking position via contractual covenants, e.g. acceleration clauses in loan agreements, which will probably mean that the merger has to be negotiated with the creditor as well, as without its consents the loan will become due immediately and will have to be refinanced, probably at less favourable terms.

20 The following provision was introduced by the amendment to the merger regulation by Council Directive 2009/109/EC.

strate (exclusive) causality — impairment due to other reasons, e.g. shifting profit margins does not give rise to the right to apply for safeguards. Second, it is not clear what is actually meant by "the claim has to be at stake".[21] Does the creditor have to demonstrate that the claim probably cannot be enforced? What probability is required (e.g. more than 50%)? Or is it sufficient to have the prognosis about the debtor's ability to discharge the debt upon maturity fairing worse than before the merger?

European company law thus leaves the Member States with considerable discretion as to the measures to be employed, which can even extend to veto rights. However, the Directive quite clearly states a general principle: creditors' interests have to be adequately protected. Additionally, the Directive provides for a minimum level of protection if creditors' interests are actually impaired; this mechanism relies on the creditors to take the initiative in such situations.

IV. National Measures

Member States have made use of the discretion provided for by Art. 99 para 1 Council Directive 2017/1132/EU to a large extent. A recent study commissioned by the European Commission — albeit in the context of cross-border mergers — gives a good impression of the varying methods Member States employ in order to protect creditors' interests.[22]

1. Institutional Creditor Protection

First, several Member States' laws contain outright prohibitions of certain types of mergers. Very often such prohibitions are enforced *ex officio* by the registering body throughout the course of the registration procedure, especially if that body is a judicial authority; quite often there is no remedy available for individual creditors. As such, prohibitions are often based on general precepts of company law, e.g. on the rules on maintenance of capital. Their importance is, however, not realised in many comparative en-

---

21 Stefan Grundmann, *Europäisches Gesellschaftsrecht* (2011), 535; see also Susanne Kalss and Christoph Klampfl, *Europäisches Gesellschaftsrecht* (2015) 69.

22 Bech-Bruun/Lexidale, *Study on the Application of the Cross-Border Merger Directive* (2013), Main Findings-31 et seq. and Detailed Country Reports.

deavours, which tend to look at specific provisions on mergers in statutory texts.[23]

A good example for such prohibitions can be provided under Austrian law. A classic technique of a leveraged buy-out is setting up a special purpose vehicle (SPV), which takes up the loan in pursuit of acquiring the target company. After the acquisition, the SPV is merged into the target company; the bank financing the acquisition thereby gets direct access to the cash flows of the target company and does not depend on distributions being made to the acquirer. However, from the point of view of the target company's creditors, this is dangerous, as, after the downstream merger, they face the bank as a competing creditor without the loan having been made for a business purpose of the target. In effect, the target company finances its own acquisition. Under Austrian doctrine and case law, such transactions are a forbidden repayment of contributions to the shareholder according to Art. 82 para 1 Austrian Act on Limited Liability Companies. As a result, such transactions are not entered into the register and therefore cannot become effective.[24] Similar approaches have been developed for other circumstances with comparable dangers to creditors.

This type of "institutional creditor protection" — which is not dependent on any particular action by a creditor — is hugely important in some Member States. Obviously, it lessens the need for individual creditor protection to some extent. It furthermore helps to overcome creditor apathy,[25] albeit at the cost of scrutiny by the registrar of even the most harmless transactions.

2. *Individual Creditor Protection*

Second, all Member States have introduced protection mechanisms, which are triggered by an application by individual creditors. Such devices may generally be applied ex ante or ex post,[26] depending on whether they can

23 Unfortunately, this weakness is also exhibited by the study carried out by Bech-Bruun/Lexidale (n. 22).

24 See Austrian Supreme Court 11.11.1999 – 6 Ob 4/99b –, SZ 72/172.

25 See above B.II.

26 For a taxonomy in relation to cross-border mergers see Bech-Bruun/Lexidale, *Study on the Application of the Cross-Border Merger Directive* (2013), Main Findings-33; see also Geert T.M.J. Raaijmakers and Thijs P.H. Olthoff, "Creditor Protection in Cross-Border Mergers: Unfinished Business" (2008) 4 Utrecht Law Review, 34 (37 et seq.).

be invoked before the shareholder meeting or afterwards, which, in some cases, may even take place after the merger has been entered into the register and thereby become effective. Obviously, protection mechanisms ex ante provide more transaction security, as the merging companies will not have to deal with unforeseen demands after giving the green light on the merger. On the other hand, allowing creditors a strong position before the merger may well give them the power to block the transaction altogether and, in any case, will often lead to time-consuming negotiations. Providing creditors with protection only after the merger has become effective is usually more transaction-friendly. At this stage, however, the merger may have already served to weaken the asset base available to creditors — ergo, protection may come too late.

As already mentioned, Art. 99 para 3 Council Directive 2017/1132/EU empowers the Member States to introduce different rules for creditors of the transferring and those of the acquiring company. This procedure is nevertheless very unusual for domestic mergers today.[27]

In essence, all Member States seem to have transposed the Directive's requirement of providing creditors with adequate safeguards if the satisfaction of their claims is at stake ("*creditor security approach*"). However, the precise content of these provisions varies considerably:

- As stated above, there is variation on whether the right to apply for safeguards can be exercised before the merger has taken effect or only afterwards. Member States seem to be divided almost evenly, although for domestic mergers, there is a slight tendency toward the ex post approach.[28] Usually, the claim has to be raised within a certain time period, which varies between one and six months after the merger or the publication of the draft terms of the merger.[29]
- In most cases, creditors can petition for safeguards only if the merger threatens the settlement of the claim and the latter is not secured. Of course, there is some variance in detail. Generally, the burden of proof for impairment lies with the creditor. However, under Spanish law, all creditors can request guarantees for claims, which are not due at the

---

27 Historically, this was different in many Member States; see above B.II. Additionally, the situationis different for cross-border mergers; see below C.IV.

28 Germany and Austria follow an ex post approach for domestic, but an ex ante approach for cross-border mergers; see below C.IV.

29 See the overview in the context of cross-border mergers at Bech-Bruun/Lexidale, *Study on the Application of the Cross-Border Merger Directive* (2013), Main Findings-33.

time of the merger unless their claims are sufficiently warranted.[30] This in turn probably makes access to safeguards easier, as it seems to imply that the burden of proof lies with the company as to the non-impairment of the claim.

- Some Member States use a gatekeeper approach, e.g. Italy[31] and Denmark.[32] Creditors cannot ask for safeguards if a report by an independent expert states that there are no grounds for providing security, especially because the position of the creditors is not impaired.

A number of Member States go further by providing creditors with the right to block the merger, either as a general rule or under specific circumstances ("*veto rights approach*"). Under UK law,[33] the court can order a creditor meeting; in that meeting, 25% of creditors (in value) can veto the merger. Similarly, under Italian law[34] opposing creditors seem to have de facto blocking power for 60 days without cause. Thereafter the court may order the merger to go ahead if there are no substantial dangers to creditors regardless of their veto. In Spain, creditors who are not sufficiently secured can block the merger and do not have to rely upon their right to petition for safeguards.[35] Other Member States have similar veto rights.[36] In practice, such rights may not be as problematic as they sound, as normally creditors do not have a strong holdout position, which they could use to renegotiate the debt. Instead, the company normally has the option to pay back the loan and refinance itself (in the new entity) if creditors overplay their hand.

Apart from veto rights, some Member States provide for other mechanisms designed to protect creditors. Under French law, the court can either

30 Art. 44 para 2 Ley 3/2009, de 3 de abril, sobre modificaciones estructurales de las sociedades mercantiles.

31 Art. 2503 Codice Civile.

32 Art. 298 para 1 Danish Companies Act (English version at https://danishbusinessauthority.dk/sites/default/files/danish_companies_act.pdf).

33 Art. 11 and Art. 14 Companies (Cross-Border Mergers) Regulations 2007; http://www.legislation.gov.uk/uksi/2007/2974/contents/made.

34 Art. 2503 Codice Civile and Bech-Bruun/Lexidale, *Study on the Application of the Cross-Border Merger Directive* (2013), IT-11.

35 Art. 44 para 2 Ley 3/2009 (n. 30).

36 For Finland see Bech-Bruun/Lexidale, *Study on the Application of the Cross-Border Merger Directive* (2013), FI-8; for Malta ibid., MT-8 et seq; for the Netherlands ibid., NL-10 et seq. and Geert T.M.J. Raaijmakers and Thijs P.H. Olthoff, "Creditor Protection in Cross-Border Mergers: Unfinished Business" (2008) 4 Utrecht Law Review, 34, 35 et seq.; for Portugal Bech-Bruun/Lexidale, *Study on the Application of the Cross-Border Merger Directive* (2013), PT-7; for Sweden ibid., SE-8.

order the company to provide security or it can accelerate the debt, which means that it has to be repaid immediately.[37] Under Polish law, the assets of the merging companies have to be administered separately until all creditors have been satisfied,[38] which, historically, was a prevalent mode of protection.[39]

V. Remarks de lege ferenda

Clearly, Art. 99 Council Directive 2017/1132/EU encourages variety. It does so by open wording ("adequate system of protection") and by its general character as a measure of minimum harmonization. It thus provides a barrier to a race to the bottom, but gives Member States discretion as to whether to introduce further measures.

One's assessment has to depend on the aim of European merger rules. If they are designed in order to provide a minimum standard for protection of (cross-border) creditors, the current situation is adequate. Member States retain freedom to maintain and find efficient or at least adequate solutions embedded into their overall approach towards company law. Cross-border creditors can rely upon national rules maintaining certain minimum standards. However, the rule deserves some criticism for not laying out the precise content of these minimum standards, making costly research into the national legal rules necessary not only for minor details, but also for central issues as to whether the protection is provided ex ante or ex post.

If one sees the aim of Art. 99 Council Directive 2017/1132/EU and of the merger rules overall in facilitating external growth via mergers,[40] then the assessment depends upon one's view as to whether such issues are best regulated at the EU level or be left to the Member States. We will not go into this controversial issue, but note that absent clear proof of the need for centralised regulation, the principle of subsidiarity as enshrined in Art. 5 para 3 TEU tips the balance for regulation at Member State level.

---

37 Art. 236-14 para 2 Code de Commerce. A similar provision exists under Belgian law; see Bech-Bruun/Lexidale, *Study on the Application of the Cross-Border Merger Directive* (2013), BE-10.

38 Art. 495 et seq. Code of Partnerships and Commercial Companies and Bech-Bruun/Lexidale, *Study on the Application of the Cross-Border Merger Directive* (2013), PL-7 et seq.

39 See e.g. Art. 243 Austrian General Commercial Code (in force until 1938).

40 Stefan Grundmann, *Europäisches Gesellschaftsrecht* (2011), 521.

If, however, the rule is designed to provide the basis for facilitating cross-border mergers,[41] it is clearly inadequate, as will be demonstrated in the next part.

C. Cross-border Mergers

I. Introduction

A cross-border merger by acquisition basically constitutes the same transaction as its domestic equivalent. The only relevant difference is that the merger is effected between two companies from different Member States. After the merger, the assets and liabilities are transferred to an acquiring company with its seat in a different Member State, which is also subject to a different company law than the transferring company. Thus, from the point of view of the transferring company' creditors, not only will the debtor change, but it will also have its seat in another jurisdiction. Similarly, although not of primary relevance in the present context, the shareholders of the company to be acquired will become members of a company subject to the law of another Member State.

II. Risks for Creditors

In general, due to the similarities of the transactions, the risks to creditors are equivalent to domestic mergers. That is, a change in the asset base coupled with a wider circle of creditors may be detrimental to the creditors of one company. For the acquiring company's creditors, there is no discernible difference between a cross-border merger and a domestic one. Furthermore, as a general rule, they will not care whether the assets are merged across the border or not, but only about the relationship between total assets and total claims. However, creditors of the transferring company face a number of additional perils due to the cross-border character of the transaction.

First, from their point of view, the applicable law actually changes. Of course, this does not refer to the law governing the company's obligation

41 Historically, this seems to have been an important issue; cf. Stefan Grundmann, *Europäisches Gesellschaftsrecht* (2011), 522.

itself, which does not change as a result of the merger.[42] However, the company will be governed by a different company law after the merger, which may be less creditor-friendly, e.g. by having more permissive rules on distribution to the shareholders. In some Member States as in Austria, all instances of distribution to members of a limited liability company (GmbH) or shareholders of a stock corporation (AG) are invalid and have to be repaid, unless the initial payment to the members was made as a result of a member's decision to distribute profits.[43] Whether profits accrue has to be determined by applying the creditor-friendly Austrian accounting rules. This, however, severely limits the sums that can be distributed. In a German GmbH,[44] such distribution is only invalid if, as a result of the distribution, the company's net assets fall below its share capital.[45] Otherwise, distribution is possible even if no profits have been amassed. As a result, a cross-border merger of an Austrian GmbH with its German equivalent is potentially detrimental to the Austrian company's creditors since the members have greater access to the company's funds after the merger than at the time the creditor entered into the transaction with the (then Austrian) company.

Second, the place of jurisdiction may change. Under Art. 4 Council Regulation 2012/1215/EU, a company can be sued at the place where it is domiciled, which according to Art. 63 of the Regulation, refers to either the statutory seat of the company, its central administration or its principal place of business. All these factors can change after the cross-border merger: the statutory seat will be one of the acquiring companies, and both its central administration and principal place of business are likely to shift as well, although this is not strictly necessary. Hence, the creditor will have to sue in another jurisdiction unless either a special jurisdiction according to Art. 7 et seq. Council Regulation 2012/1215/EU is applicable,[46] or the contract contains a provision on prorogation of jurisdiction according to Art. 25 of the Regulation. Especially for small and medium-sized creditors, this may pose additional burdens and may make pursuing a claim successfully less likely to transpire. Additionally, even large creditors may have to deal with an unfamiliar and probably less creditor-friendly court system.

---

42 See Case 483/14 7.4.2016 *KA Finanz AG* v. *Sparkassen Versicherung AG Vienna Insurance Group* ECLI:EU:C:2016:205.

43 See Art. 82 Austrian Act on Limited Liability Companies.

44 In contrast to the AG, for which the situation is the same as described for Austria.

45 See Art. 30 German Act on Limited Liability Companies.

46 E.g. place of performance according to Art. 7 para 1 (a) Council Regulation 2012/1215/EU.

Third, as far as insolvency is concerned, the cross-border merger will usually lead to a change of forum and applicable law. Both are determined by the centre of main interest (COMI; see Art. 3 para 1 and Art. 7 para 1 Council Regulation 2015/848/EU). COMI is the place where the debtor conducts the administration of its interests on a regular basis and which is ascertainable by third parties. For companies, the place of the registered office is normally presumed to be the centre of its main interests, unless it has been moved to another Member State within the 3-month period prior to the request for the opening of insolvency proceedings (Art. 3 para 1 Council Regulation 2015/848/EU). It follows, then, that a cross-border merger will, as a general rule, from the point of view of the transferring company's creditors, lead to important changes if the company subsequently becomes insolvent.

III. European Solution

Council Directive 2017/1132/EU does not address the issue of creditor protection in cross-border mergers directly. Rather, Art. 121 para 1 (b) states that each company taking part in the cross-border merger shall comply with the provisions of the national law to which it is subject. Para 2 continues by stating that these include "taking into account the cross-border nature of the merger, the protection of creditors of the merging companies".

This is generally understood to mean that Member States have to apply their law on domestic mergers,[47] which is, in turn, partially harmonised by Art. 99 Council Directive 2017/1132/EU (see above B. III.). As in a cross-border merger, the merging companies are subject to rules of different Member States before the merger becomes effective, different national regimes for creditor protection apply to each of the merging companies. As we have seen, Member States' regulatory schemes show remarkable diversity. The interplay between these different rules, moreover, causes practical problems, which will be addressed below.

It is not completely clear whether Member States may introduce different provisions for creditor protection in the cross-border context as compared to purely national transactions. On the one hand, Art. 121 para 2 Council Directive 2017/1132/EU explicitly states that the rules on creditor protection shall take into account the cross-border nature of the transac-

---

47 See Recital (3) Council Directive 2005/56/EC (the original Directive on cross-border mergers before the consolidation in Council Directive 2017/1132/EU).

tion. On the other hand, the possibility of introducing different rules in a cross-border merger is mentioned explicitly only for the protection of members (see Art. 121 para 2 second sentence Council Directive 2017/1132/EU). From a systematic perspective, this seems to imply that different provisions for creditor protection are not in line with the Directive.[48] However, these provisions were introduced during the negotiations in the Council. Given the (erratic) nature of these political processes, systematic arguments in my understanding are not conclusive. Rather, a more liberal reading seems to be appropriate according to which Member States can introduce deviating provisions as long as they take into account the cross-border nature of the merger.[49] As we have seen, it is precisely the cross-border nature of the transaction which poses additional perils to the creditors of the transferring company. Deviating provisions which are more protective for creditors are, therefore, in line with Art. 121 Council Directive 2017/1132/EU. This reading is shared at least by some Member States, which have chosen to provide creditors with additional protection in comparison to national mergers.

IV. National Measures

Following Art. 121 Council Directive 2017/1132/EU, the majority of Member States apply their rules for domestic mergers likewise for cross-border

---

48 For such a reading e.g. Susanne Kalss and Christoph Klampfl, *Europäisches Gesellschaftsrecht* (2015), 85 et seq.; Marcus Lutter, Walter Bayer and Jessica Schmidt, *Europäisches Unternehmens- und Kapitalmarktrecht* (2017), 797 et seq. Case 483/14 7.4.2016 *KA Finanz AG v. Sparkassen Versicherung AG Vienna Insurance Group* ECLI:EU:C:2016:205 does not deal with the issue, but states in para 62: "In so far as, in the case of a national merger, the Member States must act in accordance with Arts. 13 to 15 of Directive 78/855 in relation to the protection of creditors, they must therefore also adhere to those provisions in the case of a cross-border merger." This is not an endorsement of the view that Member States may not introduce more stringent protective provisions for cross-border mergers (for a different reading see Jessica Schmidt, *Cross-Border Mergers and Divisions, Transfers of Seat: Is There A Need to Legislate?* (2016) 18).

49 See Mads Andenas and Frank Wooldridge, *European Comparative Company Law* (2009), 497; Jonathan Rickford, "The Proposed Tenth Company Law Directive on Cross Border Mergers and its Impact in the UK" (2005) 16 EBLR, 1393 (1408 et seq.); Arianna Ugliano, "The New Cross-Border Merger Directive: Harmonisation of European Company Law and Free Movement" (2007) 18 EBLR, 585 (608).

mergers.[50] This leads to the overabundance of solutions mentioned above (B. IV.)

However, there is a certain tendency toward introducing more restrictive provisions for outgoing mergers.[51] Under Austrian and German law, the approach for domestic mergers is protection ex post: creditors can ask for adequate safeguards only after the merger has become effective (see above B. IV.). However, with cross-border mergers, creditors of the transferring company who can demonstrate that they are reasonably likely to be prejudiced by the cross-border merger, can apply for safeguards well before the merger is entered into the register.[52] In fact, an Austrian or German judge may not issue the pre-merger certificate unless the applicant is granted security or the claim is settled,[53] which leads to a blocking position for the creditors who are actually impaired. Additionally, under Austrian law, the creditor does not need to show the detrimental effects of the merger if the share capital plus non-distributable reserves of the acquiring company are lower than those of the transferring company, as this may lead to distribution to members which would not have been possible in the transferring company. This potential impairment is sufficient to trigger a right to receive adequate safeguards.[54]

50 See e.g. for Belgium Bech-Bruun/Lexidale, *Study on the Application of the Cross-Border Merger Directive* (2013), BE-10; for the Czech Republic ibid., CZ-13; for Denmark ibid., DK-7; for the Netherlands Geert T.M.J. Raaijmakers and Thijs P.H. Olthoff, "Creditor Protection in Cross-Border Mergers: Unfinished Business" (2008) 4 Utrecht Law Review, 34 (36).

51 Some other Member States have diverging rules for domestic and cross-border mergers as well; see e.g. for Greece Bech-Bruun/Lexidale, *Study on the Application of the Cross-Border Merger Directive* (2013), EL-7 et seq; for Ireland ibid., IE-9; for Poland ibid., PL-7 et seq.

52 See Art. 13 Austrian Act on Cross-border Mergers and Art. 122j German Act on Conversions (UmwG). Similar provisions can be found in Slovenia; cf. Bech-Bruun/Lexidale, *Study on the Application of the Cross-Border Merger Directive* (2013), SI-9.

53 See Art. 13 para 2 Austrian Act on Cross-border Mergers and Art. 122k para 1 German Act on Conversions (UmwG).

54 On the disputed issue, whether such rules are admissible under Council Directive 2017/1132/EU see above C.III.

V. Ongoing Reform of Creditor Protection in Cross-border Mergers

It is obvious that, in order to promote cross-border mobility, it is necessary to achieve a common framework in all Member States, as the transaction will be subject to the requirements of two different legal orders. The *Bech-Bruun/Lexidale* study on the implementation of the Cross-Border Merger Directive shows that the approach pursued by Art. 121 Council Directive 2017/1132/EU, namely a light-touch approach giving considerable leeway to Member States in core issues of creditor protection, did not ultimately achieve the desired result.[55] The enormous differences between Member States, e.g. on the issue of the commencement of the protection period (ex ante or ex post approach) and on the nature of the protection offered to creditors, serve to make the merger process very complex and constitute a strong deterrent to cross-border mergers. What seems to be needed is more harmonisation at least for the most critical issues.

This was also the result of a consultation carried out by the Commission in 2015,[56] in the course of which an overwhelming majority of respondents favoured further and even full harmonization with the aim of maximising certainty, while minimising procedural cost. Of course, the entire issue hinges on agreement as to the type of protection to be provided. In the course of the consultation, there was little discussion of this question. Additional consultations have resulted in a similar picture.

The Commission has reacted and brought forward a new proposal on corporate mobility,[57] which *inter alia* addresses cross-border mergers and the issue of creditor protection. It introduces detailed mechanisms for the

---

55 Bech-Bruun/Lexidale, *Study on the Application of the Cross-Border Merger Directive* (2013), Main Findings-31 et seq. See also Geert T.M.J. Raaijmakers and Thijs P.H. Olthoff, "Creditor Protection in Cross-Border Mergers: Unfinished Business" (2008) 4 Utrecht Law Review, 34, 39; Jessica Schmidt, 'EU Company Law Package 2018', Der Konzern 2018, 229 (238 et seq.).

56 For a summary see COM(2018) 241 final, 15 et seq. See also Jessica Schmidt, *Cross-Border Mergers and Divisions, Transfers of Seat: Is There A Need to Legislate?* (2018) 18 et seq. For conversions see also Carsten Gerner-Beuerle, Federico M. Muciarelli, Edmund-Philipp Schuster and Mathias Siems, "Cross-Border Reincorporations in the European Union: The Case for Comprehensive Harmonisation" (2018) 18 Journal of Corporate Law Studies 1, 34 et seq.

57 Commission, Proposal for a directive of the European Parliament and of the Council amending Directive (EU) 2017/1132 as regards cross-border conversions, mergers and divisions COM (2018) 114 final. After this contribution went into print, Parliament, Council and Commission agreed upon a modified text, which could not be taken into account here.

protection of creditors (and minority members), which follow similar lines for conversions, mergers and divisions as far as possible.[58]

The Proposal nevertheless shies away from introducing a fully harmonised framework.[59] Rather, Member States are left with the possibility of introducing additional protection devices (at least as long as they comply with primary law). Even if politically speaking, this may be a prudent move in order to achieve the necessary support from the Member States during negotiations in the Council, at a conceptual level, it is unfortunate that the Proposal is thus deprived of the benefits of full harmonisation. Member States may therefore introduce new rules on individual creditor protection or maintain their existing provisions. That is, the Proposal will not affect rules on institutional creditor protection either (see above B. IV.).

According to the Proposal, Member States may require that the board of each merging company declares that its members are unaware of any reason as to why the new company would be unable to meet due liabilities in the post-merger period. If the Member State chooses to do so, liability for false statements may be the result (Art. 126b para 1 of the Proposal). It is not completely clear why the Proposal explicitly empowers Member States to do so, as it follows a minimum harmonisation approach anyway. This seems to be a strong nudge for Member States to introduce such provisions.

More importantly, the Proposal opts for an ex ante approach.[60] The draft merger terms have to include "details on the safeguards offered to creditors" (Art. 122n of the Proposal). This is not supposed to mean that the company has to offer such safeguards, as Art. 126b para 3 (b) of the Proposal makes it clear that such safeguards are optional. Nevertheless, any safeguards offered have to be explicitly included in the terms. If the creditors are not satisfied with the terms offered, they can petition for adequate safeguards within one month of the disclosure of the draft terms (Art. 126b para 2 of the Proposal). This means that the petition has to be made on the day of the general meeting deciding on the merger, at the latest. Although the provision does not state clearly what the petitioners have to bring for-

---

58 The following discussion of the Proposal's merits is partially based on European Company Law Experts, "The Commission's 2018 Proposal on Cross-Border Mobility – An Assessment" (available: https://europeancompanylawexperts.wordpress.com/publications/the-commissions-2018-proposal-on-cross-border-mobility-an-assessment-september-2019/ and in ECFR 2019, Issue 1, in print).

59 See very clearly Explanatory Memorandum to Proposal 19.

60 See, however, Jessica Schmidt, *Cross-Border Mergers and Divisions, Transfers of Seat: Is There A Need to Legislate?* (2018) 18 et seq. (in favour of ex post protection).

ward, we infer from Art. 126b para 3 that they have to demonstrate that a reasonable likelihood exists that their rights will be unduly prejudiced.

Of course, the uncertainty about whether such claims will be made provides a major barrier to cross-border mergers. However, Art. 126b para 3 (a) provides a mechanism for reducing this uncertainty: the company may disclose a report by an independent expert which states that there is no reasonable likelihood that the creditors' rights are being unduly prejudiced.[61] Although the Proposal does not stipulate it clearly, we understand this to mean that, in this case, the creditors have no right to additional safeguards. This point stands as a major incentive for the companies to try and obtain such a report. Hence, the Proposal follows a gatekeeper approach. Yet, apart from the fact that the expert has to be "appointed or approved" by the competent authority, the rules for the appointment and the qualification of the gatekeeper are left to the Member States.

The second exception in Art. 126b para 3 (b) is more difficult to understand. The creditors are deemed not to be prejudiced if they have a claim against a third party or the company resulting from the merger of at least the same value as the original claim "and which is of a credit quality at least commensurate with the creditor's original claim immediately after completion of the merger". Additionally, the creditor has to be able to bring the claim in the same jurisdiction as the original claim. The purpose is clear: if the claim's quality is not affected by the merger or if a claim of equal credit quality is granted against a third party in the draft merger terms, then there is no justification for requesting additional safeguards. However, it is unclear who decides on the credit quality since the independent expert is not mentioned in Art. 126b para 3 (b). Is it supposed to be a decision by a credit rating agency? Or does it represent (b) just a clarification for circumstances to be taken into account by the independent expert when he/she makes his/her judgment on whether the rights of creditors are unduly prejudiced?

In any case, the Proposal does not give creditors the right to block the transaction. It likewise stops short of stating that the competent authority can only issue the pre-merger certificate if the creditors have been provided with adequate safeguards. The second issue is left to the Member States, who subsequently have to provide the detailed procedural framework. Provisions such as Art. 13 para 2 Austrian Act on Cross-border Mergers and Art. 122k para 1 German Act on Conversions (see above C. IV.) can there-

61 Supportive also Jessica Schmidt, EU Company Law Package 2018, Der Konzern 2018, 229 (239).

fore be maintained if the Proposal is actually enacted. Yet even those Member States giving creditors the right to block the transaction, e.g. by collective decision making, can maintain such rules as the Proposal does not fully harmonize the issue.

At first glance, the Proposal lacks some type of "white list" of types of safeguards deemed to provide creditors with adequate protection. This is left to the Member States, who, in turn, tend to leave the matter to the competent authorities. This is probably a wise decision, as, the adequacy of a safeguard very much depends on the factual situation a creditor is in. Any further definition would probably curtail judicial discretion without much positive effect.

In sum, the Proposal will certainly improve the regulation of creditor protection if it is enacted, even though room for improvement remains. The current negotiations in the Council will probably help to smoothen out some inconsistencies and adjust minor policy decisions, although the focus of the political discussion will most probably be on other issues, namely the issue of artificial arrangements and the board level representation of employees, especially in the context of conversions (i.e. the transfer of seat).[62] It is nevertheless very unlikely that the major structural flaw of the proposed provision —namely the lack of full harmonization —will be taken up during negotiations in the Council, as Member States tend to protect their freedom to regulate as far as possible.

D. *Concluding Remarks*

To conclude, we would like to reiterate that the current situation for domestic mergers leaves a lot of legislative freedom to Member States for purely national transactions. This is even the case if creditors from other Member States are affected. There are good arguments behind the reason why this may be a sound policy decision, the main one being that there is no single correct solution for the issue of creditor protection, but a number of possible approaches none of which have proven to be superior at this stage. Additionally, in many Member States, the protection is not achieved by a single instrument, but by a mix of different instruments, which are only partially addressed in Art. 99 Council Directive 2017/1132/EU. For example, it is hard to assess the importance and adequacy of the rules on the individual protection for creditors without taking in-

62 Cf. Art. 86a et seq. of the Proposal.

to account general company law rules and the role of registration authorities (institutional creditor protection). As a result, it seems preferable to leave Member States to follow their national, path-dependent approaches as long as certain minimum standards are fulfilled.

This argument is not convincing in the least, however, for cross-border mergers (and, in fact, for any future regulation of other cross-border transactions, like conversions or especially divisions). In these cases, diversity is counterproductive as it causes friction between different national approaches which have to be applied to the same transaction. Obviously, full harmonization would be the appropriate approach in order to minimise discrepancies between the different applicable laws. This, however, necessitates a European consensus on the type of measures providing adequate protection. Such a consensus does not seem to be forthcoming at this stage.

This is probably the main reason why the Commission in its Proposal favours a conceptually inferior, but (hopefully) more workable approach —namely more extensive material regulation on creditor protection without going so far as introducing full harmonisation. Hence, Member States may maintain their traditional approaches as long as they at least provide the protection prescribed by the European Directive. Of course, this may be more helpful to creditors than to the companies involved, as creditors will know what to expect at least, without companies having common rules to adhere to. Considering the nature of European law on mergers as a provision designed to facilitate restructurings (enabling provisions), this result is hardly optimal.

We nevertheless see no grave problem in the fact that the regimes for domestic and cross-border mergers will drift apart if the Proposal comes to be enacted.[63] The various regulations will be the result of a varied factual circumstances, which leads to the requirement for further harmonisation in the case of cross-border mergers. However, in the long run, successful regulation on creditor protection for cross-border mergers may have an indirect harmonization effect on domestic transactions as well.

63 See also Geert T.M.J. Raaijmakers and Thijs P.H. Olthoff, "Creditor Protection in Cross-Border Mergers: Unfinished Business" (2008) 4 Utrecht Law Review, 34 (38).

Bibliography

Mads Andenas and Frank Wooldridge, *European Comparative Company Law* (CUP, Cambridge, 2009).

John Armour, "Share Capital and Creditor Protection: Efficient Rules for A Modern Company Law' (2000) 63 Modern Law Review, 355.

Bech-Bruun/Lexidale, *Study on the Application of the Cross-Border Merger Directive* (Study for the Directorate General for the Internal Market and Services, the European Union, September 2013) (http://ec.europa.eu/internal_market/company/docs/mergers/131007_study-cross-border-merger-directive_en.pdf).

Paul Davies, *Introduction to Company Law* (Oxford University Press, Oxford, 2002).

Vanessa Edwards, *European Company Law* (Clarendon Press, Oxford, 1999).

Luca Enriques and Jonathan R. Macey, "Creditors Versus Capital Formation: The Case Against the European Legal Capital Rules" (2001) 86 Cornell Law Review, 1165.

European Company Law Experts, "The Commission's 2018 Proposal on Cross-Border Mobility – An Assessment" (available: https://europeancompanylawexperts.wordpress.com/publications/the-commissions-2018-proposal-on-cross-border-mobility-an-assessment-september-2019/).

Carsten Gerner-Beuerle, Federico M. Muciarelli, Edmund-Philipp Schuster and Mathias Siems, "Cross-Border Reincorporations in the European Union: The Case for Comprehensive Harmonisation" (2018) 18 Journal of Corporate Law Studies 1.

Stefan Grundmann, *Europäisches Gesellschaftsrecht* (2nd Edition, C.F. Müller, Heidelberg, 2011).

Matthias Habersack and Dirk Verse, *Europäisches Gesellschaftsrecht* (4th Edition, C.H. Beck, Munich, 2011).

Susanne Kalss and Christoph Klampfl, *Europäisches Gesellschaftsrecht* (C.H. Beck Manz, Munich, 2015).

Marcus Lutter, Walter Bayer and Jessica Schmidt, *Europäisches Unternehmens- und Kapitalmarktrecht* (6th Edition, De Gruyter, Berlin, 2017).

Peter Mankowski, "Does contract suffice to protect the creditors of a company and their interests?" in Marcus Lutter (ed), *Legal Capital in Europe* (De Gruyter Recht, Berlin, 2006), 394.

Geert T.M.J. Raaijmakers and Thijs P.H. Olthoff, "Creditor Protection in Cross-Border Mergers: Unfinished Business" (2008) 4 Utrecht Law Review, 34.

Jonathan Rickford, "The Proposed Tenth Company Law Directive on Cross-Border Mergers and its Impact in the UK" (2005) 16 EBLR, 1393.

Jessica Schmidt, *Cross-Border Mergers and Divisions, Transfers of Seat: Is There A Need to Legislate?*, Study for the JURI Committee of the European Parliament (2016) (http://www.europarl.europa.eu/cmsdata/105632/schmidt.pdf).

Jessica Schmidt, "EU Company Law Package 2018", Der Konzern 2018, 229 (Part I) and 273 (Part II).

Wolfgang Schön, "The Future of Legal Capital" (2004) 5 EBOR, 429.

Arianna Ugliano, "The New Cross-Border Merger Directive: Harmonisation of European Company Law and Free Movement" (2007) 18 EBLR, 585.

Creditor Protection in Restructurings in Serbia

Mirjana Radović[*]

Summary

A. *Introduction*

In Serbia restructurings of companies are becoming increasingly important. On the one hand, this is due to the fact that the ongoing process of transition towards market economy as well as the intended EU integration of Serbia forces companies to become more efficient in order to be able to cope with competitive pressure and market forces within the EU. In this respect, restructuring may be used as a measure for enhancing efficiency.[1] On the other hand, restructurings of companies are facilitated or stimulated by numerous legislative changes. These changes in principle contribute

---

* Associate Professor at the Faculty of Law of the University of Belgrade.

1 Take, for example, the case of Serbian Railways which underwent a partial division into three newly formed companies in 2015. See: http://serbianrailways.com/general-information, last visited 30.3.2018. A similar example is the Public Enterprise "Elektroprivreda Srbije". See: http://eps.rs/en/Pages/Main-information.aspx, last visited 30.3.2018.

to increased legal certainty and improved stakeholder protection in this field — thus, making restructurings more appealing to companies. Additionally, under the new legislation some companies are required to divide their business activities into two or more different legal entities, which makes their restructuring necessary.[2]

The term "restructuring of a company" may be interpreted widely, so as to encompass not only asset deals, but also share deals, both in and outside insolvency. Hence, the main types of restructurings include: asset deals, mergers, divisions, takeovers and reorganisations in bankruptcy. However, the analysis in the present paper shall be limited only to creditor protection in mergers and divisions under Serbian law. Therefore, asset deals, takeovers and reorganisations in bankruptcy are not going to be further elaborated. The described limited scope of analysis may be justified by reasons of simplicity and coherency. Namely, unlike asset deals or reorganisations in bankruptcy, mergers and divisions of companies are regulated at the EU level, which is why these types of restructurings are illustrative of the way Serbia implements the *acquis*. Moreover, the protection of creditors is particularly important in these two cases, as opposed to takeovers where the protection of shareholders of the target company is the legislator's main concern. Finally, in Serbia creditor protection in mergers and divisions is regulated by the same set of rules, which significantly simplifies its explanation by enabling a unified analysis.[3]

The issue of creditor protection in restructurings is highly important, but still open for debate in comparative law. Since the EU law fails to provide precise guidance in this regard, there are currently numerous different national legal regimes governing creditor protection in the Member States. Such a situation makes it even more interesting to present the Serbian approach to the subject. This paper proceeds in two parts. The first part sets forth the Serbian regulatory framework for creditor protection in mergers and divisions, which is contained in the Partnerships and Companies Act of 2011. The second part then details the mechanisms for individual creditor protection prescribed by the Serbian legislator and analyses their suit-

---

2 This is the case with banks and their financial leasing activities, which have to be separated from the banking business within a different legal entity. See: Financial Leasing Act [Zakon o finansijskom lizingu], *Official Gazette of the Republic of Serbia* No. 55/2003, 61/2005, 31/2011, 99/2011, Art. 10 para 5.

3 Partnerships and Companies Act [Zakon o privrednim društvima], *Official Gazette of the Republic of Serbia* No. 36/2011, 99/2011, 83/2014, 5/2015 (hereafter, PCA), Arts. 505 and 509-514.

ability and effectiveness in achieving the intended regulatory goals.[4] Building on the results of the previous analysis the paper concludes with an overall assessment of creditor protection in mergers and divisions in Serbia — its adequacy for protecting these stakeholders while at the same time preserving attractiveness of mergers and divisions as ways of corporate restructuring.

B. *Regulation of Creditor Protection in the Serbian Partnerships and Companies Act*

Under the Stabilisation and Association Agreement concluded with the European Communities and their Member States, Serbia has a duty to harmonise its national law with the *acquis communautaire*, especially in the areas relevant to trade.[5] Accordingly, the Serbian legislator started to implement the *acquis* regarding mergers and divisions almost twenty years ago — in the Enterprise Act of 1996.[6] However, the relevant provisions of the Enterprise Act contained only the basics, which is why they were expanded and amended in the next Partnerships and Companies Act of 2004.[7] The same trend was continued seven years later with the enactment of the new Partnerships and Companies Act of 2011 (hereafter, the PCA), which further improved the legal regime and brought it even more in line with the EU law. Hence, its solutions with regard to mergers and divisions are considered the best we have had since the beginning of the process of harmonisation. Today, this Act still constitutes the law in force in Serbia.

When it comes to creditor protection in mergers and divisions, the main purpose of the PCA was to fully and properly implement the Third and the Sixth Company Law Directive.[8] Even though these two directives were

---

4 However, explanation of specific rules on protection of certain groups of creditors, such as debenture- holders and holders of securities to which special rights are attached is left out of deliberations in this paper.

5 Stabilisation and Association Agreement between European Communities and their Member States, of the one part, and the Republic of Serbia, of the other part, *Official Journal of the European Union* L 278, 18.10.2013, pp. 16-471, Art. 72 para 3.

6 Former Enterprise Act [Zakon o preduzećima], *Official Gazette of the FRY* No. 29/96, 33/96, 29/97, 59/98, 74/99, Art. 421 ff.

7 Former Partnerships and Companies Act [Zakon o privrednim društvima], *Official Gazette of the Republic of Serbia* No. 125/2004, Art. 377 ff.

8 To be precise, the relevant provisions of the Serbian Partnerships and Companies Act were based on the Directive 2011/35/EU concerning mergers of public limited liability companies which is the successor of the former Third Company Law Di-

subsequently superseded by the single new Company Law Directive,[9] all solutions regarding creditor protection have been completely taken over by this latest codification.[10] Since the relevant provisions in the current EU law remain the same, the Serbian PCA in principle continues to be in accordance with the *acquis*. However, bearing in mind that especially in the field of creditor protection the EU lawmaker leaves many questions open and gives a lot of options to the Member States, the Serbian national legal regime has its particularities despite such minimum harmonisation.

Under the EU influence, the PCA regulates all major types of mergers and divisions: mergers by acquisition, mergers by formation of a new company, divisions by acquisition, divisions by formation of a new company and spinoffs (also known as "partial divisions").[11] In all these situations there is a company that is transferring its assets and liabilities to one or more other companies. Unfortunately, the Company Law Directive uses different terms for denoting these companies — the former is called either "a company being acquired", in case of a merger, or "a company being divided" in case of a division, whereas the latter is called either "an acquiring company", in case of a merger, or "a recipient company", in case of a division.[12] Unlike the Directive, the PCA adopted a unified terminology for both mergers and divisions, so that the term "transferring company" refers to the company being acquired/divided, whilst the term "acquiring company" covers not only an acquiring company in a merger, but also a recipient company in a division.[13] In order to avoid unnecessary complexity of the

---

rective, as well as the Directive 82/891/EEC concerning the division of public limited liability companies which is also known as the Sixth Company Law Directive. See: Directive 2011/35/EU of the European Parliament and of the Council of 5 April 2011 concerning mergers of public limited liability companies, *Official Journal of the European Union* L 110, 29.4.2011, pp. 1-11; Sixth Council Directive of 17 December 1982 based on Art. 54(3)(g) of the Treaty, concerning the division of public limited liability companies (82/891/EEC), *Official Journal of the European Communities* L 378, 31.12.1982, pp. 47-54.

9 Directive (EU) 2017/1132 relating to certain aspects of company law, *Official Journal of the European Union* L 169, 30.6.2017, pp. 46-127 (hereafter, Company Law Directive).

10 Namely, the current Company Law Directive represents merely a codification of former directives in the field of company law without any substantial changes as to their texts.

11 See: PCA, Arts. 485-489. Spinoff denotes a partial division in which a company being divided does not cease to exist after transferring a part of its assets and liabilities to one or more other companies.

12 Company Law Directive, Art. 109 para 1 and Art. 136 para 3.

13 PCA, Art. 483 para 1.

text, in the present paper the terminology embraced by the PCA shall be given preference.

The PCA contains a common set of provisions regarding creditor protection in both mergers and divisions. The only differentiation between mergers and divisions in the prescribed regime arises from the fact that in a division there are two or more acquiring companies. This in itself inevitably leads to greater complexity of the rules on liability of those acquiring companies for obligations of the transferring company. Furthermore, the PCA provisions on creditor protection are equally applicable to all types of companies (i.e. not only public limited liability companies, but also limited liability companies), as well as partnerships (i.e. general and limited partnerships). Such a scope of application is wider than the one embraced by the Company Law Directive, albeit fully in accordance with its minimum harmonisation approach. With respect to domestic mergers and divisions the relevant provisions of the Directive are aimed at regulating solely public limited liability companies.[14] However, this means that the EU rules are sometimes better suited for exactly those types of large companies. Therefore, it may not be optimal to simply transpose all these provisions to small and medium-sized enterprises, without ascertaining that this will not impair the efficiency of their restructuring.

Although under the Company Law Directive Member States are allowed to expand the application of the same set of rules to cooperatives,[15] the Serbian PCA remains silent on the issue. Despite that, the Serbian Cooperatives Act prescribes that provisions of the PCA also apply to cooperatives by way of analogy.[16] As a result, in Serbia creditors are afforded the same level of protection even in restructurings of cooperatives. In addition, the EU law empowers Member States to apply the same legal regime even to companies which are the subject of bankruptcy proceedings.[17] Hence, in Serbia this is made possible by the Bankruptcy Act, according to which mergers and divisions constitute one possible reorganisation measure for the insolvency debtor.[18] Moreover, under Serbian law, reorganisation measures are regulated by the same legal acts that generally regulate those types

14 Company Law Directive, Art. 87 para 1 and Art. 135 para 1, Annex I – Types of Companies Referred to in Arts. 2(1) and (2), Arts. 44(1) and (2), Art. 45(2), Arts. 87(1) and (2) and Art. 135(1).

15 Company Law Directive, Art. 87 para 2 and Art. 135 para 4.

16 Cooperatives Act [Zakon o zadrugama], *Official Gazette of the Republic of Serbia* No. 112/2015, Art. 13.

17 Company Law Directive, Art. 87 para 3 and Art. 135 para 4.

18 Bankruptcy Act [Zakon o stečaju], Art. 157 para 1 point 15.

of transactions outside of bankruptcy.[19] Consequently, such regulation further widens the scope of application of the relevant provisions of the PCA, which are to be applied also in cases of mergers and divisions as measures of reorganisation in bankruptcy. On the other hand, the Serbian PCA explicitly prohibits mergers or divisions where a company being acquired or ceasing to exist (i.e. the transferring company) is in liquidation, regardless of the fact that the company may not have begun to distribute its assets yet.[20]

Finally, under the PCA protection afforded to the creditors is the same for creditors of all companies involved in a merger or a division. Thus, we have not used the option given by the Company Law Directive to differentiate between creditors of the transferring company and creditors of the acquiring company in this regard.[21] In other words, the prescribed level of protection applies equally to both these groups of stakeholders.

According to the Company Law Directive, only creditors "whose claims antedate [i.e. existed before] the publication of the draft terms of merger or division and have not fallen due at the time of such publication" deserve extra protection.[22] The *ratio legis* of the first part of this provision lies in the idea that every person who becomes a creditor after the publication of the draft terms of merger (or division) knowingly and willingly takes a risk that the announced corporate change might negatively affect his position. Since all new creditors after such publication know or ought to know about the planned merger (or division), it is assumed that they can require some security from the debtor in advance, which makes additional regulatory protection unnecessary.[23] Finally, the idea behind the last part of the cited provision is that the creditors whose claims have fallen due at the time of publication of the draft terms of merger (or division) are already

---

19 Vuk Radović, *Bankruptcy Law – Volume II* [*Stečajno pravo – knjiga druga*] (2017), 232.

20 See: PCA, Art. 484 para 2.

21 Company Law Directive, Art. 99 para 3 and Art. 146 para 4.

22 See: Company Law Directive, Art. 99 para 1 and Art. 146 para 1.

23 This, of course, makes sense only for creditors whose claims arise from a contractual relationship with the debtor. Namely, only these creditors willingly and knowingly enter into an obligational relationship with their debtor. However, the same does not hold true for creditors whose claims arise from their debtor's tort liability. These creditors neither have the possibility to decide on the personality of their debtor nor are they in a position to secure their claims beforehand.

entitled to receive satisfaction and are, therefore, protected by the general rules on compulsory enforcement.[24]

Unlike the explained provision of the Company Law Directive, in Serbia all creditors whose claims antedate the registration of the merger (or division) are afforded protection.[25] In other words, if a creditor's claim existed at the time the merger or division took effect, he is protected by specific provisions of the PCA. Such a rule represents an extension of the scope of protection provided under the EU law, in two ways. On the one hand, pursuant to the cited provision of the Serbian PCA, the relevant point in time for determining the circle of protected creditors is set later than the one prescribed by the Directive. Consequently, in Serbian law protection is afforded also to creditors whose claims arise after the publication of the draft terms of merger (or division) until the registration of this corporate change.[26] On the other hand, under the afore-mentioned provision of the Serbian PCA it is irrelevant whether a creditor's claim has fallen due at the time the merger (or division) takes effect. This means that even creditors whose claims have become mature before the registration of the merger (or division) can benefit from specific protection prescribed by the PCA. Conversely, according to the Company Law Directive such creditors are excluded from the circle of protected creditors. It can be concluded that, in comparison to the *acquis*, the Serbian PCA covers a potentially larger number of creditors. Nevertheless, the described extension of the scope of application by the Serbian legislator is indisputably allowed, since the Directive contains only minimum harmonisation in this respect.[27]

---

24 Cf. Alexander Naraschewski, "Gläubigerschutz bei der Verschmelzung von GmbH", *GmbHR* 8/1998, 356 (356); Manuela Heiss, "Gläubigerschutz bei der Unternehmensspaltung", *DZWir* 1/1993, 12 (14); Seulen in Semler/Stengel, UmwG (2017), § 22 Rn. 36; Müller in Henssler/Strohn, *Gesellschaftsrecht*, UmwG § 22 Rn. 7. For a critical approach, see: Stefan Grundmann, *Europäisches Gesellschaftsrecht* (2011), 534 and 535.

25 PCA, Art. 509 para 1.

26 Regrettably, in Serbian legal theory and practice it has still not been discussed when a claim is deemed to have arisen for the purposes of these provisions.

27 Moreover, widening the scope of creditor protection is not unusual in comparative law. In Germany, for example, the circle of protected creditors is even wider, since it encompasses all creditors whose claims had their legal foundation before the date on which the division took effect. See: Karsten Schmidt, "Gläubigerschutz bei Umstrukturierungen – Zum Referentenentwurf eines Umwandlungsgesetzes", *ZGR* 1993, 366 (391); Thomas Schröer, "Sicherheitsleistung für Ansprüche aus Dauerschuldverhältnissen bei Unternehmensumwandlungen", *DB* 6/1999, 317 (318); Carsten Jaeger, "Sicherheitsleistung für Ansprüche aus Dauerschuldverhältnissen bei Kapitalherabsetzung, Verschmelzung und Beendigung

Under the Serbian PCA, two classes of creditors are explicitly excluded from the scope of application of the protective provisions. The first class covers those creditors who would fall into the first or the second payment line in case of their debtor's insolvency.[28] The second class encompasses creditors whose claims are already secured (i.e. secured creditors). Unfortunately, the Serbian lawmaker failed to explicitly insist on adequate security, as a reason for exclusion from the specifically prescribed system of creditor protection. Therefore, it is not clear whether the courts in Serbia would decline protection to every creditor whose claim was secured at the time the merger (or division) took effect, irrespective of adequacy and coverage of such security in relation to the secured claim. Both of the explained exceptions to the general scope of creditor protection are justified by the fact that the position of those creditors is considered to be already secure, which is why it is needless to apply any extra protection to them.

C. *Mechanisms for Individual Protection of Creditors*

In Serbian law institutional protection of creditors is highly underdeveloped,[29] bearing in mind that mergers and divisions involving their debtor are allowed also in cases where one or more companies participating in a restructuring are insolvent.[30] Therefore, creditors' claims may be exposed to great risks due to such corporate changes of their debtor. For this reason, the Serbian PCA focuses primarily on ensuring individual protection of creditors,[31] by prescribing various specific rights each of them may individ-

---

eines Unternehmensvertrages", *DB* 21/1996, 1069 (1069); Seulen in Semler/Stengel, UmwG (2017), § 22 Rn. 10 *et seq.* and § 133 Rn. 11; Müller in Henssler/Strohn, *Gesellschaftsrecht*, UmwG § 22 Rn. 4; Wardenbach in Henssler/Strohn, *Gesellschaftsrecht*, UmwG § 133 Rn. 4.

28 According to the Serbian Bankruptcy Act, the first line of distribution in insolvency includes employees minimum wages for the last year before insolvency, as well as minimum pension and disability insurance contributions for the last two years before insolvency, whereas the second line of distibution involves public revenues for the last three months before insolvency. See: Bankruptcy Act, Art. 54 para 4 points 1 and 2.

29 On the difference between institutional and individual creditor protection in restructurings, see: Karsten Schmidt, "Gläubigerschutz bei Umstrukturierungen – Zum Referentenentwurf eines Umwandlungsgesetzes", *ZGR* 1993, 366 (367).

30 See: PCA, Art. 484 para 2; Vuk Radović, *Bankruptcy Law – Volume II*, 232.

31 Individual creditor protection entitles individualised creditors to claims against companies involved in a restructuring. See: Karsten Schmidt, "Gläubigerschutz

ually exercise when it comes to a merger (or division) involving their debtor. Under the PCA individual protection of creditors is regulated within provisions concerning: 1. duty to inform the creditors;[32] 2. liability of the companies involved in a restructuring;[33] 3. right to obtain adequate safeguards;[34] and 4. specific judicial protection of creditors.[35] On the other hand, creditors are not given the right to challenge the shareholders' decision about the merger (or division), nor do they have the so-called "veto right" against the planned merger (or division). Since creditors cannot oppose to this corporate change (i.e. cannot block the merger/division), the Serbian legislator mainly concentrates on ensuring their adequate protection.

I. Duty to Inform the Creditors

Notwithstanding the fact that a duty to inform the creditors is not specifically prescribed by the Company Law Directive, such a duty indisputably constitutes a necessary precondition for exercising creditors' rights and, hence, for their effective protection. Namely, if the creditors do not know about the intended merger (or division), they cannot actively request adequate protection of their rights *ex ante* before such corporate change takes effect and their debtor either ceases to exist or acquires the business of the transferring company. Consequently, it is clear that the creditors need to be properly informed about the planned merger (or division) in advance.

The Serbian PCA prescribes two ways of informing the creditors about the planned merger (or division). This is done through introducing: (a) a general duty towards all the creditors; and (b) a special duty towards a specific type of creditors. A general duty to inform all the creditors about the merger (or division) burdens each company involved in a restructuring. Such a duty is performed through publication of the draft terms of merger/division on the company's website (if the company has got one) and on the

bei Umstrukturierungen – Zum Referentenentwurf eines Umwandlungsgesetzes", *ZGR* 1993, 366 (367).

32 PCA, Arts. 495 and 497.

33 PCA, Arts. 505 and 506.

34 PCA, Arts. 509 and 510.

35 PCA, Art. 511.

website of the Serbian Agency for Business Registers.[36] The truth is that the companies involved in a merger (or division) primarily owe this duty to their shareholders, but the PCA explicitly considers that the creditors are thereby informed about the intended corporate change as well.[37] The information given on the company's website and the website of the Serbian Agency for Business Registers needs to be available online at least one month before the date fixed for the general meeting which is to decide on the merger (or division). Furthermore, it should be available free of charge and without the need for identification of the person trying to gain access.[38] As a result, creditors will normally become informed about the intended merger through publication of the necessary documents on the internet.

Unlike the general duty to inform, a special duty to inform is specifically prescribed for the purpose of aiding creditor protection. Here, every company involved in a merger (or division) has a duty to inform about the planned corporate change each creditor that is known to the company and whose claim amounts to at least 2,000,000 Serbian dinars (around 17,000 euros) on the day of publication of the draft terms of merger.[39] These creditors have the right to be individually informed about the planned merger (or division) by way of a written notice which contains the same elements as the draft terms of merger/division. Moreover, such individual information also needs to reach the creditors at least one month before the date fixed for the general meeting which is to decide on the merger (or division).[40] It is worth noting that the relevant point in time for determining the circle of creditors, who have the right to be individually informed, is different from the relevant point in time for determining the creditors, who are afforded specific protection in case of a merger (or division). Namely, whereas in the former case only creditors on the day of publication of the draft terms of merger/division shall be individually informed, in the latter case even creditors whose claims arose after the day of publication of the draft terms of merger/division but before the day of registration of the merger (or division) shall be specifically protected.[41]

36 See: PCA, Art. 495 para 1. The Serbian Agency for Business Registers serves, *inter alia*, as a company register, where all Serbian companies are registered, including their corporate changes, such as mergers or divisions.

37 PCA, Art. 495 para 6.

38 PCA, Art. 495 para 2.

39 See: PCA, Art. 497 para 1.

40 *Ibid.*

41 Cf. PCA, Art. 497 para 1 and Art. 509 para 1.

II. Liability of the Companies

Prescribing liability of the companies involved in a merger (or division) for obligations of the transferring company represents an important mechanism of creditor protection. A merger or division results in a transfer of assets and liabilities from one legal entity to another without the need for creditors' consent, and, as a rule, leads to termination of the transferring company.[42] Hence, it is essential for creditors to know against which company and under which legal regime they can successfully enforce their claims after such corporate change takes effect. Bearing in mind that the Company Law Directive leaves it to the Member States to determine the date on which a merger or a division takes effect,[43] the Serbian legislator has chosen the date of registration as the relevant point in time in this regard. Thus, mergers and divisions of companies in Serbia are effectuated by registration in the Agency for Business Registers.[44] Determining the date of registration is of great legal significance, since from that moment a merger or division produces certain prescribed legal consequences — one of them being the liability of the acquiring companies for obligations of the transferring company.

In Serbian law, unlike the Company Law Directive, liability of the companies is regulated as one of the *ex lege* consequences of a merger or division, and not as a specific mechanism for individual creditor protection. In this regard, the Serbian PCA, much like the *acquis*, differentiates between: 1. liability of the successor company; and 2. liability of other acquiring (recipient) companies. In addition, the PCA contains specific rules on liability in case of a spinoff (i.e. partial division). Finally, special attention is given to liability for the so-called "forgotten obligations", that were not allocated to any of the acquiring companies by the draft terms of division.

1. *Liability of the successor company*: The successor company is the one acquiring company to which obligations of the company being acquired or divided are transferred through universal succession. Irrespective of the fact that universal succession is not explicitly mentioned by the Serbian PCA, it is undisputedly accepted as a legal consequence of every merger or div-

---

42 An exception is possible only in cases of spinoffs (i.e. partial divisions), where the company being divided continues to exist even after transferring a part of its assets and liabilities to one or more other companies.

43 Company Law Directive, Arts. 103 and 149.

44 PCA, Art. 505 para 1.

ision.[45] Universal succession results in an *en bloc* transfer of assets and liabilities of the company being acquired or divided to the acquiring company according to the draft terms of such corporate change.[46] This happens automatically (i.e. *ex lege*) on the day of registration of the merger or division.[47] In this way the afore-mentioned successor company becomes the primary debtor of a particular obligation and is liable to the creditor in the same way, or to the same extent as the former debtor (i.e. the transferring company).[48]

2. *Liability of other acquiring (recipient) companies*: Previous deliberations have shown that the draft terms of merger (or division) have a decisive role in determining which acquiring company becomes a universal successor and with regard to which obligations of the transferring company. Since in case of a merger there is only one acquiring company to which all assets and liabilities of the company being acquired are transferred, the situation is rather straightforward — the only acquiring company becomes the successor company, which is liable to all the creditors for obligations of the (now former) transferring company. However, the situation is not at all as simple in case of a division. Here, a company being divided transfers its assets and liabilities to two or more acquiring companies, so that each ac-

45 Mirko S. Vasiljević, *Company Law – The Law of Business Organizations* [*Kompanijsko pravo – Pravo privrednih društava*] (2017), 518. The relevant provisions of the Company Law Directive are interpreted the same way, so as to embrace universal succession as a way of transferring assets and liabilities in accordance with the draft terms of merger/division. See: Martin Heidenhain, "Fehlerhafte Umsetzung der Spaltungs-Richtlinie", *EuZW* 11/1995, 327 (328 and 329).

46 Cf. J.E. Goudsmit, *The Pandects – A Treatise on Roman Law and upon Its Connection with Modern Legislation* (2005), 118 and 119; Stefan Schröcker, *Datenschutz und Universalsukzession bei Verschmelzungen nach dem Umwandlungsgesetz* (2006), 41; Arndt Teichmann, "Die Spaltung von Rechtsträgern als Akt der Vermögensübertragung", *ZGR* 1993, 396 (398); Martin Heidenhain, "Fehlerhafte Umsetzung der Spaltungs-Richtlinie", *EuZW* 11/1995, 327 (328).

47 Martin Heidenhain, "Fehlerhafte Umsetzung der Spaltungs-Richtlinie", *EuZW* 11/1995, 327 (329); Harald Stingl, *Gesamtrechtsnachfolge im Gesellschaftsrecht: Verschmelzung, Umwandlung, Spaltung, Anwachsung* (2016), 2; Tatjana Jevremović Petrović, *Cross-border Mergers of Companies in the EU Law* [*Prekogranična spajanja društava u pravu EU*] (2010), 312.

48 Mirjana Radović, "Liability of the Recipient Company for Debts of the Company being Divided in Case of Divisions and Spinoffs [*Odgovornost društva sticaoca za obaveze društva prenosioca kod statusnih promena podele i izdvajanja*]" in Vuk Radović (ed.), *Harmonisation of Serbian Business Law with the European Union Law* [*Usklađivanje poslovnog prava Srbije sa pravom Evropske unije (2017)*] (2017), 145 (174).

quiring company receives merely a portion of those assets and liabilities according to the draft terms of division.[49] In other words, the successor company to which certain assets and liabilities are transferred in accordance with the draft terms of division represents only a partial universal successor of the transferring company.[50]

Bearing in mind that in case of a division the successor company acquires not all, but just a portion of assets of the previous debtor, creditors' interests would be seriously jeopardised, if we left things at that — namely, if the successor company were the only debtor creditors could turn to from now on. Being that the compensation for assets transfer resulting from a division goes directly to the shareholders and not to the transferring company itself,[51] this reduces the amount of assets creditors can use for satisfaction of their claims.[52] Additionally, the amount of cash flow, which can also be an important source for satisfying creditors' claims, is usually lower in the successor company than in the company being divided.[53] This further impairs creditors' position. Finally, after becoming creditors of the successor company, they now have to compete with this company's own creditors, which potentially diminishes their chances of obtaining satisfaction.[54] All these things coupled together pose specific risks for creditors in case their debtor decides to restructure its business through division.

There is no doubt that creditors would prefer to be able to satisfy their claims against each and every acquiring company, instead of just the successor company. Hence, from the creditors point of view, the best solution would be the unlimited joint and several liability of all acquiring com-

49 PCA, Art. 488 para 1.

50 Cf. Harald Stingl, *Gesamtrechtsnachfolge im Gesellschaftsrecht: Verschmelzung, Umwandlung, Spaltung, Anwachsung* (2016) 10; Sagasser and Bultmann in Sagasser/Bula/Brünger, *Umwandlungen*, § 18 Rn. 49.

51 Seulen in Semler/Stengel, UmwG (2017), § 133 Rn. 1.

52 Thomas Schröer, "Sicherheitsleistung für Ansprüche aus Dauerschuldverhältnissen bei Unternehmensumwandlungen", *DB* 6/1999, 317 (317); Volker Rieble, "Verschmelzung und Spaltung von Unternehmen und ihre Folgen für Schuldverhältnisse mit Dritten", *ZIP* 8/1997, 301 (302); Manuela Heiss, "Gläubigerschutz bei der Unternehmensspaltung", *DZWir* 1/1993, 12 (13).

53 Cf. Manuela Heiss, "Gläubigerschutz bei der Unternehmensspaltung", *DZWir* 1/1993, 12 and 13-14.

54 Felix Blobel and Michael Menz, "Die Auswirkungen von Schuldner- und Gläubigerwechsel auf die Spaltungshaftung nach § 133 UmwG", *NZG* 2009, 608 (608); Thomas Schröer, "Sicherheitsleistung für Ansprüche aus Dauerschuldverhältnissen bei Unternehmensumwandlungen", *DB* 6/1999, 317 (317); cf. Martin Heidenhain, "Fehlerhafte Umsetzung der Spaltungs-Richtlinie", *EuZW* 11/1995, 327 (329).

panies with regard to all obligations of the transferring company. Indeed, such a solution would enable the creditors to enforce their claims against all assets of their original debtor, notwithstanding the fact that these assets now belong to different legal persons.[55] It may be interesting to note that the afore-mentioned unlimited joint and several liability of all acquiring companies was the law in Serbia before the current PCA came into force.[56] However, nowadays it is considered as an overprotection of creditors and a barrier to effectuating a division, which makes this type of restructuring significantly less attractive to companies.[57]

For this reason, the crucial task of every legislator is to find the optimal level of creditor protection when regulating liability of the acquiring companies. This can be done through different ways of limiting liability of the acquiring companies for obligations with regard to which they did not become successors of the company being divided. However, the given task is rather complicated, especially for the Serbian lawmaker, which neither has the means nor the time and expertise to seriously deal with these issues. That is why it is only natural to look to the *acquis* for guidance in this respect. And yet, the *acquis* has failed to provide a clear and defined model for regulating liability of the companies involved in a division. Instead, the relevant provisions of the Company Law Directive offer many options to the Member States.[58] Such regulation makes it difficult to determine what, if any, minimum of creditors' protection through liability of the acquiring companies is required from the Member States.

Under the Serbian PCA, other acquiring companies, to which a particular obligation was not transferred according to the draft terms of division, are subsidiarily jointly and severally liable to the creditor.[59] In the Serbian

55 Cf. Felix Blobel and Michael Menz, "Die Auswirkungen von Schuldner- und Gläubigerwechsel auf die Spaltungshaftung nach § 133 UmwG", *NZG* 2009, 608 (609); Manuela Heiss, "Gläubigerschutz bei der Unternehmensspaltung", *DZWir* 1/1993, 12 (14).

56 Therefore, all companies involved in a division were jointly and severally liable for all obligations of the company being divided, while at the same time such liability was unlimited. See: former Partnerships and Companies Act 2004, Art. 413 para 2 and Art. 417.

57 Cf. Arndt Teichmann, "Die Spaltung von Rechtsträgern als Akt der Vermögensübertragung", *ZGR* 1993, 396 (417); Karsten Schmidt, "Gläubigerschutz bei Umstrukturierungen – Zum Referentenentwurf eines Umwandlungsgesetzes", *ZGR* 1993, 366 (388).

58 Cf. Martin Heidenhain, "Fehlerhafte Umsetzung der Spaltungs-Richtlinie", *EuZW* 11/1995, 327 (329).

59 PCA, Art. 505 para 3 point 3.

judicial practice subsidiary liability means that these companies shall be liable if the successor company does not fulfil its obligation after a written request from the creditor.[60] Hence, the creditor does not need to exhaust all legal means to obtain satisfaction (such as, litigation, judgment, compulsory execution), but is merely required to request from a successor company in writing to fulfil its obligation.[61] After the successor company fails to comply, the creditor can turn to the other acquiring companies. Lastly, the liability of other acquiring companies is limited up to the value of net assets allocated to each of those companies according to the draft terms of division.[62] The PCA explicitly prescribes that the value of net assets is calculated as the difference between the value of assets and the value of obligations transferred to that particular acquiring company in accordance with the draft terms of division.[63] The relevant moment for determining these values should be the moment in which the division takes effect.[64]

The presented regulation of liability is at first glance harmonised with the EU law. However, there is one important, additional provision, that should not be overlooked. Namely, under the PCA the rules on liability of the acquiring companies do not apply, if the creditor has otherwise obtained adequate protection (i.e. through security, contract amendments, etc.).[65] This actually means that the liability of other acquiring companies represents a secondary mechanism of creditor protection, which comes into play only when other mechanisms do not adequately protect the creditor in a particular case. In other words, such liability is construed as an alternative mechanism, which shall be overridden whenever the creditor successfully exercises his right to obtain adequate safeguards. It can be concluded, that Serbian law in this respect changed from previous mandatory unlimited joint and several liability of all acquiring companies, to current

60 M.S. Vasiljević, *Company Law – The Law of Business Organizations [Kompanijsko pravo – Pravo privrednih društava]*, (2017) 97. Similarly, the Company Law Directive prescribes that joint and several liability of the acquiring companies shall exist if the creditor of the company to which the obligation has been transferred in accordance with the draft terms of division has not obtained *satisfaction* of his claim. See: Company Law Directive, Art. 146 para 3; Martin Heidenhain, "Fehlerhafte Umsetzung der Spaltungs-Richtlinie", *EuZW* 11/1995, 327 (329).

61 Mirko S. Vasiljević, *Company Law – The Law of Business Organizations [Kompanijsko pravo – Pravo privrednih društava]*, (2017) 97.

62 PCA, Art. 505 para 3 point 3.

63 *Ibid.*

64 Cf. Manuela Heiss, "Gläubigerschutz bei der Unternehmensspaltung", *DZWir* 1/1993, 12 (15).

65 PCA, Art. 505 para 5.

limited, subsidiary liability that is conditional upon failure to provide adequate protection of creditor through other mechanisms.[66]

Finally, the question remains whether the solution adopted in Serbian law is fully in accordance with the EU law. Unfortunately, this is still open to debate, bearing in mind the ambiguity of Article 146 of the Company Law Directive, which can be interpreted in two opposite ways. On the one hand, if primacy is given to paragraph 2 of the same Article, which says that "Member States shall at least provide that [...] creditors shall be entitled to obtain adequate safeguards", we might conclude that paragraph 3, which regulates liability of the acquiring companies, is not needed whenever such minimum adequate safeguards exist. On the other hand, one might argue that paragraph 3 regulating liability of the acquiring companies is applicable in any case, irrespective of other adequate safeguards.[67] The main argument to support this interpretation lies in the explicit provision of the Company Law Directive, according to which Member States need not apply paragraph 3 where the division operation is subject to supervision of a judicial authority and a majority of creditors has agreed to forego such joint and several liability.[68] Why would the Directive have this rule, if it does not consider liability of the acquiring companies to be otherwise mandatory?

Be that as it may, the Serbian solution seems questionable in any case. Prescribing liability of the acquiring companies as merely an alternative mechanism potentially undermines the whole system of creditor protection. Looking from the employees' perspective, such regulation means that their rights against the acquiring companies will often depend on whether or not the protection they already got was "adequate". However, it goes without saying that "adequacy" is not a clear and undisputed fact, but needs to be assessed on a case-by-case basis. This fact alone can result in creditors starting a litigation against the acquiring company they actually had no right to pursue, even though their claim against the successor company might be undisputed. Furthermore, it seems that the current Serbian solution is not even in the interest of the acquiring companies, since it pre-

66 It may be interesting to note that the same solution currently exists in Croatia. See: Croatian Companies Act [*Zakon o trgovačkim društvima*] (Consolidated Version from 2011, available at: https://narodne-novine.nn.hr/clanci/sluzbeni/2011_12_152_3144.html, last visited 31.3.2018), Art. 550.o para 4.

67 Cf. Martin Heidenhain, "Fehlerhafte Umsetzung der Spaltungs-Richtlinie", *EuZW* 11/1995, 327 (329).

68 For a detailed rule see: Company Law Directive, Art. 146 para 3.

vents them from having a clear grasp of their obligations resulting from the division.

3. *Specific rules regarding spinoffs*: Since in case of a spinoff (also known as "partial division") the transferring company does not cease to exist after registration of such corporate change, there are two possible scenarios relevant to liability of the companies involved. On the one hand, if according to the draft terms of division a certain obligation is allocated to the transferring company, that company remains primarily liable to the creditors.[69] In other words, the transferring company continues to be liable in the same way and to the same extent as before the spinoff. Additionally, each acquiring company is jointly and severally liable to the creditor for the obligation of the transferring company, albeit up to the value of net assets allocated according to the draft terms of division.[70] It is interesting to note that, here, the Serbian legislator does not prescribe subsidiary liability of the acquiring companies.[71]

On the other hand, if according to the draft terms of division a certain obligation is allocated to one of the acquiring companies, that acquiring company indisputably becomes the primary debtor, who is unlimitedly liable to the creditor in the same way and to the same extent as the transferring company.[72] However, the PCA does not regulate the legal position of the transferring company in this case, nor the legal position of other acquiring companies. Bearing in mind that the spinoff represents a corporate change, which is executed voluntarily by the transferring company irrespective of the creditors' possible dissent, the transferring company should not be allowed to unilaterally limit its liability for certain obligations in

---

69 Mirjana Radović, "Liability of the Recipient Company for Debts of the Company being Divided in Case of Divisions and Spinoffs [*Odgovornost društva sticaoca za obaveze društva prenosioca kod statusnih promena podele i izdvajanja*]", 145 (174).

70 PCA, Art. 505(1)(2).

71 A similar solution existed in the former Serbian law, according to which acquiring companies were also jointly and severally liable for obligations of the transferring company in case of a spinoff. However, such liability was unlimited. See: Judgment of the Higher Commercial Court, Pz. 7604/95 from 15.12.1995, *Court Practice of Commercial Courts – Bulletin* [*Sudska praksa privrednih sudova – Bilten*] No. 1/1996, 57.

72 Mirjana Radović, "Liability of the Recipient Company for Debts of the Company being Divided in Case of Divisions and Spinoffs [*Odgovornost društva sticaoca za obaveze društva prenosioca kod statusnih promena podele i izdvajanja*]", 145 (175). Cf. PCA, Art. 505 para 1 point 1.

this way.[73] Therefore, it should be held that the liability of the transferring company to the creditor remains primary and unlimited. The stated conclusion is also in accordance with the Company Law Directive, pursuant to which limiting liability is only possible for the acquiring companies.[74] When it comes to other acquiring companies, the existing legal gap in the Serbian PCA can be filled by way of analogy with the rules on divisions. Consequently, other acquiring companies shall become subsidiarily jointly and severally liable for the given obligation of the transferring company, whereas their liability is limited to the value of net assets allocated to each of them.[75]

4. *Liability for forgotten obligations*: Under the influence of the Company Law Directive, the PCA contains specific rules with regard to the so-called forgotten obligations, i.e. the ones that were not allocated to a particular acquiring company in the draft terms of division.[76] The problem of forgotten obligations is actually only relevant to divisions, but not to spinoffs, being that in spinoffs all obligations not (explicitly or impliedly) allocated by the draft terms of division, remain with the transferring company, which continues to exist even after this corporate change.[77] Unlike that, after a division takes effect, the company being divided ceases to exist, which is why it is essential to resolve the issue of allocating forgotten obligations between the acquiring companies.

The Serbian PCA prescribes that all acquiring companies shall be jointly and severally liable for forgotten obligations, although their liability is limited to the value of net assets allocated to each of those companies.[78] Since the Company Law Directive gives Member States the option to limit

---

73 Mirjana Radović, "Liability of the Recipient Company for Debts of the Company being Divided in Case of Divisions and Spinoffs [*Odgovornost društva sticaoca za obaveze društva prenosioca kod statusnih promena podele i izdvajanja*]", 145 (175).

74 Company Law Directive, Art. 146 para 3.

75 PCA, Art. 505 para 3 point 3.

76 Cf. Martin Heidenhain, "Spaltungsvertrag und Spaltungsplan", *NJW* 44/1995, 2873 (2878); Seulen in Semler/Stengel, *UmwG* (2017), § 133 Rn. 37; Arndt Teichmann, "Die Spaltung von Rechtsträgern als Akt der Vermögensübertragung", *ZGR* 1993, 396 (414); Volker Rieble, "Verschmelzung und Spaltung von Unternehmen und ihre Folgen für Schuldverhältnisse mit Dritten", *ZIP* 8/1997, 301 (303); Karsten Schmidt, "Gläubigerschutz bei Umstrukturierungen – Zum Referentenentwurf eines Umwandlungsgesetzes", *ZGR* 1993, 366 (387).

77 Cf. Seulen in Semler/Stengel, UmwG 4. A., § 133 Rn. 37.

78 PCA, Art. 506 para 2.

the liability of acquiring companies in case of forgotten obligations,[79] it can be concluded that the Serbian law is in that sense completely harmonised with the EU law. Nevertheless, the adopted solution seems doubtful and unjustified. Namely, limiting liability of the acquiring companies for forgotten obligations of the transferring company potentially impairs the position of those creditors, who most likely did not have the chance to require some other protective measure beforehand — that is, before the division took effect and their debtor ceased to exist.[80] As a consequence, these very creditors are confined to satisfying their claims only up to the value of net assets of the company that was divided. However, this value is fixed in the moment company being divided ceased to exist and, therefore, cannot be subsequently increased even in case of business success of the acquiring companies. Such an outcome is contrary to the fundamental understanding of divisions, which are based on continuity of an enterprise, rather than its liquidation.

III. Right to Obtain Adequate Safeguards

Given that the liability of companies involved in a merger or division is regulated as merely an alternative mechanism of creditor protection, the main set of rules creditors can rely upon when such a corporate change jeopardises their chances of satisfaction concerns the right to obtain adequate safeguards. Thus, the Serbian PCA enables those creditors who believe that the merger (or division) will negatively affect satisfaction of their claims to require obtaining adequate safeguards.[81] As with all other mechanisms of creditor protection, here, again the protected group of creditors are the ones whose claims existed at the time of registration of the merger or division.[82] In contrast to the approach embraced by the Company Law Directive, under the Serbian PCA even creditors, whose claims have already fallen due at the time the merger or division takes effect, are afforded

79 Company Law Directive, Art. 137 para 3 subpara 2.

80 Mirjana Radović, "Liability of the Recipient Company for Debts of the Company being Divided in Case of Divisions and Spinoffs [*Odgovornost društva sticaoca za obaveze društva prenosioca kod statusnih promena podele i izdvajanja*]", 145 (176).

81 PCA, Art. 509 para 1.

82 *Ibid.* Cf. Thomas Schröer, "Sicherheitsleistung für Ansprüche aus Dauerschuldverhältnissen bei Unternehmensumwandlungen", *DB* 6/1999, 317 (318).

protection through the right to obtain adequate safeguards.[83] Hence, although creditors with matured claims can already commence compulsory enforcement proceedings against the debtor, this is not perceived as an obstacle for them to request additional (adequate) safeguards.

There are two exempt groups of creditors, that are not granted the right to obtain adequate safeguards in case of a merger (or division) involving their debtor. The first group encompasses creditors that would fall into the first or the second tier of distribution if their debtor went bankrupt.[84] It is not clear why the Serbian legislator considers this group of creditors to be "safe" from any risks in case of a merger or division involving their debtor. Quite the contrary, there are numerous examples in practice, where bankruptcy estate was found to be insufficient even for covering the costs of bankruptcy proceedings, let alone satisfying creditors of the first and the second tier of distribution. In that sense, it seems more justified to adopt the same solution as in Germany, according to which the right to obtain adequate safeguards is denied to those creditors, who have priority in satisfying their claims from the funds which are specially designated for creditor protection and supervised by the State.[85] The second group of exempt creditors covers all secured creditors.[86] Unfortunately, the PCA does not specify that only creditors whose security is *adequate* are exempt from protection, but instead refers to all secured creditors.[87] Such use of words may cause problems in practice if, for example, a creditor does have some form of security, yet not enough to cover his entire claim, or has a security that will no longer be adequate after a merger or division of his debtor is exe-

83 Cf. Company Law Directive, Art. 99 paras 1-2 and Art. 146 paras 1-2; Seulen in Semler/Stengel, UmwG (2017), § 133 Rn. 119.

84 PCA, Art. 509 para 2. Under the Serbian Bankruptcy Act, the first two tiers of distribution in bankruptcy proceedings cover creditors with claims such as: employees' minimum wages for the last year before insolvency, minimum contributions for pension and disability insurance for the last two years before insolvency, and public revenues for the last three months before insolvency. See: Bankruptcy Act, Art. 54 para 4 points 1 and 2.

85 Alexander Naraschewski, "Gläubigerschutz bei der Verschmelzung von GmbH", *GmbHR* 8/1998, 356 (356); Thomas Schröer, "Sicherheitsleistung für Ansprüche aus Dauerschuldverhältnissen bei Unternehmensumwandlungen", *DB* 6/1999, 317 (319); Seulen in Semler/Stengel, UmwG (2017), § 22 Rn. 58; Müller in Henssler/Strohn, *Gesellschaftsrecht*, UmwG § 22 Rn. 2 and 8.

86 PCA, Art. 510 para 2 point 2; cf. Manuela Heiss, "Gläubigerschutz bei der Unternehmensspaltung", *DZWir* 1/1993, 12 (14).

87 Cf. Alexander Naraschewski, "Gläubigerschutz bei der Verschmelzung von GmbH", *GmbHR* 8/1998, 356 (356); Seulen in Semler/Stengel, UmwG (2017), § 22 Rn. 60; Müller in Henssler/Strohn, *Gesellschaftsrecht*, UmwG § 22 Rn. 9.

cuted. It seems that the described "minor" deficiency of the legislation may be easily overcome by proper interpretation of the law. This, however, sets too much expectation on Serbian judges, who in principle avoid being "creative" when it comes to interpreting legal rules in company law matters.

The creditors who, based on the previous analysis, do have the right to obtain adequate safeguards, may exercise this right against all companies involved in a merger or division — i.e. not only the transferring company, but also the acquiring companies.[88] However, there are several conditions that need to be fulfilled in order for the creditor to successfully exercise this right. Firstly, the financial situation of the companies involved in the merger (or division) needs to be such that this corporate change jeopardises satisfaction of the creditor's claim.[89] In other words, there needs to be causality between the merger (or division) and the increased risk that the claim will not be satisfied.[90] Secondly, in a particular case adequate safeguards have to be necessary for putting the creditor in a position not less favourable than the one he had before the merger (or division).[91] Thirdly, the creditor has to explicitly request obtaining adequate safeguards from the company.[92] Finally, fourthly, such request needs to be sent to the company within 30 days from the date of publication of the draft terms of merger/division.[93]

The first two of the afore-mentioned conditions are not really precise, but have to be separately assessed and determined in each case — that is, for each claim of the creditor. Furthermore, the burden of proof that these conditions are met lies on the creditor.[94] In that sense, it does not suffice if the creditor merely demonstrates the probability of his claim being jeopardised by the merger (or division).[95] This significantly reduces his chances of succeeding in the intention to obtain adequate safeguards from the

---

88 PCA, Art. 510 para 1. Cf. Müller in Henssler/Strohn, *Gesellschaftsrecht*, UmwG § 22 Rn. 3; Seulen in Semler/Stengel, UmwG (2017), § 133 Rn. 123.

89 *Ibid.*

90 Cf.: Stefan Grundmann, *Europäisches Gesellschaftsrecht*, 535; Seulen in Semler/Stengel, UmwG (2017), § 22 Rn. 20 and 34.

91 PCA, Art. 510 para 1.

92 PCA, Art. 509 para 1.

93 *Ibid.*

94 See: Civil Procedure Act [Zakon o parničnom postupku], *Official Gazette of the Republic of Serbia* No. 72/2011, 49/2013, 74/2013, 55/2014, Art. 228.

95 Contrary to the Serbian solution, German law eases the burden of proof by requesting the creditor to merely show that the merger (or division) will probably jeopardise satisfaction of his claim. See: Alexander Naraschewski, "Gläubiger-

company. Even so, if the creditor somehow manages to prove that all the prescribed conditions are fulfilled, the PCA offers an open list of adequate safeguards he may obtain from the company. These safeguards are enumerated in the PCA only by way of example and encompass: different types of security (i.e. pledge, lien, mortgage, surety or guarantee), contract amendments or cancellation, separate management of assets of the transferring company until the creditor's claim is satisfied in full, etc.[96] However, the legislator failed to clarify whether the creditor or the company is entitled to choose between the many possible types of safeguards. Bearing in mind the nature of those safeguards, it seems that opting for one or several of them needs to be based on an out-of-court agreement between the creditor and the company. Otherwise, the creditor is advised to seek judicial protection, which is specially prescribed for that purpose.

IV. Judicial Protection

In case the creditor does not obtain adequate safeguards, despite exercising this right against the company, the PCA prescribes specific rules on his judicial protection. It goes without saying that the creditor can turn to court for protection of his rights even in other situations (e.g. for damages because he was not duly informed about the merger or division, or for damages because the successor company did not fulfil its obligation, etc.). However, such situations fall under the general rules on civil procedure. On the other hand, when the creditor's right to obtain adequate safeguards is violated, there are specific procedural rules regarding his judicial protection.

First and foremost, a creditor may file a claim to the court, only if he failed to obtain adequate safeguards from the company within 15 days after the date of requesting such safeguards.[97] Another specific provision regarding creditor's judicial protection concerns an interim measure that the

schutz bei der Verschmelzung von GmbH", *GmbHR* 8/1998, 356 (356); Karsten Schmidt, "Gläubigerschutz bei Umstrukturierungen – Zum Referentenentwurf eines Umwandlungsgesetzes", *ZGR* 1993, 366 (382); Thomas Schröer, "Sicherheitsleistung für Ansprüche aus Dauerschuldverhältnissen bei Unternehmensumwandlungen", *DB* 6/1999, 317 (317); Seulen in Semler/Stengel, UmwG (2017), § 22 Rn. 20 and 35; Müller in Henssler/Strohn, *Gesellschaftsrecht*, UmwG § 22 Rn. 10.

96 PCA, Art. 509 para 2.

97 PCA, Art. 511 para 1.

court can adopt. Namely, under the PCA the court is allowed to temporarily prohibit the execution of the planned merger or division upon request.[98] The said measure is taken provisionally while the court continues its examination of the case and, thus, constitutes a valuable tool of creditor protection. However, the courts need to be cautious when deciding on this measure, bearing in mind that it may not serve as a disguised veto right of the creditors, that would enable them to have a say on the merger or division. For this reason, the PCA prescribes that the interim measure can be adopted only if this is necessary and justified in order to protect the creditor.[99] The two conditions regarding necessity and justification need to be interpreted strictly, so that the prohibition of executing a merger would remain merely an exception to the general rule that creditors cannot decide on the merger or division nor interfere with its execution.

Unfortunately, when regulating further conditions for adopting the afore-mentioned interim measure, the legislator obviously made a mistake, by requiring that it can be adopted only "at the request of the company".[100] Clearly, it is illogical that the company would ever request the prohibition of executing the planned merger or division — quite the contrary, this request should come from the very creditor asking for judicial protection. Nevertheless, up to now Serbian courts tended to rigorously stick to the legal text in all procedural matters. One can only assume that they would do the same also in this case. Regrettably, such an outcome completely annuls all the benefits from introducing this specific interim measure in the first place.

D. Conclusion

The current Serbian regulation of creditor protection in restructurings is in principle harmonised with the EU Company Law Directive. However, being that the Directive leaves room for creativity of national legislators in this respect, the solutions adopted in Serbia are somewhat specific in comparison to other European jurisdictions. Generally speaking, the Serbian legislator focuses primarily on mechanisms for individual creditor protection, rather than ensuring adequate institutional protection. Unfortunately, the adopted legislation suffers from two major deficiencies. On the one

98 PCA, Art. 511 para 3.
99 *Ibid.*
100 *Ibid.*

hand, the liability of acquiring companies for obligations of the transferring company is prescribed as merely an alternative mechanism of creditor protection, which shall be applied only if a particular creditor has not otherwise obtained adequate protection. Such a rule raises concerns with regard to legal uncertainty both for the creditor and the acquiring company. On the other hand, the right of a creditor to obtain adequate safeguards is not sufficiently guaranteed under the Serbian PCA. Firstly, creditors are required to request adequate safeguards within a rather short time frame (i.e. 30 days from the date of publication of the draft terms of merger/division). Secondly, the burden of proving all prescribed conditions for exercising the right to obtain adequate safeguards completely lies on the creditor. Lastly, thirdly, the creditor cannot block the merger (or division) until obtaining adequate safeguards, even if the satisfaction of his claim is seriously jeopardised by this corporate change, since the PCA requires the company (i.e. the debtor) to request the adoption of such an interim measure from the court.

Bibliography

Felix Blobel and Michael Menz, "Die Auswirkungen von Schuldner- und Gläubigerwechsel auf die Spaltungshaftung nach § 133 UmwG", *NZG* 2009, 608.

J.E. Goudsmit, *The Pandects – A Treatise on Roman Law and upon Its Connection with Modern Legislation* (The Lawbook Exchange, Clark (New Jersey), 2005).

Stefan Grundmann, *Europäisches Gesellschaftsrecht* (2. Auflage, C.F. Müller Verlag, Heidelberg, 2011).

Martin Heidenhain, "Fehlerhafte Umsetzung der Spaltungs-Richtlinie", *EuZW* 11/1995, 327.

Martin Heidenhain, "Spaltungsvertrag und Spaltungsplan", *NJW* 44/1995, 2873.

Manuela Heiss, "Gläubigerschutz bei der Unternehmensspaltung", *DZWir* 1/1993, 12.

Martin Henssler and Lutz Strohn (eds.), *Gesellschaftsrecht* (3. Auflage, C.H. Beck, München, 2016) [cited as: Author, in: Henssler/Strohn, *Gesellschaftsrecht*].

Carsten Jaeger, "Sicherheitsleistung für Ansprüche aus Dauerschuldverhältnissen bei Kapitalherabsetzung, Verschmelzung und Beendigung eines Unternehmensvertrages", *DB* 21/1996, 1069.

Tatjana Jevremović Petrović, *Cross-Border Mergers of Companies in the EU Law* [*Prekogranična spajanja društava u pravu EU*] (Belgrade, 2010).

Alexander Naraschewski, "Gläubigerschutz bei der Verschmelzung von GmbH", *GmbHR* 8/1998, 356.

Mirjana Radović, "Liability of the Recipient Company for Debts of the Company being Divided in Case of Divisions and Spinoffs [*Odgovornost društva sticaoca za obaveze društva prenosioca kod statusnih promena podele i izdvajanja*]", in: Vuk Radović (ed.), *Harmonisation of Serbian Business Law with the European Union Law* [*Usklađivanje poslovnog prava Srbije sa pravom Evropske unije (2017)*] (Belgrade, 2017), 145.

Vuk Radović, *Bankruptcy Law – Volume II* [*Stečajno pravo – knjiga druga*] (Belgrade, 2017).

Volker Rieble, "Verschmelzung und Spaltung von Unternehmen und ihre Folgen für Schuldverhältnisse mit Dritten", *ZIP* 8/1997, 301.

Bernd Sagasser, Thomas Bula and Thomas R. Brünger (Hrsg.), *Umwandlungen: Verschmelzung – Spaltung – Formwechsel – Vermögensübertragung* (4. Auflage, Verlag C.H. Beck, München, 2011) [cited as: Author, in: Sagasser/Bula/Brünger, Umwandlungen].

Karsten Schmidt, "Gläubigerschutz bei Umstrukturierungen – Zum Referentenentwurf eines Umwandlungsgesetzes", *ZGR* 1993, 366.

Johannes Semler, Arndt Stengel (Hrsg.), *Umwandlungsgesetz* (4. Auflage, C.H. Beck, München, 2017) [cited as: Author, in: Semler/Stengel, UmwG (2017)].

Stefan Schröcker, *Datenschutz und Universalsukzession bei Verschmelzungen nach dem Umwandlungsgesetz* (Wiesbaden, 2006).

Thomas Schröer, "Sicherheitsleistung für Ansprüche aus Dauerschuldverhältnissen bei Unternehmensumwandlungen", *DB* 6/1999, 317.

Harald Stingl, *Gesamtrechtsnachfolge im Gesellschaftsrecht: Verschmelzung, Umwandlung, Spaltung, Anwachsung* (1. Auflage, Linde Verlag, Wien, 2016).

Arndt Teichmann, "Die Spaltung von Rechtsträgern als Akt der Vermögensübertragung", *ZGR* 1993, 396.

Mirko S. Vasiljević, *Company Law – The Law of Business Organizations* [*Kompanijsko pravo – Pravo privrednih društava*] (10th edition, Belgrade, 2017).

Shareholders Protection in Mergers and Divisions in Serbian Law

Vuk Radović[*]

Summary

A. General Overview on Structural Modifications in Serbian Law

Modern Serbian regulations in the domain of company law, from the *Law on Enterprises* of 1996 to the current *Law on Partnerships and Companies* of 2011, regulate the subject of structural modifications.[1] European Union

---

* Professor at the Faculty of Law, University of Belgrade.

1 Zakon o preduzećima – ZOP [Law on Enterprises], *Official Gazette of the Federal Republic of Yugoslavia* No. 29/1996, Arts. 421-435; Zakon o privrednim društvima – ZOPD 2004 [Law on Partnerships and Companies], *Official Gazette of the Republic of Serbia* No. 125/2004, Arts. 377-425; Zakon o privrednim društvima – ZOPD

regulations have had the greatest impact on Serbian solutions in this field,[2] primarily its Third Directive on Mergers[3] and Sixth Directive on Divisions.[4] A moderate, but not insignificant influence was also exerted by US law, and was predominantly manifested in the introduction of the right of dissenting shareholders in structural modifications procedures.

Structural modifications include diverse and complex procedures in which one company (transferring company) transfers its assets and liabilities to another company (acquiring company), whereby members of the transferring company become members of the acquiring company by acquiring shares in the acquiring company (so-called exchange of shares) instead of shares in the transferring company. The minimal rule is that there must be at least one transferring company and one acquiring company (two participants), while the maximum number of participants has not been set. Companies of different legal form can take part in structural modifications (e.g. joint stock company and limited liability company), as well as public and private companies. The only legal limitation is that companies undergoing bankruptcy or liquidation procedures cannot take part in structural modifications, unless such change is being conducted as a reorganization measure in conformity with bankruptcy law.[5]

2011 [Law on Partnerships and Companies], *Official Gazette of the Republic of Serbia* No. 36/2011, 99/2011, 83/2014 and 5/2015, Arts. 483-514.

2 See more Ivica Jankovec, "Statusne promene preduzeća prema pravu Evropske unije" [Structural modification of enterprises in the law of the European Union] (2001) 5-8 Pravo i privreda, 60-69.

3 Third Council Directive 78/855/EEC of 9 October 1978 based on Art. 54(3)(g) of the Treaty concerning mergers of public limited liability companies, *OJ* L 295, 20.10.1978. Codified version of Third Directive, which included all the amendments adopted in the meantime, was adopted in April 2011. See Directive 2011/35/EU of the European Parliament and of the Council of 5 April 2011 concerning mergers of public limited liability companies (codification), *OJ* L 110, 29.4.2011.

4 Sixth Council Directive of 17 December 1982 based on Art. 54(3)(g) of the Treaty, concerning the division of public limited liability companies (82/891/EEC), *OJ* L 378, 31.12.1982.

5 ZOPD 2011, Art. 484. Law on Bankruptcy has included structural modifications among enumerated reorganization measures. See Zakon o stečaju [Law on Bankruptcy], *Official Gazette of the Republic of Serbia* No. 104/2009, 99/2011, 83/2014 and 113/2017, Art. 157, para 1, subpara 15. More about this reorganization measure see Vuk Radović, *Stečajno pravo – knjiga druga (pobijanje pravnih radnji stečajnog dužnika, reorganizacija, međunarodni stečaj, реорганизација, stečaj povezanih društava)* [Bankruptcy law – part II (avoidance powers, reorganization, international bankruptcy, bankruptcy of corporate groups] (2017), 232-234.

Serbian law provides four structural modifications: merger by acquisition, merger by formation of a new company, division and spinoff – partial division (hereafter mergers and divisions). It has accepted the *numerus clausus* concept, whereby only the four changes stipulated and regulated by law are called structural modifications. This does not mean that other types of status changes are not allowed *a priori*, but only that they do not fall under the legal term *structural modifications*,[6] and that they are governed by general company law rules.

In Serbian law, rules dealing with mergers and divisions apply to all types of partnerships and companies. This points to evident non-compliance with Community law, which links merger and division regulations to joint stock companies only (national mergers and divisions) or to all companies (cross-border mergers).[7] Although expanding the personal domain of application of EU Company law rules at the national level is not bad in itself, the justifiability of linking partnerships (general partnerships and limited partnerships) with such rules is disputable in the case of mergers and divisions. Moreover, in Serbian law, other regulations additionally expand the subjective domain of application of merger and division provisions, so that they are applied to some other types of business entities as well.[8]

Company law regulations concerning mergers and divisions predominantly boil down to protecting the members of participating companies. The reason for this should be sought in the need to protect the interests of such persons who may be jeopardized in a number of ways within the merger and division procedure. As a rule, mergers and divisions fall under the category of so-called fundamental corporate changes which were traditionally subject to prior approval from all members of every participating company. Rules prescribed by company law were eventually liberalized,

6 Jakša Barbić, *Pravo društava – knjiga druga – društva kapitala – Svezak I. Dioničko društvo* [Law on business organizations – Book 2 – Companies – Vol. I. Joint stock company] (2010), 1404.

7 Directive 2005/56/EC of the European Parliament and of the Council of 26 October 2005 on cross-border mergers of limited liability companies, *OJ* L 310, 25.11.2005, Art. 2. About the reasons for broadening personal scope of application in case of cross-border mergers in comparison to the rules contained in Third and Sixth directive see Tatjana Jevremović Petrović, "Statusne promene" [Structural modifications] in Mirko Vasiljević, Vuk Radović and Tatjana Jevremović Petrović (eds), *Kompanijsko pravo Evropske unije* [Company law of the European Union] (2012), 297-298.

8 Zakon o zadrugama [Law on Cooperatives], *Official Gazette of the Republic of Serbia* No. 112/2015, Arts. 13 and 65.

with unanimity giving way to the qualified majority for decision-making by the general meeting of shareholders. Cancellation of the *de facto* veto right resulted in the strengthening of other shareholders' rights, and the subsequent increase of regulations governing this field. Agency problems thwarting mergers and divisions (the relationship between directors and shareholders in dispersed share ownership systems and the relationship between majority and minority shareholders in concentrated share ownership systems)[9] have triggered the emergence of numerous shareholders' rights even in countries that have not had the above-mentioned legislative shift from unanimity to majority decision-making.

Shareholders' rights related to mergers and divisions are always of an individual character, since minimum participation in the share capital or a minimum percentage of voting rights are not prerequisites for obtaining them. These rights may be divided based on the following criteria: (1) based on their objective – rights can be related to informing, voting, exiting the company and compensation for damages; (2) with respect to whom they are exercised – these may be rights exercised with respect to the company of which the persons involved were members, with respect to the acquiring company regardless of whether or not such persons were its members, with respect to the management and auditor of the merger or division; (3) based on whether the member needs to fulfill any special condition for their utilization, rights may be classified as conditional and unconditional; (4) based on their consequences, rights may be divided into those that have effect only with respect to the member utilizing them and those whose effect extends to other members in the same legal position; and (5) based on their content, rights can be of a pecuniary nature, a non-pecuniary nature or mixed, etc.

However, regardless of the legal significance of each of the above-mentioned divisions, the division of member rights based on the time when they are being exercised is considered central today. According to this criterion, in case of merger or division all member rights may be divided into *ex ante* and *ex post* rights, and in that respect, it is possible to speak of prior and subsequent protection of members. Prior protection is integrated into the merger or division procedure, while subsequent protection is detached from this procedure and is implemented upon its completion.

9 See more Edward Rock, Paul Davies, Hideki Kanda, Reinier Kraakman and Wolf-Georg Ringe, "Fundamental Changes" in Reinier Kraakman *et al.*, *The Anatomy of Corporate Law: A Comparative and Functional Approach* (2017), 185-190.

B. Prior (ex ante) Protection of Members

Prior protection encompasses diverse legal mechanisms designed to protect members of the participating companies prior to the merger or division. In this respect, Serbian law has predominantly followed the solutions accepted in the European Union, initially with the adoption of its Third and Sixth Directive and subsequently substituted by its Directive on Company Law in June 2017 (hereafter Directive).[10]

The *ex ante* protection of members is rather diffused, but boils down to two main issues: keeping members informed (so-called information model),[11] and decision-making by the general meeting (so-called shareholder decision-making model). The basic postulate is that the final decision on merger or division needs to be passed by the general meeting. In order to ensure that the members' right to decide on the merger and division assumes its full value, it is necessary to strengthen the members' right to be informed before the general meeting with a special set of rules, because general rules on information are insufficient in this particular case. The management is thereby required to prepare a number of documents accompanying the merger or division, and members are afforded the right to inspect them. Verifications of the merger contract or division plan carried out by a public notary and the Business Registers Agency are considered to be a form of prior protection of members as well.

I. Mandatory Internal Acts and Documents Accompanying Merger and Division

1. Draft Merger Contract and Division Plan

In Serbian law, a contract is the legal basis for every structural modification involving at least two participants.[12] The contractual concept has been in-

10 Directive (EU) 2017/1132 of the European Parliament and of the Council of 14 June 2017 relating to certain aspects of company law – Company Law Directive, *OJ* L 169, 30.6.2017.

11 About predominance of the information model in community law dealing with mergers and divisions see Stefan Grundmann, *European Company Law – Organization, Finance and Capital Markets* (2007), 556-557.

12 ZOPD 2011, Art. 491, para 1. See Nebojša Jovanović, "Pripajanje akcionarskih društava" [Merger by acquisition between joint stock companies] (1999) 11-12 Pravo i privreda, 36.

troduced with the adoption of the *Law on Enterprises* of 1996,[13] and was considered an advancement with respect to the then existing concept of unilateral decisions passed by the general meetings of each participating company.[14] However, regardless of the fact that the contract serves as legal ground for structural modification, it is not sufficient, as the adoption of separate general meeting decisions in each participating company is also mandatory, so that the matter exceeds the framework of contract law and enters the domain of company law.

The structural modification contract (hereafter merger contract) has a mixed legal nature, both contractual and status based. This is a specific contract rendering legal effect in the domain of both the contract law and company law. Namely, the legal consequences of a merger do not arise based on the contract only, but on the law as well. Moreover, only some effects of merger can be determined by a contract, while others are defined by law beforehand and therefore cannot be deviated from.[15]

Under the influence of European regulations, Serbian law stipulates the obligation of preparing a draft merger contract first, and then concluding the contract on merger itself. Unlike the EU Directive, which uses the neutral term *draft terms of merger* (ger. *Verschmelzungsplan*, fr. *projet de fusion*),[16] Serbian law has opted for the term *draft merger contract, i.e. draft structural modification contract* (sr. *ugovor o statusnoj promeni*).

The first issue concerning Serbian law is that it speaks about a draft that is drawn up by the board of directors in one-tier system or supervisory board in two-tier system. The wording of the law is such that it suggests that this document is prepared by the management body of each individual company, meaning that each company may formulate its draft separately. From that perspective, the draft represents a unilateral decision of the board of directors (supervisory board) of a company participating in the merger. Such solution is contrary to the idea of the EU Directive, whereby the draft is drawn up jointly by the administrative or management bodies

---

13 ZOP, Art. 423, para 1.

14 See Mirko Vasiljević, *Komentar Zakona o preduzećima*, (1996), 383.

15 See more Tatjana Jevremović Petrović, "Ugovor o statusnoj promeni – trenutak zaključenja, kontrola i drugi povezani problemi", in Vuk Radović (ed), *Usklađivanje poslovnog prava Srbije sa pravom EU – 2015*, (2015), 100-101.

16 The use of a neutral term was supposed to encompass different practices of the Member States with respect to the manner of conducting mergers. At that point in time, some States required company managements to prepare a contract or a draft contract on merger prior to the general meeting, while others prohibited the conclusion of contract before obtaining the general meeting's approval regarding merger. See Vanessa Edwards, *EC Company Law* (1999), 103.

of companies participating in the merger, and only after successfully concluded negotiations.[17]

The problem is intensified even further by the fact that Serbian law speaks about the minimum content and form of a merger contract,[18] and not about the minimum content and form of the draft, which is not in conformity with solutions established by EU Company law. Furthermore, the publishing requirement is linked to the draft contract on merger, which is a concept adopted by the Directive as well. Finally, Serbian law stipulates that the merger contract be concluded before or after the adoption of the general meeting decision. Depending on when the contract is concluded, the general meeting will either be approving the draft merger contract (when there is no contract) or a merger contract (when the contract has been concluded before the general meeting).

The Serbian solutions presented above are incoherent and inconsistent. One of the possibilities for them to be rectified is to take the stand that the draft merger contract is not a unilateral document of each individual board of directors (supervisory board) of the participating companies, but a contract concluded between the board of directors (supervisory board) of different companies. Although such interpretation would be in accordance with the *acquis communautaire*, it still could not be accepted, not only because of the explicit provision speaking about the preparation of this document by the board of directors (supervisory board) expressed in its singular form, but because of other provisions of the Law as well (e.g. the provision on publication speaks about *drafts* in plural form). Regardless of the above, these imprecisions do not trigger problems in practice, because the draft contracts of participating companies are always identical and are the result of negotiations between the company administrative or management bodies.

Ex ante informing members of the participating companies is conducted in two ways: by prescribing the minimum content of the draft merger contract and by its mandatory publication.

Minimum content of the draft contract. The draft merger contract must have a certain minimum content.[19] The legislator wishes to prevent having

17 Cf. Stefan Grundmann, *European Company Law* (2007), 557.

18 See Tatjana Jevremović Petrović "Ugovor o statusnoj promeni – trenutak zaključenja, kontrola i drugi povezani problemi", in Vuk Radović (ed), *Usklađivanje poslovnog prava Srbije sa pravom EU – 2015*, (2015), 111.

19 Company Law Directive, Art. 91, para 2.

important issues left open.[20] The gist of this provision has a rationale greatly similar to that of the pre-contractual information obligation.

The most significant and most disputable element of the drafts' content is the share exchange ratio. In simple terms, this ratio is determined by comparing the net assets of the companies taking part in the merger. If we were to say that the ratio of the net assets of the transferring company and the acquiring company was 1:2, it would mean that one share of the acquiring company is obtained for two shares of the transferring company. However, in practice, it can hardly be imagined that every member of the transferring company will be entitled to a precise (rounded) amount of acquiring company shares. Instead, it is more realistic to expect that a significant number of members are afforded the right to a certain percentage of the shares. In this example, a person holding five shares of the transferring company is entitled to 2.5 shares of the acquiring company. In that case, they will receive two shares and an appropriate amount in cash for the remaining half share. Under the influence of EU law, Serbian law stipulates that a member of a transferring company may also receive cash payments, whereas the total amount of such payments to all members must not exceed 10% of the total nominal value or accounting value of the shares acquired by members of the transferring company.[21] This can help overcome the inability to provide each member of the transferring company with a specific number of shares.[22] It can be concluded that freeze-out (cash-out) mergers are not allowed in Serbian law.[23] Furthermore, one should not neglect the possibility that each member of the transferring company agrees within the merger procedure to a different exchange ratio than that previously established. Finally, the right to a proportional exchange is not afforded to members who exercise appraisal right (the right to exit the company), because they are entitled to receiving payment of the market value of their shares.

20 See Nebojša Jovanović, "Pripajanje akcionarskih društava", (1999) 11-12, *Pravo i privreda*, 36.

21 ZOPD 2011, Art. 483, para 3; Company Law Directive, Art. 89, para 1 and Art. 90, para 1.

22 Cf. Marco Ventoruzzo, "Freeze-Outs: Transcontinental Analysis and Reform Proposals" (2010), 50(4) *Virginia Journal of International Law*, 878.

23 The same applies to Montenegrin law. See Dragan Radonjić, *Pravo privrednih društava* [The Law of Partnerships and Companies] (2008), 396-397. For the extensive analysis of unavailability of cash-out mergers in Europe see Marco Ventoruzzo, 877-879.

Serbian law does not explicitly prescribe the minimum content of the draft merger contract, but only that of the merger contract.[24] This legal gap needs to be bridged with the use of analogy – application of the provision on the minimum content of the merger contract should be extended to the draft contract as well. The use of analogy is justifiable in this case, because the draft contract must not in any respect differ from the concluded merger contract.

Obligation to publish the draft contract. The Law on Partnerships and Companies recognizes prior and subsequent publication of the draft merger contract.[25] Prior publication refers to the company's obligation to publish the draft contract on its website, if it has one, and to submit a copy of that draft contract to the Business Registers Agency for publication on its website not later than one month prior to the date of the general meeting in which the decision on the merger or division is to be passed. Subsequently, the drafts need to be published and made available continually for not less than 60 days from the date of the general meeting in which the decision on merger or division was passed, while access to the drafts must be made possible to all interested parties, without identification and payment of fees. Serbia has thus made use of the option stipulated by the Directive which enables Member States to introduce the requirement of making information on the draft contract available for a specific period after the general meeting. Hence, Serbian solutions are in conformity with the minimum Community rules and even exceed them partially.

If only one company participates in the structural modification, the boards of directors, i.e. supervisory boards adopt a division plan.[26] This plan is basically subject to the same rules as those applicable to the draft merger contract (minimum content, form, mandatory auxiliary documents, publication, members' right of inspection, general meeting's approval, etc). Unlike the draft contract, the division plan does not have a contractual character, but rather represents a unilateral company law based act of a company taking part in structural modification.

24 See ZOPD 2011, Art. 491, para 2.

25 ZOPD 2011, Art. 495. Cf. Company Law Directive, Art. 92. See Zlatko Stefanović, Bojan Stanivuk, *Komentar Zakona o privrednim društvima* [Commentary on Law on Partnerships and Companies] (2012), 500.

26 Division plan can be used only in certain divisions (for example, division by formation of a new company) or spinoffs (for example, spinoff by formation of a new company).

2. *Board Report on Merger or Division*

Every merger and division must be accompanied by a written report of the administrative or management bodies of each of the participating companies. The report is drawn up by the board of directors in a one-tier system or by the executive board in a two-tier system (hereafter board).[27] Although the law does not mention this, the boards of all companies taking part in the merger or division are allowed to prepare a joint report.[28]

In this report, the board is required to justify the proposed merger or division in detail, providing the following in particular: (1) the desired objectives of the merger or division; (2) an analysis of expected economic effects for the companies participating in the merger or division; (3) an explanation of the legal consequences; (4) rationale for the share exchange ratio; (5) information on amendments to the merger contract (division plan), if such amendments were made based on the auditor's report on mergers and divisions; and (6) information on significant changes in the assets and liabilities of the companies taking part in the merger or division that have occurred after the date on which the financial statements were prepared.[29] The report must be produced in written form and must be written in a way that it may be understood by an average shareholder of the company.[30]

The Serbian solution deviates from the EU law in three ways.

Firstly, a description of special issues that have arisen with respect to the assessment process is missing as one of the mandatory elements of the report.

Secondly, the last required element of the report is imprecise and essentially does not match the provisions of Community law. According to the Serbian solution, the board of each company is required to include in its report information on significant changes that had taken place in each of the participating companies after the date on which the financial statements were prepared. According to the Directive, the administrative or management bodies of each of the companies involved must inform their company's general meeting, as well as the administrative or management

---

27 In two-tier system the report has to be subsequently submitted to the supervisory board for adoption.

28 Cf. Croatian Zakon o trgovačkim društvima – ZTD [Law on Partnerships and Companies], *Official Gazette of the Republic of Croatia* No. 111/93, 34/99, 121/99, 52/00, 118/03, 107/07, 146/08, 137/09, 125/11, 152/11, 111/12, 68/13 and 110/15, Art. 514, para 3.

29 ZOPD 2011, Art. 494.

30 Stefan Grundmann, *European Company Law*, (2007) 558.

bodies of the other companies involved, which will in turn inform their respective general meetings, of any significant change in the assets or liabilities that has occurred between the date of preparation of the draft terms on merger (division plan) and the date of the general meeting.[31] The above points to the existence of multiple differences.

(1) According to the Directive, the administrative or management body needs to inform both the general meeting of its own company, and the administrative or management bodies of other companies involved in the merger or division, while Serbian law requires the company board to inform its general meeting only.
(2) The Directive requires the administrative or management bodies to cite in their report all significant changes that have occurred within the company in which they are exercising their function, as well as information they receive from the managements of other companies involved. Serbian law requires the company board to state in its report all changes that have taken place in each of the companies participating in the merger or division, regardless of whether this is related to its own company or whether the information was previously received from the boards of other companies.
(3) Community law takes the date of the preparation of the draft merger contract (division plan) as a relevant starting date for tracking changes, which is a logical solution, because the draft is presented to the general meeting which votes on it, while Serbian law uses the date on which financial statement is made, which may even be significant before the date of the preparation of the draft contract.

Thirdly, the Directive offers Member States the option not to require the preparation of the board report in the event that all those who have the right to vote in each of the companies involved so agree, but does oblige Member States to do so when dealing with cases of merger by acquisition of a subsidiary company by a parent company which is its only member, or merger by acquisition of a subsidiary by a parent company holding 90% or more of the voting capital in the subsidiary, along with requirements for the fulfillment of other conditions.[32] In Serbian law, there are two exceptions: the first is related to situations when an acquiring company holds not less than 90% of the transferring company's share capital rendering at least 90% of the voting rights, while the second is related to cases when all

31 Company Law Directive, Art. 95, para 2.
32 Company Law Directive, Art. 95, para 3 and Arts. 110-115.

the members of that company agree.[33] The latter exception reflects evident deviation from the Community regime, because Serbian law regards this exception with respect to a specific company, and requires the consent of all members of that company, as opposed to Community law which requires the consent of all members of all the companies taking part in the merger or division. Hence, in Serbian law, the exception is related only to the company in which consent has been acquired, while European law applies the exception to all participating companies, so that it is impossible to have a situation in which the board of one company is not required to prepare a report, while the boards of other companies are required to do so. The Community system is better, because it is not based only on the communication between the board and general meeting of a specific company, but also establishes communication channels between the board of one merger (division) participant and other participants in the process.

3. Expert's Report on Merger or Division

Apart from the board's report, a written expert's report must also accompany each merger or division.[34] If the draft merger contract (division plan) and the board report are treated as the first instrument of member protection within the framework of the information model, then the expert report may be regarded as the second instrument of protection.[35]

According to Serbian law, the expert is appointed by the competent court in a non-contentious procedure at the request of each company participating in the merger or division. Hence, the basic rule is that there are as many experts and as many reports as there are companies taking part in the structural modifications.

If a number of companies participate in the merger or division, the competent court may appoint a single expert at the joint request of all those companies, and the expert will consequently prepare a joint merger (division) report for all.[36] In that case, the expert is required to draw up and submit the joint report to all participating companies within a time period set by the court, but not longer than two months from the date of

---

33 ZOPD 2011, Art. 490, para 6 and Art. 501, para 2.

34 ZOPD 2011, Art. 493; Company Law Directive, Art. 96.

35 Stefan Grundmann, *European Company Law* (2007), 559.

36 Because of its efficiency, in practice this is the most widely used option. See Zlatko Stefanović, Bojan Stanivuk, *Komentar Zakona o privrednim društvima* (2012), 498.

the expert's appointment. It is unclear why the legislator has set a time limit for the preparation of the joint report only, and not for individual reports as well. This provision is superfluous, because every report, be it individual or joint, must be available to company shareholders for a certain time period prior to the general meeting in order to enable them to exercise their inspection right. The law does not stipulate that the same expert may be appointed at the request of the participating companies, who would then prepare separate reports for each company.[37] Most probably, this should be left to the rules dealing with conflict of interest.[38]

The expert prepares the report in written form. Although it covers the entire draft merger contract (division plan), the report must also include the expert's opinion on whether the share exchange ratio is fair and reasonable. In the report justification, the expert must particularly state: (1) which valuation methods were used in determining the proposed ratio for the exchange shares, and which weights were assigned to the values obtained with the application of those methods; (2) whether the applied methods and weights were appropriate for the circumstances of the particular case, and what the exchange ratio would have been if other weights were assigned; and (3) which circumstances impeded the valuation and examination, if any. The absence of an expert's report renders the general meeting's decision on merger (division) voidable.[39]

The expert is authorized to request the companies taking part of the merger or division to provide all information and documents needed for the successful preparation of the report, as well as to conduct all other necessary activities to verify the veracity of the data and documents obtained from those companies. Such a broad right afforded to experts guarantees that they will be able to get informed adequately.[40]

Like in the case of the company board's report, Serbian law stipulates two exceptions to the requirement to conduct a merger (division) examination: (1) when the acquiring company holds 90% of the share capital and 90% of the voting rights in the transferring company; and (2) if all members of all companies involved in the merger (division) agree so. The latter exception is characterized by two limitations: (a) it does not apply to public joint stock companies, so they can be exempt from the obligation of

---

37 Cf. Croatian ZTD, Art. 515, para 2.

38 John Temple Lang, "Three EEC Draft Directives on Company Law – Capital, Mergers and Management" (1972) 7 *Irish Jurist*, 316.

39 Jakša Barbić, *Pravo društava – knjiga druga – društva kapitala – Svezak I. Dioničko društvo* (2010), 1416.

40 Stefan Grundmann, *European Company Law* (2007), 560.

providing an expert's report only in case the conditions concerning the first exception are fulfilled (the public joint stock company is the acquiring company holding 90% of the share capital and 90% of the voting rights in the transferring company); and (b) unlike in the case of a similar exception concerning the obligation to set up a board report, the legislator opted for the proper concept, requiring the consent of the shareholders of all companies involved. The dilemma remains as to why this exception does not apply to public joint stock companies, and why the rules concerning consent are different for the board's report and the expert's report.

4. *Financial Statements*

Every merger and division must be accompanied by audited financial statements as at a date preceding the date of the adoption of the general meeting decision on merger (division) by not more than six months. For this purpose, companies may use the following documents: (1) the most recent annual financial statements, with auditor's opinion, if not more than six months have passed from the end of the financial year to the date of the adoption of the general meeting's decision on merger or division; and (2) semi-annual financial statements, with auditor's opinion, if more than six months have passed from the end of the financial year to the date of the adoption of the general meeting's decision on merger or division. Apart from these options, companies may also compile new financial statements, with auditor's opinion. In that case, they do not need to conduct a new inventory of their entire assets and can rely on items contained in their most recent audited annual financial statement, taking into account significant changes in asset value that have occurred from the date on which the most recent statements were drawn up, and that are not visible in business records.[41] EU law emphasizes that the new statement must be drawn up on a date not earlier than the first day of the third month preceding the date of the draft terms of merger (division). It also stipulated that the statement must be drawn up using the same methods and the same layout as the last annual balance sheet. Serbian law does not have similar provisions.

The above-mentioned financial statements are not necessary if all members of the company taking part in the merger or division so agree. Once again, like in the case of the board report on merger (division), and contrary to Community law, this exception applies to each individual compa-

41 ZOPD 2011, Art. 490, paras 1-3; Company Law Directive, Art. 97, paras 1-2.

ny, because consent is not sought from all shareholders of every participant in the merger or division.

II. Shareholders' Right to Inspect Documents

The company conducting the merger or division is required to enable its shareholders to inspect the following documents in the company headquarters:[42]

(1) the draft merger contract (division plan);
(2) the expert's report on the merger (division) examination;
(3) the board's report on merger (division);
(4) financial statements, with auditor's opinion, as at a date preceding the date of the adoption of the general meeting decision on merger (division) by not more than six months;
(5) annual financial statements for the past three years for the each of the companies taking part in the corporate change, with auditors' opinions if the statements were audited;
(6) proposal for a decision on amendments to the articles of incorporation (or bye-laws) of the acquiring company, and if the merger (division) results in the formation of a new company, proposal for the articles of incorporation, as well as the proposal for the bye-laws if the company concerned is a joint stock company;[43]
(7) list of shareholders of the transferring company, with an indication of the par value of their shares in the acquiring company, as well as of the shares they will be acquiring in the acquiring company;
(8) list of employees of the transferring company whose employment will continue in the acquiring company; and
(9) proposal for the general meeting's decision on merger (division).

Members must be allowed to exercise their inspection right for not less than one month prior to the date of the general meeting in which a decision on merger or division is to be passed. The company does not need to

42 ZOPD 2011, Art. 496. Cf. Company Law Directive, Art. 97, para 1.

43 In Serbia, each joint stock company must have two founding acts: the articles of incorporation and the bye-laws. The articles of incorporation is used only for the registration purposes, and cannot be changed afterwards. In practice, the bye-laws are the major document of a joint stock company and it can be changed via absolute majority vote by the general meeting of shareholders. See ZOPD 2011, Arts. 11-12 and 246-247.

fulfill this requirement if the relevant documents have been published in way in which the draft merger contract (division plan) is published.

Every member has the right to copy these documents free of charge. Exceptionally, the company is not required to provide free copies if all interested persons are enabled, without the need for their identification, to get free downloads of such documents from the company register's website.

Slight discrepancies are evident between Serbian and Community law with regard to the two exceptions mentioned above – the first concerning the lack of obligation on the part of the company to enable shareholders to inspect relevant documents in its headquarters, and the second regarding situations when shareholders are not entitled to free copies. The Directive applies the same standard in both cases – if all the documents were available to the shareholders on the company's website and the shareholders were able to access them free of charge. The standards are somewhat different in Serbian law, but the thing that both laws have in common is that companies are exempt from this requirement in case the documents are published on the Business Registers Agency's website.

III. Voting by the General Meeting of Shareholders

1. General Rules

The requirement of having a decision passed by the general meeting represents the last form of *ex ante* shareholder protection. The general meeting's approval is an indispensible precondition for the validity of merger or division.

Just like EU law, Serbian law speaks about the consent (approval) of the general meeting. Hence, the question arises as to who is competent for the decision on merger or division. Theoretically, approval only means that this is an additional necessary condition for merger (division) implementation, whereby competence for the adoption of the decision is not transferred from the board to the general meeting. Only the board can propose the adoption of such a decision to the general meeting, since the preparation of the draft merger contract (division plan) is also under its competence, and this document and its publication is a necessary step of the procedure. However, the final decision on merger or division is passed by the general meeting. Therefore, in order for the merger contract or division plan to be valid, it is necessary to have the approval of both the managing bodies and the general meeting of each of the companies involved. Such approval is given in different ways. The board gives its approval by concluding a draft merger contract (draft division plan) or merger contract (division plan) with the boards of other participants in the merger (division), meaning that the contractual nature of merger (division) is prevalent in the initial phases of the procedure. Then the general meeting of each company passes a decision on merger (division) independently, which points to the company law nature of merger (division). This leads to two conclusions: firstly, merger (division) has a mixed legal nature, and secondly, competence for passing a decision on merger (division) is shared between the board and the general meeting of shareholders, whereby the first phase is within the competence of the board, and the second phase is within the competence of the general meeting.

In order to carry out a proposed merger or division, approval must be given by the general meetings of each of the participating companies. If the general meeting of one of the companies fails to give its approval, the concluded merger contract cannot have legal effect (if it has been concluded before the date of the general meeting) or the merger contract cannot be concluded (if only a draft contract existed before the date on which the general meeting was held). In other words, the contract cannot have validity only among the companies whose general meetings have expressed their approval because the draft contract, i.e. contract was concluded between specific parties, and every party to the contract needs to give its approval.[44] Consenting companies have only one option – to initiate a new merger or division procedure, implying that the phases concluded earlier on (e.g. publication of draft merger contract) must be repeated.[45]

Today, it is quite common to require some form of qualified majority for decision-making in order to adopt a merger (division) decision.[46] The basic rule laid down by EU law is that the decision must be adopted by a majority of not less than two-thirds of the votes of the shareholders present

44 Cf. Jakša Barbić, *Pravo društava – knjiga druga – društva kapitala – Svezak I. Dioničko društvo* (2010), 1416.

45 Cf. Nebojša Jovanović, "Pripajanje akcionarskih društava" (1999) 11-12, *Pravo i privreda*, 35.

46 Edward Rock, Paul Davies, Hideki Kanda, Reinier Kraakman and Wolf-Georg Ringe, "Fundamental Changes" in Reinier Kraakman et al., *The Anatomy of Corporate Law: A Comparative and Functional Approach* (2017), 184. Before Third and Sixth directive, the approval of a merger by shareholders was unknown in British and Irish law. See John Temple Lang, "Three EEC Draft Directives on Company Law – Capital, Mergers and Management" (1972) 7 *Irish Jurist*, 315.

(qualified relative majority).[47] Alternatively, Member States may prescribe that a simple majority is sufficient if at least half of the capital is represented.[48] Many countries have adopted stricter standards than those of the Community. Hence, Germany, Austria and Croatia require three-quarters of the votes of shareholders present,[49] while France stipulates a two-third majority along with the fulfillment of an additional condition — a minimum quorum of a quarter of all voting shares. Italian and Japanese law also have solutions similar to the French model, the difference being that the minimum quorum is lower in Italy (one-fifth of all voting shares)[50] and higher in Japan (one-third of all voting shares).

Serbian law basically accepts German solution, as it stipulates that the decision is adopted by a three-quarter majority vote of the shareholders present.[51] However, what characterize Serbian law are high quorum thresholds for general meetings.[52] Namely, a quorum constitutes a simple majority of the total number of votes (over 50% of the voting shares). If a meeting is adjourned for lack of quorum, a reconvened (repeated) meeting may be held, with a quorum of one-third of the total number of votes. Hence, a quorum constitutes one-half or one-third of the total number of votes, depending on whether it is the initial or reconvened meeting. In the case of reconvened general meetings of public joint stock companies, an additional condition is applied — decisions adopted in these meetings require a majority of not less than one-quarter of the total voting power entitled to vote.[53] Rules on the majority and quorum may be amended in a joint stock company's bye-laws, but only towards a stricter regime, i.e. only a larger majority or quorum may be set with respect to that prescribed by law. This indicates that Serbian standards exceed European standards in

47 Cf. Montenegrin Zakon o privrednim društvima – ZOPD [Law on Partnerships and Companies], *Official Gazette of the Republic of Montenegro* No. 6/2002, 17/2007, 80/2008, 40/2010, 36/2011, 40/2011, Art. 22, para 4.

48 Company Law Directive, Art. 93, para 1.

49 German Umwandlungsgesetz – UmwG, *BGBl.* I S. 3210, 1995 I S. 428, with the latest amendments from July 17, 2017 in *BGBl.* I S. 2434, § 65, para 1; Austrian Bundesgesetz über Aktiengesellschaften (Aktiengesetz – AktG), *BGBl.* Nr. 98/1965, with the latest amendments in *BGBl.* I Nr. 107/2017, § 221, para 2; Croatian ZTD, Art. 516, para 2.

50 This rule applies only to listed Italian companies, while in non-listed companies relative majority is sufficient. See Italian Codice civile (March 16, 1942, n. 262, with latest amendments from December 7, 2016, n. 291), Arts. 2368-2369.

51 ZOPD 2011, Art. 498, para 2.

52 ZOPD 2011, Arts. 351 and 353.

53 ZOPD 2011, Art. 354.

this respect. However, from the standpoint of promoting a company's restructuring through structural modifications, large quorums and majorities for decision-making have a discouraging effect.

Identical rules concerning the quorum apply to limited liability companies as well.[54] However, there is a difference with regard to the decision-making majority. Namely, the general meeting of a limited liability company decides on mergers and divisions with a two-third majority of the total number of votes of all members. The articles of incorporation may prescribe a different decision-making majority, but not smaller than a simple majority of the total number of votes. Despite the fact that a qualified majority is required for decision-making on merger or division in both types of companies, there are three differences: first of all, the majority stands at three-quarters in joint stock companies and two-quarters in limited liability companies; secondly, a qualified relative majority (majority of those present) is required in joint stock companies, while a qualified absolute majority (the majority of all) is necessary in limited liability companies; thirdly, in joint stock companies, the prescribed majority represents a minimum standard, whereas in limited liability companies it represents a solution that is assumed and may be deviated from towards a stricter or milder regime, but not moving below a majority of the total number of votes. Judging by all the above, it is obvious that the threshold for the adoption of a decision on merger or division in limited liability companies is higher, because the absolute majority condition must be fulfilled by all means.

German, Austrian and Croatian law allow companies to prescribe through their articles of association other conditions for the adoption of general meeting decisions on merger or division (e.g. that the decision must be passed twice in a row, in two separate sessions or that the minimum quorum condition must be fulfilled).[55] In Serbian law, this would not be allowed, not only because it has not been prescribed explicitly, but also because additional conditions are primarily related to the introduction of a compulsory quorum for the adoption of a decision, and in Serbian law, this matter has already been regulated by general rules for every general meeting decision.

In the event that a company has issued one or more classes of preferred shares, Serbian law, just like comparative law, accepts the concept of voting

54 ZOPD 2011, Art. 208.

55 German UmwG, § 65, para 1; Austrian AktG, § 221, para 2; Croatian ZTD, Art. 516, para 2.

by classes.[56] The law lists situations when the holders of such shares have the right to vote. All these situations are essentially related to the loss, diminishment or change of any right conferred on preferred shareholders, which will often be the case during mergers and divisions.[57] In such situations, holders of each class of preferred share vote in the general meeting, but separately from the holders of ordinary shares and separately from other classes of preference shares. The merger (division) decision is deemed adopted when holders of every class of shares have voted for it, with a proper quorum and majority for decision-making.

Patterned after the EU Directive, Serbian Company Law stipulates that the general meeting is required to do the following simultaneously with the adoption of the decision on merger or division: (1) adopt amendments to the articles of incorporation or the bye-laws in the case of a joint stock company, if that company continues to operate after the merger of division; and (2) adopt the articles of incorporation of the company formed as a result of the merger or division, as well as its bye-laws if it is a joint stock company.[58] Therefore, along with the approval of the merger or division, the general meeting also approves the constitutive documents of the company that is being founded or amendments to the constitutive documents of the company that will continue existing. In practical terms, the question may arise as to whether this involves one decision rendering approval for both the merger (division) and the constitutive documents, or two separate decisions. In Serbia, this issue is particularly topical considering the difference between the majority needed for decision-making on the adoption of new articles of incorporation/bye-laws or amendments to the existing articles of incorporation/by-laws (absolute majority of all votes), and the majority needed for the adoption of the decision on merger or division. If these were to be separate items on the agenda, subject to different majority requirements for decision-making, situations could arise when shareholders would pass a decision on merger or division, but would then be unable to pass a decision on amendments to the existing or adoption of new articles of incorporation, i.e. by-laws. Here is a practical example to demonstrate what this would look like: the meeting is attended by shareholders

---

56 Company Law Directive, Art. 93, para 2; German UmwG, § 65, para 2; Austrian AktG, § 221, para 3; Croatian ZTD, Art. 516, para 3; Montenegrin ZOPD, Art. 22, para 4; ZOPD 2011, Art. 255, para 1.

57 Situations prescribed by law when preferred shareholders have the right to vote basically match what Community law refers to when it says "rights are affected by the transaction".

58 ZOPD 2011, Art. 498, para 4. Cf. Company Law Directive, Art. 93, para 3.

holding 60% of the voting shares and 45% of those holding voting shares cast their vote in favor of the merger or division and amendments to the by-laws, the condition for the adoption of the decision on merger or division (three-quarter majority of the shareholders present) is fulfilled, but not the condition for amendments to the by-laws (50% of all voting shares). If the stand that these are two separate items of the agenda were to be accepted, it would be best to require that the same majority be applied for both decisions – the majority prescribed for merger (division) decisions. Another possibility would be to treat the two decisions as a whole, and consequently make unified decisions within the same agenda item. This interpretation is desirable for at least three reasons: firstly, it is closest to the linguistic interpretation of "simultaneous" passing of decisions stipulated by law; secondly, according to the Directive, the general meeting's decision encompasses both the approval for merger (division) and the approval for the amendment of constitutive documents; and thirdly, the issue of a majority for decision-making would not be raised in this case, because the majority prescribed for merger (division) decisions would be applied without any doubt.

Finally, if as a result of the merger or division some members of the transferring company become members of the acquiring company, who are jointly and severally liable for its obligations, then the decision on merger or division can only be made with their approval.[59]

2. *Simplified Merger (Division) Procedure as a Derogation from the Requirement of Approval by the Shareholders*

The Directive has allowed, and in some situations even obligated Member States not to require approval by the general meeting of the acquiring company if certain conditions are fulfilled.[60] This procedure is "designed to facilitate merging a subsidiary with and into a parent corporation that owns a substantive percentage of the subsidiary's shares".[61] Serbia has accepted this possibility by way of regulating the so-called *simplified merger (division) procedure*,[62] referred to in comparative law as *upstream merger*.[63] The simpli-

59 ZOPD 2011, Art. 498, para 3.
60 Company Law Directive, Arts. 94 and 110-115.
61 Marco Ventoruzzo, "Freeze-Outs: Transcontinental Analysis and Reform Proposals" (2010) 50(4), *Virginia Journal of International Law*, 877.
62 ZOPD 2011, Art. 501. Cf. Montenegrin ZOPD, Art. 22b.
63 See Robert W. Hamilton, *The Law of Corporations* (2000), 622.

fication boils down to the requirement of obtaining approval from the general meeting of the transferring company only, while the decision on merger or division in the acquiring company is passed by the board. Apart from derogating from the rule on the general meeting's approval, the acquiring company is not required to draw up and submit to the general meeting for approval neither the board's report, nor the auditor's report on merger (division). Finally, if the acquiring company is the sole member of the transferring company, the merger contract does not contain information on the exchange of shares. This rule is understandable, because all shares of the transferring company belong to the acquiring company, so that the distribution of shares of the transferring company is not an issue.[64]

In Serbian law, the simplified merger (division) procedure is allowed if: (1) the acquiring company holds not less than 90% of the share capital of the transferring company and not less than 90% of the voting shares in the transferring company; (2) if the acquiring company publishes the draft merger contract (division plan) not later than one month prior to the date set for the acquiring company's general meeting, wherein the decision on the merger (division) is to be made; (3) the acquiring company has made documents related to the merger (division) available to its members in that period; and (4) if one or more members of the acquiring company who hold shares accounting for at least 5% of the share capital do not demand that a general meeting be convened in order to pass a decision on merger or division.

When it comes to simplification of the merger (division) procedure, *acquis* recognizes three distinct regimes:[65] the first is applied when the acquiring company is the only shareholder of the transferring company; the second regime is related to situations when the acquiring company holds not less than 90% of the voting capital of the transferring company; while the third regime is of a general character, as it requires no holdings on the part of the acquiring company in the share capital of the transferring company. Every subsequent regime implies a lesser degree of derogation from general rules, but the one thing they all have in common is that they do not require a decision by the acquiring company's general meeting. The first two regimes are binding on the Member States, while the third is optional. Serbian law has adopted the second regime only. However it has

---

64 Jakša Barbić, *Pravo društava – knjiga druga – društva kapitala – Svezak I. Dioničko društvo* (2010), 1410.

65 See more Nebojša Jovanović, "Posebni slučajevi pripajanja akcionarskih društava" [Special cases of merger by acquisition between joint stock companies] (1999) 5-8 *Pravo i privreda*, 112-121.

narrowed down the rule compared to Community law. Namely, the simplified merger (division) procedure in Serbian law assumes that the acquiring company holds not less than 90% of the share capital and 90% of the voting rights in the transferring company, while the Directive requires only 90% of the voting rights. *Pro future*, harmonization with EU law should be more extensive, particularly considering the derogated rules on structural modifications between the parent and fully dependent company.

IV. *Preliminary Control of Merger Contract (Division Plan)*

In comparative law, merger contract control is regulated in different ways.[66] Depending on when it is being conducted, it can be preliminary or subsequent. In Serbian law, preliminary control is carried out on two levels: the first represents control conducted by a notary public, while the second is related to control executed by a registrar.

1. *Control by a Notary Public*

Control conducted by a notary public within the merger (division) procedure may be limited or broad. Limited control is provided by the company law. It is a rule and comes down to signature certification (notarization). In contrast, broader control is regulated by the law on public notaries and comes down to merger contract solemnization.

Signature certification. The merger contract is concluded in written form and is certified in conformity with the law.[67] Certification (legalization) is mandatory, meaning that it cannot be ruled out by internal acts of the company.[68] It is performed by the notary public in the notary public office.[69] With the act of certification, the notary public confirms that the submitters of the merger contract, whose identity has been validated prior to the certification, have signed the submitted contract in the notary's pres-

66 See more Tatjana Jevremović Petrović, "Ugovor o statusnoj promeni – trenutak zaključenja, kontrola i drugi povezani problemi", in Vuk Radović (ed), *Usklađivanje poslovnog prava Srbije sa pravom EU – 2015* (2015), 136.

67 ZOPD 2011, Art. 491, para 4.

68 Dejan Đurđević, *Javnobeležnička delatnost* (2014), 180.

69 Zakon o overavanju potpisa, rukopisa i prepisa [Law on certification of signatures, documents and copies], *Official Gazette of the Republic of Serbia* No. 93/2014 and 22/2015, Arts. 1 and 3.

ence (signature certification in the more narrow sense) or have acknowledged that the signatures placed on the contract beforehand are theirs.[70] In this manner, only the authenticity of the merger contract is confirmed.[71]

Through signature certification, the notary public conducts so-called limited preventive protection.[72] He needs to get acquainted with the content of the merger contract to a degree that is necessary in order to fill in the entries in the notarial register, but is not accountable for it. The notary public is required to refuse signature certification if certain reasons prescribed by law apparently exist in a particular case (e.g. the contract contains a prohibited legal transaction or the certification helps achieve certain objectives that are not allowed).[73] It is not important how the notary has learned about the existence of circumstances requiring certification refusal. What is important is that he is in possession of such information. Hence, the relatively narrow preventive legal control conducted by the notary public may be broadened in this particular case.[74]

Solemnization. The second form of control performed by the notary public is not prescribed by company law, but by the Law on public notaries and is applied only if specific conditions are fulfilled. According to this law, a real estate sales contract is concluded in the form of a notarized (solemnized) document – so-called certification of non-public document (solemnization).[75] In contrast to legalization, where only the legalization clause has the power of evidence of a public document, the entire document has the power of evidence of a public document in the case of solemnization.[76] This leads to the conclusion that merger contract solemnization is required whenever a merger or division results in the transfer of immovable property from the transferring company to the acquiring company, which is not rare in practice.

The fact that solemnization is conducted instead of legalization also has a significant consequence in terms of control. Namely, in the solemnization process, the notary public is required to examine whether the pro-

---

70 Zakon o overavanju potpisa, rukopisa i prepisa, Art. 5, para 1.

71 Cf. Dejan Đurđević, *Javnobeležnička delatnost* (2014), 178.

72 Dejan Đurđević, *Javnobeležnička delatnost* (2014), 186.

73 Zakon o overavanju potpisa, rukopisa i prepisa, Art. 11.

74 See more Tatjana Jevremović Petrović, Ugovor o statusnoj promeni – trenutak zaključenja, kontrola i drugi povezani problemi', in Vuk Radović (ed), *Usklađivanje poslovnog prava Srbije sa pravom EU – 2015* (2015), 139-140.

75 Zakon o javnom beležništvu [Law on public notaries], *Official Gazette of the Republic of Serbia* No. 31/2011, 85/2012, 19/2013, 55/2014, 93/2014, 121/2014, 6/2015 and 106/2015, Art. 93.

76 Dejan Đurđević, *Javnobeležnička delatnost* (2014), 229.

posed structural modification is permissible, i.e. whether it is contrary to mandatory rules, public policy and good customs, and if he determines that it is not permissible, he is required to refuse contract certification in a written decision.[77] This enables a more comprehensive control of the merger contract, which is not reduced to the mere examination of formal conditions only, but focuses on significant material conditions for the validity of this contract as well.[78] Furthermore, the notary public does not examine the merger contract only, but also numerous other documents which are considered part of the merger contract as stipulated by the company law (e.g. proposal for a decision on amendments to the articles of incorporation or by-laws of the acquiring company).[79]

2. *Control Conducted by Registrar*

Apart for the notary public, the registrar of the Business Registers Agency also conducts merger and division control. Since the formality principle is applied in the registration procedure, the registrar makes decisions based on the facts contained in the registration application, the attached document and registered data, without having to verify the accuracy of the data presented in the application, the validity of the attached documents and the correctness and legality of the procedures in which the documents were issued.[80] This leads to the conclusion that the merger (division) control conducted by the registrar is weak, and comes down to mere examination of formal conditions for registration (e.g. whether all necessary documents have been attached, whether the application was filed by an authorized person, etc.).

---

77 Zakon o javnom beležništvu, Art. 93đ.

78 Tatjana Jevremović Petrović, "Ugovor o statusnoj promeni – trenutak zaključenja, kontrola i drugi povezani problemi", in Vuk Radović (ed), *Usklađivanje poslovnog prava Srbije sa pravom EU – 2015* (2015), 141.

79 ZOPD 2011, Art. 491, para 3. Cf. Tatjana Jevremović Petrović, "Ugovor o statusnoj promeni – trenutak zaključenja, kontrola i drugi povezani problemi", in Vuk Radović (ed), *Usklađivanje poslovnog prava Srbije sa pravom EU – 2015* (2015), 141.

80 Zakon o postupku registraciji u Agenciji za privredne registre [Law on registration procedure in the Business Registers Agency], *Official Gazette of the Republic of Serbia* No. 99/2011 and 83/2014, Art. 3, para 3.

C. Subsequent (ex post) Protection of Members

Subsequent member protection encompasses all rights rendered to members of the participating companies after the merger or division has been carried out. According to Serbian law, members are guaranteed four rights: the right to exit the company, the right to additional payment, the right to avoid the decision of the general meeting and the right to take legal action against members of the board for damages. The two latter rules have been incorporated into Serbian law under the influence of the EU's Third Directive; the right to exit a company originates from the United States, while the right to additional payment is characteristic of most European legislations. Unlike the *ex ante* protection of members, which is basically integrated into the merger and division procedure, *ex post* rights are diverse and some of them are, by sheer logics, mutually exclusive. In essence, the right to exit the company is a right that is out of sync with all others.

I. The Right of Dissenting Shareholders to Exit the Company (Appraisal Right)

In Serbian law, mergers and divisions are considered to be fundamental corporate changes, which give their members the right to exit the company. In essence, this is an American approach, which is characterized by a very broad concept of dissenting shareholders' rights. Contrary to that, a different solution dominates in Europe (for example, in Germany, Austria, Italy, France, Spain), where shareholders are not given the right to exit the company in case of a merger or division. In these legal systems, shareholders are bound by the decision on merger or division, whilst they have the right to exit the company only under the condition that the merger or division is followed by at least one of the enumerated legal consequences (for example, if a merger leads to the change in corporate form of a participating company or results in restrictions on transferability of shares).

According to the Serbian company law, a shareholder has a right to exit the company if he votes against or sustains from voting on the decision on merger or division.[81] Apart from dissenting shareholders, the law broadens the scope of persons who have the right to exit the company with share-

81 ZOPD 2011, Art. 474, para 1, subpara 2.

holders that have not participated in the general meeting on which a decision on merger or division was adopted.[82]

This right is guaranteed to shareholders of the transferring company only.[83] Therefore, shareholders of the acquiring company do not have appraisal rights. From comparative law perspective, this limitation is not unusual.[84]

Dissenting shareholders in case of mergers and divisions have the right to obtain payment of the market value of their shares from the company.[85] This is contrary to the general rule on appraisal rights in Serbian law, according to which a dissenting shareholder has the right to one of the highest of three values (book value, market value and estimated value), on a day when the decision to convene the general meeting of shareholders was made.[86]

II. The Right to Additional Payment[87]

For shareholders of companies participating in a merger or division the question of adequacy of the share exchange ratio is of the utmost importance. A shareholder, who is damaged by the determined ratio, has a right to additional payment. This right is limited in four ways.

Firstly, as in the case of appraisal rights, this right is given only to shareholders of the transferring company, but not to the shareholders of the acquiring company. The identical approach is accepted in German and Croa-

---

82 For extensive critic of this approach see Vuk Radović, "Uslovi za ostvarivanje prava nesaglasnih akcionara" [Conditions for exercising shareholder's right to appraisal] (2017) 4-6 Pravo i privreda, 62-65.

83 ZOPD 2011, Art. 508.

84 See German UmwG, § 29; Austrian AktG, § 234b.

85 Market value is legally defined term. See ZOPD 2011, Art. 259.

86 Basically, in Serbia there are two regimes of appraisal rights. First regime is *lex generalis*, always applicable if there are no other rules (ZOPD 2011, Arts. 474-477). Second regime (*lex specialis*) applies only to mergers and divisions. The most important distinction between these two sets of norms is in determining the "fair value" of shares. More about general regime see Vuk Radović, "Odmeravanje visine naknade nesaglasnim akcionarima" [Dissenting shareholders' right to a fair value of shares] in Vuk Radović (ed), *Usklađivanje poslovnog prava Srbije sa pravom EU – 2017* [Harmonization of the Serbian Business Law with the Business Law of the European Union – 2017] (2017), 64-90.

87 ZOPD 2011, Art. 507.

tian law.[88] On the other hand, Austrian law does not recognize this personal limitation.

Secondly, the amount of additional payment cannot exceed 10% of nominal value of exchanged shares in the transferring company.

Thirdly, shareholders of the transferring company can receive payment only in cash. A similar rule is accepted in Germany.[89] Conversely, Austrian and Croatian law allow the company to issue additional shares as a form of compensation, instead of rendering cash payments.[90] Theoretically speaking, this approach is more acceptable, since it gives more flexibility to companies, which can be very important especially in cases where participants in a merger or division are facing liquidity problems.

Fourthly, a shareholder claiming that the share exchange ratio is not adequate, can initiate judicial proceedings against the acquiring company within 30 days from the day of publication of the draft merger contract or division plan, requesting cash payment. Practically speaking, shareholders have to initiate judicial proceedings, although it is still not certain whether the general meeting will approve the merger or division. Hence, a much better solution would be for the 30 days deadline to start from the day when the general meeting adopts the decision or the day when the merger or division takes legal effect. In any case, the court needs to wait until the general meeting's decision is adopted, since otherwise the case has to be dismissed. Thus, shareholders who are not satisfied with the determined share exchange ratio are placed at a disadvantage, because they risk bearing all judicial costs in case the general meeting's decision is subsequently not adopted.

In contrast to the solution prevailing in comparative law, in Serbia the shareholder does not have to vote against the general meeting's decision or to show, in some other way, disagreement with the proposed merger or division in order to have the right to additional payment. This is a logical consequence of the above-mentioned rule regarding the beginning of deadline from which the shareholder has the right to initiate judicial proceedings.

If the court finds that all conditions are met for exercising the right to additional payment, in its judgment it shall instruct the acquiring company to make proportionate additional payment to all shareholders of the transferring company, whose shares have been exchanged for shares of the acquiring company, regardless of the fact whether or not they initiated ju-

88 See German UmwG, § 14, para 2; Croatian ZTD, Art. 532, para 2.

89 See German UmwG, § 15, para 1.

90 See Austrian AktG, § 225c; Croatian ZTD, Art. 532, para 5.

dicial proceedings or voted in favor of the decision on merger or division. A similar effect of the court judgment in this regard is not very common in comparative law.

The standard for determining the value of shares is based on the market value. The right to additional payment exists when the market value of shares which a member received in the acquiring company is less than the market value of shares that shareholder had in the transferring company. The shareholder has the right to payment equaling the difference between these two values. From all of the above-stated, it can be concluded that the same standards are applied to determining the value of shares for the purposes of the appraisal right and the right to additional payment.

III. The Right to Challenge the Decision of the General Meeting

The general meeting's decision on merger or division can be challenged on the basis of general rules on the avoidance of general meeting decisions. However, Serbian Law on partnerships and companies provides several special rules for avoidance of these decisions.

First of all, in proceedings involving suits for the avoidance of a merger (division) decision, the court will give the defendant sufficient time to eliminate the reasons for avoidance, if the reasons are remediable.[91] The possibility of reconvening the general meeting wherein a new decision on merger or division would be passed would represent a remediable reason, while action taken by bodies of the company that has ceased to exist would be deemed irremediable.[92]

Secondly, the court is required to submit its final and enforceable decision annulling the decision on merger or division to the company register for publication.

---

91 This provision has obviously been written under the influence of the Second company law directive, which requires courts to leave sufficient time for status regulation before implementation of liquidation proceedings, in case the number of members drops below the minimal number prescribed by law. See V. Edwards, 115.

92 Tatjana Jevremović Petrović, "Pobijanje odluke skupštine o statusnoj promeni" [Avoidance of general meetings' decision on the statutory merger] in Vuk Radović (ed), *Usklađivanje poslovnog prava Srbije sa pravom EU – 2017* [Harmonization of the Serbian Business Law with the Business Law of the European Union – 2017] (2017), 114.

Thirdly, the annulment of the general meeting's decision has no effect on the rights and obligations of the acquiring company in connection to the merger or division, which have arisen after the legal consequences of this corporate change have occurred, but prior to the date of publication of the decision by the registrar. All companies that have participated in the merger or division bear unlimited joint and several liability for those obligations. Community law prescribes identical rules.[93]

Fourthly, the decision on merger or division cannot be challenged on the grounds of inadequate share exchange ratio.[94] The reason for the exclusion of these grounds for challenging should be sought in the fact that the merger or division procedure also demands the participation of experts who are required to give their opinion on the fairness and reasonability of the share exchange ratio.[95] Hence, member protection on these grounds is integrated into the very procedure. The way in which the expert is appointed is an additional argument in this direction. Namely, according to Serbian law, the expert is appointed by the court, so that it would be uneconomical and inexpedient to allow challenging on these grounds considering that the court would have to engage an expert within the framework of avoidance proceedings to give his opinion on the adequacy of the defined exchange ratio. After all, the objective of this rule is to ensure the efficiency of merger (division) implementation.[96] Finally, the inability to challenge on these grounds is in sync with the right to additional payment. A member who is unsatisfied with the defined exchange ratio may vote against the general meeting's decision on merger or division, and if the decision is passed, he may exercise other rights, like the right to exit the company or the right to additional payment.

In Serbian law, a particular issue in proceedings for the avoidance of merger (division) decisions involves passive legitimization. If a transferring company has ceased to exist as a result of merger (division), it cannot be denoted as the defendant, meaning that the decisions of such companies cannot be challenged. *Pro futuro*, special rules should be introduced to en-

---

93 Company Law Directive, Art. 108, para 1, subparas g-h.

94 See also German UmwG, § 14, para 2; Austrian AktG, § 225b.

95 See more Mirko Vasiljević, *Vodič za čitanje Zakona o privrednim društvima* [Guide for reading Law on partnerships and companies] (2004), 559 and 567; Tatjana Jevremović Petrović, "Pobijanje odluke skupštine o statusnoj promeni", in Vuk Radović (ed), *Usklađivanje poslovnog prava Srbije sa pravom EU – 2017* (2017), 109-110.

96 Mirko Vasiljević, *Vodič za čitanje Zakona o privrednim društvima* (2004), 559.

able proceedings for the avoidance of decisions made by such companies as well.

IV. Liability for Damages

The law establishes direct joint and several liability of the members of the board of directors in a one-tier system, i.e. members of the supervisory board in a two-tier system, towards shareholders of that company, for any damage caused intentionally or through gross negligence in the preparation and implementation of a merger or division.[97] This liability is applied in each company participating in the merger or division, regardless of whether it is an acquiring company or a transferring company. A member of the company may take legal action for compensation on these grounds within a period of three years from the date of publication of merger (division) registration. These grounds for liability are not applied in the event that a subsidiary is merged with its sole member.

The solutions presented above have served as a basis for the establishment of so-called special individual action which differs from so-called general individual action. According to the general rules of Serbian company law, a company member is entitled to bring individual legal action against persons who owe special duties to the company (duty of care and duty of loyalty), demanding compensation for damages caused by breach of special duties owed to the company.[98] Apart from time frames for taking legal action[99] and the circle of persons against whom such action may be taken,[100] the basic difference between general and special individual legal action is that general legal action takes breach of duties as grounds for liability, while special legal action focuses on damage caused intentionally or through gross negligence in the course of merger or division preparation and implementation, regardless of whether or not this has led to a breach

97 ZOPD 2011, Art. 514.

98 ЗОПД 2011, Art. 78.

99 The time period for taking general individual action is subjective-objective (within six months from the date of learning of such breach, but not later than five years from the date of the breach), and in the case of special individual legal action it is objective (within three years from the registration publication).

100 Concept of persons who owe special duties to the company is broader, since it includes, besides members of the board of directors in one-tier system and members of the supervisory board in two-tier system, legal representatives, commercial procurators and liquidators. See ZOPD 2011, Art. 61, para 1, subparas 4-5.

of duties prescribed by law. It is debatable just how necessary it was to introduce special individual legal action into Serbian law considering that, as a rule, damage caused by willful misconduct during the preparation and implementation of merger or division also represents a breach of the duty of care.

The Serbian company law differs from European law in two aspects. Firstly, the EU Directive only speaks about liability of members of the administrative or management bodies towards the shareholders of the transferring company,[101] while Serbian law extends this rule to the acquiring company as well. This derogation is in conformity with Community law, which sets only minimum rules in this domain. The second difference is of greater proportion, and involves the Directive's rule establishing direct civil liability of the expert responsible for preparing the expert report on merger or division, towards members of the transferring company.[102] Serbian law does not have a similar rule, and such liability does not arise based on general rules.

Members of the administrative or managing bodies, and according to European law the merger (division) expert as well, are indisputably liable towards the company on whose behalf they conducted their activities. Extension of this liability towards company members as well enables compensation for damages even in situations when the company ceases to exist as a result of the merger or division.[103]

Bibliography

Jakša Barbić, *Pravo društava – knjiga druga – društva kapitala – Svezak I. Dioničko društvo* [Law on business organizations – Book 2 – Companies – Vol. I. Joint stock company] (5th Edition, Organizator, Zagreb, 2010).

Dejan Đurđević, *Javnobeležnička delatnost* [Public notary activity] (Dosije studio, Belgrade, 2014).

Vanessa Edwards, *EC Company Law* (Oxford University Press, Oxford, 1999).

Stefan Grundmann, *European Company Law – Organization, Finance and Capital Markets* (Intersentia, Antwerpen – Oxford, 2007).

Robert W. Hamilton, *The Law of Corporations* (5th ed., West group, St. Paul, Minn., 2000).

101 Company Law Directive, Art. 106.

102 Company Law Directive, Art. 107.

103 Cf. Stefan Grundmann, 5 *European Company Law* (2007), 64.

Ivica Jankovec, "Statusne promene preduzeća prema pravu Evropske unije" [Structural modification of enterprises in the law of the European Union] (2001) 5-8 Pravo i privreda, 60-69 ž.

Tatjana Jevremović Petrović, "Statusne promene" [Structural modifications] in Mirko Vasiljević, Vuk Radović and Tatjana Jevremović Petrović (eds), *Kompanijsko pravo Evropske unije* [Company law of the European Union] (Faculty of Law University of Belgrade, Belgrade, 2012), 283-350.

Tatjana Jevremović Petrović, "Ugovor o statusnoj promeni – trenutak zaključenja, kontrola i drugi povezani problemi" [Merger contract (terms of merger) – contracting, merger control and other connected issues] in Vuk Radović (ed), *Usklađivanje poslovnog prava Srbije sa pravom EU – 2015* [Harmonization of the Serbian Business Law with the Business Law of the European Union – 2015] (Faculty of Law University of Belgrade, Belgrade, 2015), 94-147.

Tatjana Jevremović Petrović, "Pobijanje odluke skupštine o statusnoj promeni" [Avoidance of general meetings' decision on the statutory merger] in Vuk Radović (ed), *Usklađivanje poslovnog prava Srbije sa pravom EU – 2017* [Harmonization of the Serbian Business Law with the Business Law of the European Union – 2017] (Faculty of Law University of Belgrade, Belgrade, 2017), 91-122.

Nebojša Jovanović, "Pripajanje akcionarskih društava" [Merger by acquisition between joint stock companies] (1999) 11-12 Pravo i privreda, 22-58.

Nebojša Jovanović, "Posebni slučajevi pripajanja akcionarskih društava" [Special cases of merger by acquisition between joint stock companies] (1999) 5-8 Pravo i privreda, 112-121.

Reinier Kraakman *et al.*, *The Anatomy of Corporate Law: A Comparative and Functional Approach* (3rd ed., Oxford University Press, New York, 2017).

John Temple Lang, "Three EEC Draft Directives on Company Law – Capital, Mergers and Management" (1972) 7 *Irish Jurist*, 306-328.

Dragan Radonjić, *Pravo privrednih društava* [The Law of Partnerships and Companies] (Pobjeda, Podgorica, 2008).

Vuk Radović, "Uslovi za ostvarivanje prava nesaglasnih akcionara" [Conditions for exercising shareholder's right to appraisal] (2017) 4-6 Pravo i privreda, 49-70.

Vuk Radović, "Odmeravanje visine naknade nesaglasnim akcionarima" [Dissenting shareholders' right to a fair value of shares] in Vuk Radović (ed), *Usklađivanje poslovnog prava Srbije sa pravom EU – 2017* [Harmonization of the Serbian Business Law with the Business Law of the European Union – 2017] (Faculty of Law University of Belgrade, Belgrade, 2017), 64-90.

Vuk Radović, *Stečajno pravo – knjiga druga (pobijanje pravnih radnji stečajnog dužnika, reorganizacija, međunarodni stečaj, реорганизацuја, stečaj povezanih društava)* [Bankruptcy law – part II (avoidance powers, reorganization, international bankruptcy, bankruptcy of corporate groups] (Faculty of Law University of Belgrade, Belgrade, 2017).

Zlatko Stefanović, Bojan Stanivuk, *Komentar Zakona o privrednim društvima* [Commentary on Law on Partnerships and Companies] (Paragrag Co, Novi Sad, 2012).

Mirko Vasiljević, *Komentar Zakona o preduzećima* [Commentary on Law on enterprises] (The Business Lawyers Association of the Federal Republic of Yugoslavia, Belgrade, 1996).

Mirko Vasiljević, *Vodič za čitanje Zakona o privrednim društvima* [Guide for reading Law on partnerships and companies] (The Business Lawyers Association of the Republic of Serbia and Montenegro, Belgrade, 2004).

Marco Ventoruzzo, "Freeze-Outs: Transcontinental Analysis and Reform Proposals" (2010) 50(4) *Virginia Journal of International Law*, 841-917.

Employee Participation in the Boards and Corporate Restructuring – The Perspective of EU Law

Achim Seifert[*]

Summary

* Professor of Private Law, German and European Labour Law & Comparative Law at the Friedrich-Schiller-University of Jena.

A. Corporate Restructuring as Challenge for Employee Participation in the Boards

Employee participation in company boards,[1] as it has been developed in a number of EU Member States in their national laws,[2] depends on the legal form of business in which the company is organised. In most of the Member States which have established employee participation schemes, board-level representation is limited to public limited companies,[3] only in few Member States employee participation schemes are extended to other legal forms such as private limited companies, cooperatives[4] or mutual associations.[5] Due to this limitation of employee participation to determined legal forms of business, the rules on employee representation in the boards have never become a company law [*Unternehmensrecht*], *i.e.* a set of rules that applies to all companies of a minimum size, independently from their legal form.[6]

1 Pursuant to the definition of Art. 2k Directive 2001/86/EC of 8 October 2001 complementing the Statute for a European Company with regard to the involvement of employees in the European company (O.J.E.C. 2001 L 294/22), "participation" means the influence of the body representative of the employees and/or the employees' representatives in the affairs of a company by way of the right to elect or appoint some of the members of the company's supervisory or administrative organ, or the right to recommend and/or oppose the appointment of some or all of the members of the company's supervisory or administrative organ".

2 For an overview of the different models of employee participation in the boards see Achim Seifert, Employee Participation at Board Level in Europe, in Jürgen Basedow, Chen Su, Matteo Fornasier and Ulla Liukkunen (eds), *Employee Participation and Collective Bargaining in Europe and China*, (2016), 209-236 with further references.

3 See e.g. Arts. 225-27 et seq. French Commercial Code; Art. L. 426-1 Labour Code of Luxembourg.

4 Cf. S. 1(1) of the German Act on Employee Participation [*Mitbestimmungsgesetz (MitbestG)*] and S. 1(1) of the German Act on Employee Participation in supervisory boards by one-third [*Drittelbeteiligungsgesetz (DrittelbG)*]; see also Arts. 110(1) and (5) of the Austrian Works Constitution Act [*Arbeitsverfassungsgesetz*] and Art. 2:263(2) Dutch Civil Code [*Buergerlijk Wetboek*].

5 Cf. S. 1(1) No. 4 DrittelbG and Art. 110(5) No. 2 Arbeitsverfassungsgesetz.

6 The debate on the establishing of such *Unternehmensrecht* has been relevant for the evolution of employee participation in Germany. For a brief overview see Achim Seifert, Unternehmensinteresse und Aufsichtsratsmitbestimmung im Spannungsverhältnis, in: Ulrich Jürgens, Dieter Sadowski, Folke Schuppert & Manfred Weiss (eds), Perspektiven der Corporate Governance – Bestimmungsverfahren unternehmerischer Entscheidungsprozesse und Mitwirkung der Arbeitnehmer (2007), 258 (262-3) with further references.

This only fragmentary character of national employee participation schemes which results from their implementation into the structures of corporate law may be considered as the Achilles' tendon of employee participation since it opens to companies many options to avoid existing statutory employee participation schemes. Corporate restructuring, *i.e.* the corporate reorganization of the company by means of mergers, division operations or conversions, may be used by companies, covered by a statutory employee participation scheme, in order to escape from employee participation. Such avoidance strategies have been observed in the Member States of the EU providing statutory duties for certain legal forms to establish an employee representation within the boards. The example par excellence for such avoidance strategies is probably the escape from employee participation in Germany since the German Act of employee participation [*Mitbestimmungsgesetz*] guarantees even an equal representation of shareholders and employees in the supervisory boards of public limited companies, private limited companies and cooperatives employing 2,000 or more employees. The principle of contractual freedom in corporate law and the vested rights of employees to participate through their representatives in the management of the company may therefore be in a state of tension.

This also applies to the European level. The EU has not been able to establish a harmonized model of employee representation in the boards covering all corporations of a minimum size within the Internal Market. The proposal of the European Commission for a so-called Fifth Directive on Company Law which comprised provisions on board-level participation of employees by one-third in the supervisory boards of public limited companies with 500 or more employees has not been adopted by the Council:[7] leaving aside that the Draft Fifth Directive only provided an employee representation of one-third in the supervisory boards, its scope of application was limited to public limited companies and did not cover other legal forms of business such as private limited companies. In the end, this

7 Proposition d'une cinquième directive tendant à coordonner les garanties qui sont exigées dans les États membres des sociétés, au sens de l'article 58 paragraphe 2 du traité, pour protéger les intérêts, tant des associés que des tiers en ce qui concerne la structure des société anonymes ainsi que les pouvoirs et obligations de leurs organes, J.O.C.E.E. 1972 C 131/49. See also the amended proposal for a Fifth Directive founded on Art. 54(3) (g) of the EEC Treaty concerning the structure of public limited companies and the powers and obligations of their organs, O.J.C.E.E. 1983 C 240/2.

project has been silently buried.[8] The main reasons for this failure were the refusal of the German Government which was afraid that the German model of paritarian employee participation would not be acceptable anymore, and other Member States where the idea of an employee representation in the boards as such is strongly rejected.[9]

As a result, statutory employee participation schemes under the national laws of the EU Member States are exposed to corporate restructuring operations which may weaken or avoid them. Regarding the company law side, Directive (EU) 2017/1132 relating to certain aspects of company law addresses various forms of corporate restructuring, namely national as well as cross-border mergers and divisions of limited liability companies. Additionally, the "Company Law Package" of the European Commission of April 2018 which contains *inter alia* a "Proposal for a Directive amending Directive (EU) 2017/1132 as regards cross-border conversions, mergers and divisions" will complete the already existing rules on employee participation in the event of corporate restructuring operations.

The purpose of the following paper is to critically analyse the effects different operations of corporate restructuring may have on employee participation schemes under the national laws of the Member States. Since there are no general principles or rules addressing the fate of employee participation schemes in the event of corporate restructuring operations, it will be necessary to examine separately the different forms of corporate restructuring for which the EU has established a regulatory framework. Also the above mentioned reform proposal of the European Commission regarding Directive (EU) 2017/1132 ("Company Law Package") shall be taken into consideration as far as it addresses corporate restructuring operations such as cross-border divisions and cross-border conversions.[10] In a first step, the impact of cross-border mergers shall be examined. Secondly, division operations and their potential effect on employee participation schemes shall

8 For an assessment of the controversy on the Fifth Directive of Company Law see Thomas Abeltshauser, *Strukturalternativen für eine europäische Unternehmensverfassung: eine rechtsvergleichende Untersuchung zum 5. Gesellschaftsrechtlichen EG-Richtlinienvorschlag*, (1990).

9 This is notably the case for the UK: for a fuller analysis see Achim Seifert, Employee Participation at Board Level in Europe, in Jürgen Basedow, Chen Su, Matteo Fornasier and Ulla Liukkunen (eds), *Employee Participation and Collective Bargaining in Europe and China*, (2016), 209 (217-8), with further references.

10 At the time of writing of this paper, however, neither the European Parliament, nor the Council have taken a decision on the Commission Proposal. The following paper will therefore be focusing on the Commission Proposal as far as the reform is concerned.

be analysed, and in a third step, a closer look shall be given to employee participation schemes in the frame of cross-border conversions.

B. Mergers

As far as employee participation is concerned, Directive (EU) 2017/1132 provides different rules for national mergers and for cross-border mergers.[11] Both sets of rules need to be examined in the present context.

I. National Mergers

Already in 1978, the national rules of the Member States on national mergers of public limited liability companies have been harmonised.[12] This *acquis communautaire* now builds Chapter 1 of Title 2 Directive (EU) 2017/1132 relating to certain aspects of company law. Neither Directive 2017/1132, nor its predecessors comprise rules on the fate of employee participation schemes in the event of a national merger operation between public limited liability companies. This lack is without relevance however, since the public limited liability company resulting from the merger (*e.g.* a German *Aktiengesellschaft* or a Luxembourgian *société anonyme*) will be covered by the statutory employee participation scheme in the same way as one or several of the corporations which have participated in the merger operation when the statutory threshold for the application of an employee participation scheme has been reached.

Only when the company resulting from a national merger is organised in a legal form to which the employee participation scheme of that Member State does not apply, the merger may be used as avoidance strategy. Such mergers have not been harmonised by the rules of Directive (EU) 2017/1132 on national mergers yet. The persistence of a statutory employee participation scheme, existing in one or more of the companies participat-

11 For a definition of the two types of merger, i.e. the merger by acquisition and the merger by the formation of a new company, see Arts. 89 and 90 Directive (EU) 2017/1132.

12 Cf. Third Council Directive 78/855/EEC of 9 October 1978 based on Art. 54(3)(g) of the Treaty concerning mergers of public limited liability companies, O.J.E.E.C. 1978 L 295/36. This Directive has been repealed by Directive 2011/35/EU of the European Parliament and of the Council of 5 April 2011 concerning mergers of public limited liability companies, O.J.E.U. 2011 L 110/1.

ing in a merger, therefore depends on whether statutory law covers different legal forms of business and not only one of them (e.g. public limited liability companies). A private limited company [*société à responsabilité limitée*] under Luxembourgian law, for instance, resulting from a national merger in which a public limited liability company [*société anonyme*] with a board co-determined by one-third[13] has participated will not be co-determined after the merger since the statutory employee participation scheme of the Grand-Duchy only applies to public limited liability companies and not to other legal forms of business.[14]

II. Cross-Border Mergers

By far much more dangerous for employee participation schemes under the laws of Member States are cross-border mergers. Such operations may undermine existing employee participation structures in companies participating in them. In the event that a corporation, covered by a statutory board-level representation scheme, is going to be merged in another corporation, established according to the rules of another Member State and not providing such employee participation scheme, the employees may lose their participation rights by a cross-border merger. Due to these risks of cross-border mergers for existing employee participation schemes, namely Germany refused to adopt the Directive on cross-border mergers as long as the instrument does not comprise rules which sufficiently safeguard an existing board-level representation of employees in at least one of the participating companies.[15] The fear was great that companies may use European company law in order to avoid employee participation schemes under national law. Employee participation was therefore the main obstacle to the adoption of the Directive on cross-border mergers. Directive 2005/56/EC of 26 October 2005 on cross-border mergers[16] could only be voted after adopting the negotiation model of Directive 2001/86/EC supplementing the Statute for a European company with regard to the involvement of em-

---

13 Cf. Art. L. 426-1 Labour Code of Luxembourg.

14 For a critical analysis of this lack of protection, see Achim Seifert, Comment recodifier le dialogue social au sein de l'entreprise?, Journal des tribunaux Luxembourg 2011, 117, 121.

15 On this controversy cf. Matthias Habersack and Dirk Verse, *Europäisches Gesellschaftsrecht*, (2011), § 8, para 52 with further references.

16 O.J.E.C. 2005 L 28/40.

ployees.[17] The rules of Directive 2005/56/EC on cross-border mergers have been replaced by Articles 118 to 134 of Directive (EU) 2017/1132 of 14 June 2017 relating to certain aspects of company law (codification).[18] As far as employee participation is concerned, Article 133 of Directive (EU) 2017/1132 replaces Article 16 of Directive 2005/56/EC, but without substantive changes.

1. *Duty to Negotiate an Agreement on Employee Involvement*

Article 133(1) of Directive (EU) 2017/1132 provides as conflict of laws rule that the rules on employee participation, if any, in the Member State where it has its registered office shall apply to the company resulting from the cross-border merger. As a result, the law of the real seat of the company applies. However, the second paragraph of this Article comprises three derogations from this principle. If the requirements of one of these three exceptions are fulfilled, employee participation in the company resulting from the cross-border merger shall be negotiated with the employees, similar to the negotiations on employee involvement in the SE.

The first case of derogation is that at least one of the merging companies has, in the six months prior to the publication of the draft terms of the cross-border merger, an average number of employees that exceeds 500 and is operating under an employee participation system within the meaning of point (k) of Article 2 of Directive 2001/86/EC.[19] Secondly, there is a duty to negotiate employee participation when the national law applicable to the company resulting from the cross-border merger does not offer at least the same level of employee participation as operated in the merging companies.[20] And finally, the law of the seat State does not apply when the national law applicable to the company resulting from the cross-border merger does not guarantee to employees of the company who are employed in other Member States the same level of employee participation as is provid-

17 Cf. Art. 16 Directive 2005/56/EC.

18 O.J.E.U. 2017 L 169/46.

19 Cf. Art. 133(2), phrase 1 Directive (EU) 2017/1132.

20 Cf. Art. 133(2)(a) Directive (EU) 2017/1132. Pursuant to this rule, the level of employee participation is measured by reference to the proportion of employee representatives amongst the members of the administrative or supervisory organ or their committees or of the management group which covers the profit units of the company, subject to employee representation.

ed for those employees who are employed in the Member State where the company resulting from the cross-border merger has its registered office.[21]

2. Procedure

Article 133 of Directive (EU) 2017/1132 essentially picks up the negotiation model of Directive 2001/86/EC of 8 October 2001 supplementing the Statute for a European company with regard to the involvement of employees. The management of the participating corporations and a special negotiating body (SNB) shall therefore negotiate an agreement on employee involvement in the company resulting from the cross-border merger. There are only two cases when no negotiations take place: When the SNB decides by a qualified majority not to open negotiations or to terminate negotiations already opened,[22] or when the relevant organs of the merging companies choose without any prior negotiation to be directly subject to the standard rules for participation of the Member State in which the company resulting from the cross-border merger is to have its registered office.[23] In the latter case, Management may reduce transaction costs by avoiding the complex and time consuming negotiation procedure as provided by Article 133 of Directive (EU) 2017/1132; in this respect, the rules on cross-border mergers go beyond the rules on the European Company, since Directive 2001/86/EC does not give Management the power to sidestep the negotiation model.

The cross-border merger may not be registered unless an agreement on arrangements for employee involvement has been concluded or the standard rules apply since the negotiations have failed or the relevant organs of the merging companies have chosen without any prior negotiation to be directly subject to the standard rules for participation or a decision of the SNB pursuant to Article 133(4)(b) of Directive (EU) 2017/1132 has been taken.[24] By this, compliance with the negotiation procedure under Article 133 of Directive (EU) 2017/1132 is ensured.

---

21 Art. 133(2)(c) Directive (EU) 2017/1132.

22 Cf. Art. 133(4)(b) Directive (EU) 2017/1132. The provision requires for such decision of the SNB "a majority of two thirds of its members representing at least two thirds of the employees, including the votes of members representing employees in at least two different Member States".

23 Cf. Art. 133(4)(a) Directive (EU) 2017/1132.

24 Cf. Art. 133(3) Directive 2005/56/EC in conjunction with Arts. 12(2) to (4) Regulation (EC) No. 2157/2001.

a) Negotiation of an Agreement on Employee Participation

Neither Article 133 of Directive (EU) 2017/1132, nor Directive 2001/86/EC provide a more concrete framework for the negotiations between the SNB and the management of the companies participating in the cross-border merger. Article 4(1) of Directive 2001/86/EC only obliges the parties to "negotiate in a spirit of cooperation with a view to reaching an agreement on arrangements for the involvement of the employees". However, in most cases, the parties reach such agreement.

b) Application of the Standard Rules

The Standard Rules of Directive (EU) 2017/1132 apply when the parties so agree or when no agreement has been concluded after six months of negotiation and the competent organ of each of the participating companies has decided to accept the application of the standard rules.[25] Furthermore, as has already been mentioned above, the relevant organs of the merging companies may skip the negotiation procedure and thereby accelerate the merger procedure.[26]

The underlying principle of the Standard Rules is the "before and after principle".[27] Thus, the highest level of employee participation which has been practised in one or several companies participating in the cross-border merger shall be maintained for the company resulting from the cross-border merger. However, Article 133(3)(e) of Directive 2017/1132 considerably softens this principle and differs from the Standard Rules of Directive 2001/86/EC. Article 7(2)(b) of Directive 2001/86/EC only requires that in the case of a merger, before registration of the SE, one or more forms of participation applied in one or more of the participating companies were covering at least 25 percent of the total number of employees in all companies which participated in the merger. Article 133 of Directive (EU) 2017/1132 raises this relatively low percentage from 24 to 33 1/3 percent. By this, the scope of application of the Standard Rules is reduced in cases of cross-border mergers. There is no convincing justification for this threshold under Directive (EU) 2017/1132. This derogation from the Stan-

---

25 Cf. Art. 133(3)(e) Directive (EU) 2017/1132, read together with Arts. 7(1)(a) and (b) Directive 2001/86/EC.

26 Cf. Art. 133(4)(a) Directive (EU) 2017/1132.

27 See e.g. Stefan Grundmann, *European Company Law*, (2012) § 33, para 57.

dard Rules of the SE law is not consistent given that also an SE may be established by a cross-border merger.[28]

3. *Reform*

The "Company Law Package" of the European Commission proposes only two rather peripheral changes of Article 133 of Directive (EU) 2017/1132 regarding employee participation in the event of a cross-border merger.

The proposed new Article 133(7) of Directive (EU) 2017/1132 extends the already existing prohibition of abuse of rights. Currently, Article 133(7) excludes that during three years following the cross-border merger, the company performs a subsequent domestic merger which would result in an undermining of the system of employee participation. The Commission Proposal extends this clause to all possible subsequent domestic operations (*i.e.* mergers, divisions and conversions) in a period of three years following the cross-border merger and would thereby exclude that an employee participation scheme existing in one of the participating companies is jeopardized by a cross-border merger and any posterior restructuring operation within this period.

Secondly, the European Commission proposes to supplement the provisions on employee participation by a new Article 133(8) pursuant to which "a company shall communicate to its employees whether it chooses to apply standard rules for participation or whether it enters into negotiations within the SNB"; the exact time for the information procedure remains however unclear.[29] If the company wants to negotiate an agreement with the SNB, it shall inform its employees about the outcome of the negotiations without undue delay.

C. *Divisions*

Also divisions of companies may undermine existing board-level representation schemes in the companies concerned.[30] A division may result in a

28 Cf. Art. 2(1) and Art. 17 et seq. of Directive 2001/86/EC.

29 For a critical assessment of Art. 133(8) of the Commission Proposal see Jessica Schmidt, EU Company Law Package 2018 – Mehr Digitalisierung und Mobilität von Gesellschaften (Teil 1) –, Der Konzern 2018, 229 (244).

30 For a definition of the different types of divisions operations cf. Art. 135 Directive (EU) 2017/1132.

reduction of the number of employees of a corporation covered by a statutory employee participation scheme and may therefore have the effect that its workforce remains below the statutory threshold for the application of the rules on employee participation.[31] Also in the context of divisions, it shall be distinguished between (national) divisions of companies within one and the same Member State and cross-border divisions.

I. National Divisions of Limited Liability Companies

Directive (EU) 2017/1132 only partially addresses the protection of employees in a division operation. According to Article 145 Directive (EU) 2017/1132, protection of the rights of the employees of each of the companies involved in a division shall be regulated in accordance with Directive 2001/23/EC on transfer of undertakings.[32] Article 3(1) of this Directive provides, however, only the transfer of "the transferor's rights and obligations arising from a contract of employment or from an employment relationship existing on the date of a transfer [...] to the transferee". It does not safeguard therefore a board-level representation scheme existing in the company of the transferor. Consequently, there is no provision in the Directive which deals with the maintenance of an existing board-level representation scheme in the company that is divided.[33] As a result of this only

31 E.g. 500 employees under S. 1(1) of the German DrittelbG or 1,000 employees under Art. L. 426-1 Labour Code of Luxembourg.

32 Directive 2001/23/EC of 12 March 2001 on the approximation of the laws of the Member States relating to the safeguarding of employees' rights in the event of transfers of undertakings, businesses or parts of undertakings or businesses, O.J.E.C. 2001 L 82/16.

33 According to Art. 2(1)(c) Directive 2001/23/EC, "'representatives of employees' [...] shall mean the representatives of the employees provided for by the laws or practices of the Member States". The wording of this provision, as well as the fact that Art. 2(c) Directive 77/187/CEE – the first Directive on transfer of undertakings – explicitly excluded "members of administrative, governing or supervisory bodies of companies who represent employees on such bodies in certain Member States" from its scope of application, could speak in favour of the applicability of Directive 2001/23/CE to employee participation in the boards. But if one takes into account the elaboration of Directive 2001/23/CE, the difference in the wording between the two provisions may be explained by the Commission's intention to harmonize the definition of "representatives of employees" with that of Art. 1(1)(b) Directive 98/59/CE. By adopting Art. 2(1)(c) Directive 2001/23/CE, the European legislator has not pursued the purpose to change the enlarge the meaning of the term "representatives of employees" and has not had the intention

fragmentary regulation of employee rights in Article 145 of Directive (EU) 2017/1132, division operations may weaken existing board-level employee representation schemes under the national laws of the Member States.

Only few Member States have resolved this problem by national law. Section 325(1) of the German Act on corporate restructuring [*Umwandlungsgesetz*], for instance, provides that an employee participation scheme, existing prior to the division operation, shall be maintained for a period of five years after the division even though the statutory threshold for employee participation is not met anymore. This rule does not apply, however, when the number of employees in the dividing company has been reduced to less than one-fourth of the statutory threshold. But even beyond the expiration of this period, employee participation may be maintained in the dividing company when the dividing company and the companies resulting from the division constitute a group of companies which often is the case. As a matter of fact, the German Acts on employee participation comprise rules which impute employees of the dependent companies of a group for purposes of calculation of the threshold to the holding company.[34] These provisions primarily make sure that employee participation takes place where the important decisions within the group are taken. But they also prevent that divisions within the group may have the effect that statutory employee participation schemes are not applicable anymore. On the contrary, in the Austrian system, for example, which does not provide a statutory threshold for employee participation in the supervisory boards of public limited liability companies, private limited companies and some other legal forms of business, such provisions do not make any sense: however, the effects of divisions on employee participation are indirectly softened by Sections 110(6) and (6a) of the Works Constitution Act [*Arbeitsverfassungsgesetz*] according to which all works councils of a group of companies participate in the election of the representatives on the supervisory council of the holding company.

---

to include employees' representatives in the boards in the scope of application of the Directive. Cf. e.g. Timon Grau and Felix Hartmann, Betriebsübergang in: Ulrich Preis and Adam Sagan (eds), *Europäisches Arbeitsrecht: Grundlagen, Richtlinien, Folgen für das deutsche Recht*, (2015), § 11, para. 169.

34 Cf. S. 5(1) MitbestG and S. 2(2) DrittelbG. S. 2(2) DrittelbG limits however such imputation of employees of the subsidiaries to the holding to the case that the holding exercises its dominant influence over the subsidiaries pursuant to a domination agreement between them [*Beherrschungsvertrag*] under S. 291 of the Act on public limited companies [*Aktiengesetz*]: This considerably limits the scope of application of this imputation rule.

It is worth to be noted, however, that most of the national systems of board-level employee representation do not provide such rules for groups of companies.[35] In these Member States, national board-level representation systems may be easily jeopardised by divisions operated within one and the same Member State.

II. Cross-Border Divisions: The Proposal of the European Commission

The EU has not established yet a legal framework for cross-border divisions even though these operations are protected by freedom of establishment under Article 49 TFEU.[36] The Commission's Company Law Package of April 2018 tries to fill in this legal gap by proposing to include in Directive (EU) 2017/1132 a new chapter on cross-border divisions of public limited liability companies.[37]

1. The Negotiation Model

Concerning employee participation in the boards, Article 160n of the Commission Proposal picks up the negotiation model as it is provided by Directive 2001/86/EC for the establishing of a SE and of Article 133 of Directive (EU) 2017/1132 for cross-border mergers.[38] Nonetheless, the Commission Proposal differs in some respects from the negotiation model as provided by Article 133 of Directive (EU) 2017/1132 for cross-border mergers.

A first difference concerns the duty to negotiate an agreement on employee participation. In contrast to Article 133(2) of Directive (EU) 2017/1132, the threshold does not amount to 500 employees but to an av-

35 See e.g. Art. 225-27-1 French Commercial Code and Art. L. 426-1 et seq. Labour Code of Luxembourg.

36 In this sense ECJ, case C-411/03, 13.12.2005, *SEVIC Systems AG*, ECR 2005, I-10805, para. 19: "Cross-border merger operations, *like other company transformation operations*, respond to the needs for cooperation and consolidation between companies established in different Member States. They constitute particular methods of exercise of the freedom of establishment […] and are therefore amongst those economic activities in respect of which Member States are required to comply with the freedom of establishment laid down by Article 43 EC."

37 See Arts. 160a to 160w Commission Proposal for a Directive amending Directive (EU) 2017/1132.

38 For details cf. supra B.II. with further references.

erage number of employees equivalent to four-fifths of the applicable threshold, laid down in the law of the Member State of the company being divided, which triggers the participation of employees.[39] This probably takes into consideration that statutory thresholds for employee participation in some Member States are below 500 and has to be welcomed.[40] Furthermore, this rule aims at avoiding abuses by reducing temporarily the number of employees below the statutory threshold for the applicable employee participation scheme.

Interestingly, Article 160n(4) of the Commission Proposal for a Directive amending Directive (EU) 2017/1132 does not make reference to Article 133(4)(a) of Directive (EU) 2017/1132. As a result, the relevant organs of the dividing companies may not choose without any prior negotiation to be directly subject to the standard rules for participation. The reason for this omission is not revealed by the explanatory memorandum of the Commission and remains therefore unclear. It strengthens the negotiation procedure but may prolongate the period of time necessary to operate a cross-border division.

A third difference to the cross-border merger procedure under Article 133 of Directive (EU) 2017/1132 refers to the decision of the SNB not to open negotiations or to terminate negotiations already opened: like the procedure for cross-border mergers, a majority of two- thirds of its members representing at least two-thirds of the employees is required. However, Article 160n(4)(a) of the Commission Proposal for a Directive amending Directive (EU) 2017/1132 seems to skip the cross-border element required for the cross-border merger ("at least two-thirds of the employees, including the votes of members representing employees employed in at least two Member States"). The explanatory memorandum does not give an explanation for this derogation. The proposed rule would obviously facilitate to terminate already started negotiations on employee participation or to avoid such negotiations in the event of cross-border divisions.[41] Nonetheless the proposal is not convincing as it is not consistent with the idea of

---

39 Cf. Art. 160n(2) Commission Proposal for a Directive amending Directive (EU) 2017/1132.

40 In Sweden, for example, there is a threshold of 25 employees for board-level representation. Cf. Anders Victorin, Employee Participation on the company board: The Swedish experience, in Theodor Baums and Peter Ulmer (eds), *Employees' Co-Determination in the Member States of the European Union* (2004), 125.

41 In this sense, Jessica Schmidt, EU Company Law Package 2018 – Mehr Digitalisierung und Mobilität von Gesellschaften (Teil 1) –, Der Konzern 2018.

the negotiation procedure to take sufficiently into account the interests of the workforces of the company employed in different Member States.

Finally, Article 160n(4)(c) of the Commission Proposal for a Directive amending Directive (EU) 2017/1132 provides a transitional arrangement for employee participation in the dividing company: "The rules on participation that applied prior to the cross-border division continue to apply until the date of application of any subsequently agreed rules" or [...] until the application of the Standard Rules. This proposed rule has only a limited relevance. It maintains the existing employee participation scheme after the cross-border division operation has become effective and avoids a period of absence of employee participation until new employee representatives under Article 160n of the Commission Proposal for a Directive amending Directive (EU) 2017/1132 have been elected.

The competent authorities in the destination Member State of the operation shall ensure that arrangements for employee participation in the recipient companies have been determined in accordance with Article 160n of the Commission Proposal for a Directive amending Directive (EU) 2017/1132.[42] This means that the competent authority of the destination Member State(s) shall verify whether the company has complied with the procedure under Article 160n and cannot register the conversion before compliance with the rules on employee participation has been accomplished.

2. *Abusive Cross-Border Divisions*

These negative effects of cross-border divisions may perhaps be relativized by Article 160d(3) of the Commission Proposal for a Directive amending Directive (EU) 2017/1132 which prohibits the Member States to authorize a cross-border division "when it determines, after an examination of the specific case and having regard to all relevant facts and circumstances, that it constitutes an artificial arrangement aimed at [...] unduly prejudicing the legal or contractual rights of employees [...]". Recital 40 makes explicitly clear that also the circumvention of rules on employee participation may be an abusive purpose under Article 160d(3) of the Commission Proposal for a Directive amending Directive (EU) 2017/1132. However, the same Recital 40 clarifies that this provision, derogating from freedom of estab-

---

42 Cf. Art. 160r(1) Commission Proposal for a Directive amending Directive (EU) 2017/1132.

lishment under Article 49 TFEU, "must be interpreted strictly and must be based on an individual assessment of all relevant circumstances".[43]

The exact relevance of this provision for employee participation schemes remains unclear: especially, the explanatory Memorandum of the Commission Proposal does not reveal concrete elements which allow discerning, whether a cross-border division operation constitutes an abuse of freedom of establishment or not. The division as such may not be considered as an abuse of rights under Article 160d(3) of the Commission Proposal for a Directive amending Directive (EU) 2017/1132. There need to be further factual elements in a specific case which allow to qualify a cross-border division operation as an artificial arrangement under this provision. The wording of the provision but also the abuse of rights as it is understood in the national laws of the Member States[44] suggests that there must be malicious intention on the company's side which plans the cross-border division operation. A cross-border division may therefore be considered as abusive when its exclusive purpose is to avoid employee participation in the company.

At first sight, it seems to be difficult to proof that a cross-border division operation has the exclusive purpose to unduly prejudice an existing employee participation scheme in the company. The efficiency of this prohibition of abusive practices will essentially depend on the report, the independent expert shall deliver under Article 160i(3)(f) of the Commission Proposal for a Directive amending Directive (EU) 2017/1132. As a matter of fact, his or her report shall also comprise "a description of all factual elements necessary for the competent authority [...] to carry out an in-depth assessment to determine whether the intended cross-border division constitutes an artificial arrangement".[45] In addition, there is a duty for public disclosure of the draft terms of the cross-border division and the report of the

43 See also Recital 7 Commission Proposal for a Directive amending Directive (EU) 2017/1132.

44 Only a few significant examples from the national law of the Member States will suffice: for the *théorie de l'abus des droits* under French law see Jean Carbonnier, *Droit Civil – Tome 4: Les obligations* (2000), paras 232 et seq; for the German doctrine of abuse of rights [*Rechtsmissbrauchslehre*] cf. Manfred Wolf and Jörg Neuner, *Allgemeiner Teil des Bürgerlichen Rechtes*, (2016), § 20, paras 75 et seq. In the common law countries, the doctrine of abuse of rights is unknown but functional equivalents can be found in a number of malice rules in tort law: see e.g. Simon Deakin, Angus Johnston and Basil Markesinis, *Tort Law*, (2013), 431 et seq.

45 Art. 160i(3)(f) Commission Proposal for a Directive amending Directive (EU) 2017/1132.

independent expert.[46] Furthermore, the competent authority of the company being divided shall assess whether the cross-border division constitutes an artificial arrangement under Article 160d(3) of the Commission Proposal for a Directive amending Directive (EU) 2017/1132 and shall carry out an in-depth assessment of all relevant facts and circumstances.[47] Article 160p(1) lists a number of circumstances to be taken into account by the competent authority when assessing the operation. Only the intent of the cross-border division and the number of employees (employed by the dividing company before and after the division) may be relevant for the assessment whether the operation constitutes an artificial arrangement to circumvent existing employee participation schemes. However, Article 160p(1), subparagraph (2) emphasizes that these elements "may be only considered as indicative factors in the overall assessment and therefore shall not be considered in isolation".

According to Recital 40 of the Commission Proposal for a Directive amending Directive (EU) 2017/1132, "a procedural and substantive framework which describes the margin of discretion and allows for the diversity of approaches by Member States whilst at the same time setting out the requirements to streamline the actions to be taken by national authorities to fight abuses in conformity with Union law should be laid down". The contours of such a procedural and substantive framework remain however cryptic.

D. *Cross-Border Conversions*

Regarding cross-border conversions of companies within the Internal Market, the EU has neither established a legal framework even though the ECJ has ruled in *Vale Epítési kft* and in *Polbud* that freedom of establishment under Article 49 TFEU also covers cross-border conversions.[48] This may change in the near future since the Company Law Package proposed by the European Commission in April 2018 provides rules for cross-border

---

46 Cf. Art. 160j(1) Commission Proposal for a Directive amending Directive (EU) 2017/1132.

47 Cf. Art. 160p(1) Commission Proposal for a Directive amending Directive (EU) 2017/1132.

48 ECJ, Case 378/10, 12.07.2012, *Vale Építési kft*, ECLI:EU:C:2012:440. See also ECR, Case 210/06, 16.12.2008, *Cartesio Oktató és Szolgáltató bt.*, ECLI:EU:C:2008:723, Para. 111 as obiter dictum and ECR, Case 106/16, 25.10.2017, *Polbud — Wykonawstwo sp. z o.o., in liquidation*, ECLI:EU:C:2017:804, paras 46 et seq.

conversions.[49] According to Article 86b(2) of the Commission Proposal for a Directive amending Directive (EU) 2017/1132, "cross-border conversions" are operations "whereby a company, without being dissolved, wound up or going into liquidation, converts the legal form under which it is registered in a departure Member State into a legal form of a company of a destination Member State and transfers at least its registered office into the destination Member State whilst retaining its legal personality". Article 86l of the Commission Proposal for a Directive amending Directive (EU) 2017/1132 essentially extends the negotiation model for cross-border mergers to cross-border conversions. For the details, reference is therefore made to the chapters on employee participation in the context of cross-border mergers and of cross-border divisions.[50] Thus, the procedure foreseen under Article 86l of the Commission Proposal differs in the same way as Article 160i of the Commission Proposal for a Directive amending Directive (EU) 2017/1132 from the procedure for cross-border mergers as provided by Article 133 of Directive (EU) 2017/1132. Moreover, like Article 160d(3) of the Commission Proposal concerning cross-border divisions, Article 86c(3) of the Commission Proposal for a Directive amending Directive (EU) 2017/1132 prohibits abuses of the right to convert companies across the borders of the Member States.[51]

E. The Use of Legal Forms under the Law of Another Member State

In its seminal judgments in the cases *Centros*,[52] *Überseering*[53] and *Inspire Art*[54] the ECJ has recognized that freedom of establishment under Article 49 TFEU also guarantees a mutual recognition of the legal forms of the national legal orders of Member States.[55] Corporations, established according to the rules of another Member State, which are moving to the Federal Re-

---

49 Cf. Arts. 86a to 86u Commission Proposal.

50 See supra B.II. and C.II.

51 For more details see supra C.II.

52 ECJ, Case 212/97, 9.03.1999, *Centros Ltd v. Erhvervs- og Selskabsstyrelsen*, ECR 1999, I-1459.

53 ECJ, Case 208/00, 5.11.2002, *Überseering BV v. Nordic Construction Company Baumanagement GmbH (NCC)*, ECR 2002, I-9919.

54 ECJ, Case 167/01, 30.09.2003, *Kamer van Koophandel en Fabrieken voor Amsterdam v. Inspire Art Ltd.*, ECR 2003, I-10955.

55 For an assessment of this case law of the ECJ on freedom of establishment see Stefan Grundmann, *European Company Law*, (2012), § 25, paras 23 et seq., with further references.

public of Germany, are therefore recognized in the same way as legal forms under German law. As a result, a corporation established under English law such as a private limited company (Ltd.) may transfer its seat from the territory of the United Kingdom to the Federal Republic of Germany without losing its legal identity and may act in Germany in the same way as a *Gesellschaft mit beschränkter Haftung* (*GmbH*) under German law.

I. Circumvention of National Employee Participation Schemes

The risks of this new understanding of freedom of establishment for employee board-level representation schemes under national law are obvious. It opens the door for companies to circumvent national employee board-level representation schemes in the Member States.

These may establish a corporation under a national law which does not provide an employee representation in the boards and may thereafter transfer its seat to Germany. According to a recent study of the German Hans-Böckler-Foundation, this practice has been increasing over the last years.[56] In June 2014, there were 94 companies with more than 500 employees in Germany to which German participation law could not be applied due to the fact that these companies were organised in the legal form of another Member State. In most cases, companies were organised as corporations corresponding to the German *Aktiengesellschaft* (*AG*) or *Gesellschaft mit beschränkter Haftung* (*GmbH*). Often, the foreign corporation becomes the holding of companies covered by one of the German Acts on board-level employee representation. In principle, German law provides that, for purposes of the calculation of the statutory threshold for employee participation, the employees of the whole group are considered to be employees of the group holding.[57] However, this rule only applies to group holdings organised in a legal form of business under German law which is covered by one of the German Acts on employee board-level representation.[58] In some cases, foreign corporations with seat in Germany have the legal form of a partnership limited by shares [*Kommanditgesellschaft auf Aktien*]. But sometimes, the German law of employee participation is circumvented by the

56 See Sebastian Sick, Der deutschen Mitbestimmung entzogen: Unternehmen mit ausländischer Rechtsform nehmen zu, in *Mitbestimmungsförderung, Report No. 8* (2015).

57 Cf. S. 5(1) Mitbestimmungsgesetz and S. 2(2) Drittelbeteiligungsgesetz.

58 See e.g. Hellmut Wißmann, Georg Kleinsorge and Claudia Schubert, *Mitbestimmungsrecht – Kommentar*, (2017), § 5 MitbestG, para 17 with further references.

use of a foreign corporation becoming the partner with unlimited liability [*Kommanditist*] in a private limited partnership [*Kommanditgesellschaft*] (*e.g.* a "Limited (Ltd.) & *Co.KG*" or a *besloten vennootschap met beperkte aansprakelijkheid (B.V.)* & Co.KG"). For a German *GmbH & Co.KG*, Section 4(1) of the Act on Employee Participation imputes the employees of the private limited partnership to the *GmbH*. But also this rule only applies to corporations under German law and not to corporations established according to the rules of the law of another Member State.[59]

It must be feared that this recent development to the detriment of employee board-level representation under German law will be continuing in the next years and will further expose statutory employee participation schemes under German law to erosion.

II. Strategies to Maintain Existing Board-Level Representation Schemes

There are mainly two policy strategies which may be pursued to protect existing employee participation schemes in these cases.

1. Harmonization of the National Laws of the Member States

One strategy to cope with the problems raised by the increasing mobility of corporations within the Internal Market might be a harmonization of the national law of the Member States concerning the effects of a transfer of the registered office of a company on employee participation schemes. Such Directive could provide the safeguard of existing board-level representation schemes in cases of cross-border transfers of a company's registered office, similar to the model of a negotiated employee participation, underlying Directive 2001/86/EC for the SE or of Article 133 of Directive 2017/1132/EU for cross-border mergers.[60] But up to now, there have been no initiatives on EU level addressing this problem. The proposals for a so-called Fourteenth Company Law Directive on the cross-border transfer of the company seat, discussed since forty years, only deals with cross-border transfers of seat linked with a change of the legal form of the company;

---

59 Cf. Wißmann, Kleinsorge and Schubert, *Mitbestimmungsrecht*, § 1 MitbestG, paras 17 et seq. with further references.

60 In this direction Christoph Teichmann, Mitbestimmungserstreckung für Auslandsgesellschaften, ZIP 2016, 899 (903 et seq.).

also the "Company Law Package" of the European Commission only addresses cross-border conversions.[61]

2. *Extension of National Board-Level Representation Schemes to Foreign Corporations*

Another policy option might be the extension of already existing statutory employee participation schemes to foreign corporations transferring their seat to another Member State in which certain legal forms of business under national law are submitted to such employee participation (e.g. Germany). The adoption of such an "Extension Act" has been claimed by various groups in the German Parliament[62] and by some labour law authors.[63] Also the coalition agreement between the Christian Democratic Parties (*CDU & CSU*) and the Social Democratic Party (*SPD*) of 7 February 2018 which defines the programme of the Federal Government for this legislature, goes in this direction: all three Government parties agree upon that the German system of board-level representation shall be safeguarded in the event of cross-border transfers of seat.[64] Even though the coalition agreement does not explicitly mention the adoption of an act extending the German employee participation scheme to foreign corporations with seat in Germany, it expresses a political will of the government majority to address the problem. At this stage, there are no concrete legislative proposals though.

61 Cf. supra D.

62 Cf. SPD-Bundestagsfraktion, Gesetzesantrag "Demokratische Teilhabe von Belegschaften und ihren Vertretern an unternehmerischen Entscheidungen" stärken of 16 June 2010, Bundestagsdrucksachen (BT-Drs.) 17/2122; Bundestagsfraktion der Partei Die LINKE of 21 April 2010 "Unternehmensmitbestimmung lückenlos garantieren", BT-Drs. 17/1413; Bundestagsfraktion BÜNDNIS 90/DIE GRÜNEN of 9 November 2016 "Unternehmensmitbestimmung stärken – Grauzonen schließen", BT-Drs. 18/10253; see also minor interpellation (Kleine Anfrage) der Bundestagsfraktion BÜNDNIS 90/DIE GRÜNEN of 15 April 2016 – "Politischer Handlungsbedarf – 40 Jahr Unternehmensmitbestimmung", BT-Drs. 18/8182.

63 Cf. e.g. Weiss and Seifert, Der europarechtliche Rahmen für ein Mitbestimmungserstreckungsgesetz, ZGR 2009, 542, 545 with further references.

64 Koalitionsvertrag zwischen CDU, CSU und SPD, Ein neuer Aufbruch für Europa – Eine neue Dynamik für Deutschland – Ein neuer Zusammenhalt für unser Land, 52. In the same vein, the resolution of the Federal Council [*Bundesrat*], "Mitbestimmung zukunftsfest gestalten" of 10 February 2017, BT-Drs. 740/16.

In the event that legislature adopts such an extension act, this would have to respect the requirements of the principle of freedom of establishment under Article 49 TFEU since it would interfere in the internal structure of corporations established under the law of another Member State. This aspect can only be indicated in the present context without a more in-depth analysis.[65] But in principle, such an extension of national employee participation schemes to corporations, established under the law of another Member State which have transferred their registered office to the Member State where a statutory employee participation scheme applies to corporations under the law of this Member State may be in accordance with Article 49 TFEU. According to the constant case law of the ECJ, restrictions on freedom of establishment may be justified if they are applied in a non-discriminatory manner (i), pursue a legitimate public interest (ii), are appropriate (iii) and necessary in order to attain the objective (iv).[66] The Court has recognized that also the protection of workers may constitute a legitimate interest, justifying restrictions on fundamental freedoms of the Treaty, and allows therefore also national measures of the Member States aiming at safeguarding the application of employee participation schemes. As to the necessity test (iv), the Member States shall make sure that such an extension of employee participation schemes is limited to foreign legal forms of business which correspond to the legal forms covered by the national employee participation scheme. In addition, such national extension act shall not apply to foreign companies with registered office in this Member State which are already covered by an employee participation scheme.

F. *Concluding Remarks*

Up to now, EU company law has only established a fragmentary legal framework for corporate restructuring operations. This may change if the European Commission's "Company Law Package" of April 2018 will be adopted, which comprises *inter alia* a proposal for a harmonization of the national provisions on cross-border divisions and cross-border conversions.

65 For a fuller analysis of this complex question see Manfred Weiss and Achim Seifert, Der europarechtliche Rahmen für ein "Mitbestimmungserstreckungsgesetz", ZGR 2009, 542 ff.; for a summary see also Achim Seifert, Unternehmensmitbestimmung und Unionsrecht, in Ingrid Schmidt (ed) *Jahrbuch des Arbeitsrechts* 55 (2018), 23 (37 et seq.).

66 Cf. e.g. ECJ, Case 167/01, 30.09.2003, *Kamer van Koophandel en Fabrieken voor Amsterdam v. Inspire Art Ltd.*, ECR 2003 I-10155, para 133 with further references.

There is no doubt that this would strengthen freedom of establishment under Article 49 TFEU.

As to the *acquis communautaire* regarding corporate restructuring, employee participation schemes under the national laws of EU Member States are only imperfectly protected in the context of corporate restructuring operations. Especially national divisions may be used to escape from employee participation scheme which are applicable to companies: Directive (EU) 2017/1132 does not provide rules for the safeguarding of statutory employee participation schemes existing in the dividing company. Thus, there is a lack of protection. As for national mergers, an escape from employee participation is possible in the event that the company resulting from the merger is not a public limited liability company, which is not covered by the statutory employee participation scheme applicable before the merger; this lack of protection is due to the limited scope of harmonization of the national laws of mergers.

As far as cross-border restructuring operations are concerned, it becomes apparent that the model of a negotiated employee participation, underlying Directive 2001/86/EC of 8 October 2001 supplementing the Statute for a European company with regard to the involvement of employee, is becoming the policy of the EU to resolve the conflict between employee participation and party autonomy in corporate restructuring operations. Thus, employee participation schemes under national law are contractualized and are therefore not forming anymore part of the public policy applying to the companies involved in a corporate restructuring operation. *De lege lata*, the rules of Directive (EU) 2017/1132 on cross-border mergers illustrate this policy of the Union. *De lege ferenda*, the "Company Law Package" of the European Commission goes in the same direction regarding cross-border divisions and cross-border conversions.

Even though this policy is in line with the path the EU has taken since the adoption of Directive 2001/86/EC, it also reveals deficiencies. Thus, the existing negotiation models and those proposed by the European Commission in the context of the "Company Law Package" differ from each other (*e.g.* concerning the applicability of the standard rules or with regard to posterior changes of an agreement on employee participation). Furthermore, the proposal of the Commission to prohibit abusive cross-border divisions and cross-border conversions is not extended to cross-border mergers. There is no reason for this fragmentation. What is needed instead is a clear and comprehensive legal framework for employee participation covering all different types of corporate restructuring operations within the Internal Market.

Furthermore, the Union has not yet addressed the erosion of national employee participation schemes (especially in Germany) resulting from the use of legal forms of other Member States, which are not covered by an employee participation scheme. Given that an unanimous decision of the Council is required in the field of employee participation,[67] it is not to be expected that the Union will deal with this problem in the near future.

In view of these deficiencies, it is certainly not exaggerated to say that there still is much to do in order to balance contractual freedom in corporate law with the safeguarding of employee participation under the national laws of Member States. It remains to be seen whether the Company Law Package, which still is on the way, may contribute to the solution of this challenge. In any event, the Commission Proposal for a Directive amending Directive (EU) 2017/1132 does not go far enough to resolve these problems.

Bibliography

Thomas Abeltshauser, *Strukturalternativen für eine europäische Unternehmensverfassung: eine rechtsvergleichende Untersuchung zum 5. Gesellschaftsrechtlichen EG-Richtlinienvorschlag*, (Berlin 1990).

Jean Carbonnier, *Droit Civil – Tome 4: Les obligations*, (22nd edition, 2000).

Simon Deakin, Angus Johnston and Basil Markesinis, *Tort Law*, (7th edition, Oxford, 2013).

Stefan Grundmann, *European Company Law*, (2nd edition, 2012).

Matthias Habersack and Dirk Verse, *Europäisches Gesellschaftsrecht*, (4th edition, München, 2011).

Ulrich Preis and Adam Sagan (eds), *Europäisches Arbeitsrecht: Grundlagen, Richtlinien, Folgen für das deutsche Recht*, (2015).

Jessica Schmidt, EU Company Law Package 2018 – Mehr Digitalisierung und Mobilität von Gesellschaften (Teil 1) –, Der Konzern 2018, 229.

Achim Seifert, Unternehmensinteresse und Aufsichtsratsmitbestimmung im Spannungsverhältnis, in Ulrich Jürgens, Dieter Sadowski, Folke Schuppert and Manfred Weiss (eds), *Perspektiven der Corporate Governance – Bestimmungsverfahren unternehmerischer Entscheidungsprozesse und Mitwirkung der Arbeitnehmer* (Baden-Baden 2007), 258.

67 Art. 153(1)(f), read together with paragraph (2), subparagraph (3) TFEU requires unanimity for decisions of the Council regarding measures in the field of "representation and collective defence of the interests of workers and employers, including co-determination […]".

Achim Seifert, Comment recodifier le dialogue social au sein de l'entreprise?, Journal des tribunaux Luxembourg 2011, 117

Achim Seifert, Employee Participation at Board Level in Europe, in Jürgen Basedow, Chen Su, Matteo Fornasier and Ulla Liukkunen (eds.), *Employee Participation and Collective Bargaining in Europe and China*, (Tübingen, 2016), 209.

Achim Seifert, Unternehmensmitbestimmung und Unionsrecht, in Ingrid Schmidt (ed.) *Jahrbuch des Arbeitsrechts* 55 (Berlin, 2018), 23.

Sebastian Sick, Der deutschen Mitbestimmung entzogen: Unternehmen mit ausländischer Rechtsform nehmen zu, in *Mitbestimmungsförderung, Report No. 8* (Hans-Böckler-Stiftung, February 2015).

Christoph Teichmann, Mitbestimmungserstreckung für Auslandsgesellschaften, ZIP 2016, 899.

Anders Victorin, Employee Participation on the Company Board: The Swedish Experience, in Theodor Baums and Peter Ulmer (eds.), *Employees' Co-Determination in the Member States of the European Union*, (Heidelberg, 2004).

Manfred Weiss and Achim Seifert, Der europarechtliche Rahmen für ein "Mitbestimmungserstreckungsgesetz", ZGR 2009, 542.

Hellmut Wißmann, Georg Kleinsorge and Claudia Schubert, *Mitbestimmungsrecht – Kommentar*, (5th edition, München, 2017).

Manfred Wolf and Jörg Neuner, *Allgemeiner Teil des Bürgerlichen Rechts*, (11th edition, München, 2016).

European Regulations

Proposition d'une cinquième directive tendant à coordonner les garanties qui sont exigées dans les États membres des sociétés, au sens de l'article 58 paragraphe 2 du traité, pour protéger les intérêts, tant des associés que des tiers en ce qui concerne la structure des société anonymes ainsi que les pouvoirs et obligations de leurs organes, J.O.C.E.E. 1972 C 131/49.

Third Council Directive 78/855/EEC of 9 October 1978 based on Article 54(3)(g) of the Treaty concerning mergers of public limited liability companies, O.J.E.E.C. 1978 L 295/36.

Amended proposal for a Fifth Directive founded on Article 54(3)(g) of the EEC Treaty concerning the structure of public limited companies and the powers and obligations of their organs, O.J.C.E.E. 1983 C 240/2.

Directive 2001/23/EC of 12 March 2001 on the approximation of the laws of the Member States relating to the safeguarding of employees' rights in the event of transfers of undertakings, businesses or parts of undertakings or businesses, O.J.E.C. 2001 L 82/16.

Directive 2001/86/EC of 8 October 2001 complementing the Statute for a European Company with regard to the involvement of employees in the European company (O.J.E.C. 2001 L 294/22).

Directive on cross-border mergers: Directive 2005/56/EC of 26 October 2005 on cross-border mergers, O.J.E.C. 2005 L 28/40.

Directive 2011/35/EU of the European Parliament and of the Council of 5 April 2011 concerning mergers of public limited liability companies, O.J.E.U. 2011 L 110/1.

Directive (EU) 2017/1132 of 14 June 2017 relating to certain aspects of company law (codification), O.J.E.U. 2017 L 169/46.

Employee Participation in Cross-Border Mergers – European Rules, Risks and Loopholes

Erika Kovács[*]

Summary

* Assistant Professor at the Vienna University of Business and Economics (WU).

A. Introduction

The regulation of employee participation in various kinds of cross-border corporate restructuring of the company (meaning especially merger, division and seat transfer between Member States) has been an extremely sensitive issue in the history of the European Union. Due to the inherent tension between the corporate cross-border mobility, on the one hand, and the protection of employees' participation rights, on the other, arriving at a legal solution has long proven to be impossible. The difficulty of achieving any compromise also goes back to the extremely varying employee participation schemes in the Member States (MS).[1] The two extremes constitute Germany, on the one side, with parity participation in public limited companies (plc, *Aktiengesellschaft*) of over 2000 employees, and, Great Britain, on the other, completely lacking any employee participation system whatsoever. This situation coupled with the lack of consensus on possible European legislation on employee participation, served to obstruct the harmonization process of the mobility of companies for several decades.[2] The breakthrough was finally achieved with the adoption of the negotiation model in the Directive 94/45/EC on European Works Council and the elaboration of the so-called "before and after" principle in the Directive 2001/86/EC on the involvement of employees in the European company.[3] The regulation on employee participation in the European company served as a model on participation in case of cross-border mergers. Art. 16 of the Directive 2005/56/EC on cross-border mergers of limited liability companies[4] features slightly amended rules compared to the regulation on the Directive 2001/86/EC. These rules have been transferred into Art. 133 of the Directive 2017/1132/EC[5] without any contextual changes, the goal of which was to consolidate and codify the six European Directives on corpo-

1 For an overview of the employee participation systems in the Member States see: Aline Conchon, *Board-Level Employee Representation Rights in Europe – Facts and Trends*, ETUI report (2011), 10-16.

2 See the legislation procedure in detail: Maximilian Fuchs and Franz Marhold, *Europäisches Arbeitsrecht* (2018), 444-448.

3 Council Directive 2001/86/EC of 8 October 2001 supplementing the Statute for a European company with regard to the involvement of employees, OJ L 294, 10.11.2001, 22-32.

4 Directive 2005/56/EC of the European Parliament and of the Council of 26 October 2005 on cross-border mergers of limited liability companies, OJ L 310, 25.11.2005, 1-9 (no longer in force).

5 Directive (EU) 2017/1132 of the European Parliament and of the Council of 14 June 2017 relating to certain aspects of company law, OJ L 169, 30.6.2017, 46-127.

rate law into one single document. In April 2018, the European Commission put forward a proposal[6] (in the following Proposal) designed to implement marginal changes in the existing rules on cross-border mergers and to introduce new rules on cross-border conversion and division.

In the following, I will give a critical overview on the major rules of employee participation in cross-border merger regulated in Art. 133 of the Directive 2017/1132. First, I will outline the concept of board-level employee representation at the European level, followed by analysis of the three cases which trigger the application of the special rules on employee participation. In part D, I will address some weaknesses in the negotiation procedure. Part E provides a critical assessment of the Proposal regarding employee participation. The focus of Part F is on options for evading the application of employee participation rules in cross-border mergers. The paper ends with concluding remarks.

B. The Concept of the Board-Level Employee Representation

In order to illustrate the purpose of the regulation, I would like to highlight the example of a German limited liability company with more than 2000 employees and an Italian company that merged with an Austrian company. The company resulting from the cross-border merger will have its registered seat in Austria. What happens with the employee participation rights in such a case? Without any special rules on this situation, the national rules of the registered seat of the company, i.e. Austrian rules, would govern the employee participation with two major adverse consequences for the employees. First, the Italian employees would be excluded from the board-level representation, as according to the Austrian law, only employees employed in the territory of Austria have the right to actively elect representatives in the supervisory board and be elected to it themselves. The Italian employees would not have any representation in the supervisory board of the company. The second consequence would be the reduction of board-level representation, since in Germany, half of the supervisory board was composed of employees' representatives and in Austria, only one-third of the members of the supervisory board are employees.

6 Proposal for a Directive of the European Parliament and of the Council amending Directive (EU) 2017/1132 as regards cross-border conversions, mergers and divisions, COM(2018) 241 final.

The goal of the EU regulation on board-level employee representation is to impede both adverse outcomes.

The first and major aim of the European rules on employee participation is to hinder companies from misusing cross-border mergers for the express purpose of reducing the level of representation. Member States with comparatively high levels of employee participation have expressed legitimate concern that cross-border mergers eliminate or restrict the existing participation rights at the company level (this phenomenon is called "escape from the co-determination"). Additionally, making cross-border mergers possible through European regulation without appropriate protection of the employees' participation system could trigger a "race to the bottom" between the Member States and lead to an overall reduction in the level of employee participation in the entire EU. To counter this, the Directive aims at securing employees' acquired rights as regards involvement in company decisions by the application of the "before and after" principle in the process of the cross-border merger.[7] This means that employees' rights in force before the cross-border merger provide the basis for their participation rights after the merger.

The second, less specifically stated goal of the EU regulation is to give employees a voice and involve them in decision-making even beyond their respective national borders. This follows from the third case of application of the specific rules on employee participation.

The major concept of employee participation in cross-border merger seems to be very simple at first glance, but proves to be the opposite once applied in practise. The main rule is the seat principle, wherein the national rules of the MS apply, and the company resulting from the cross-border merger has its registered office. In practise, this general rule applies very rarely, but usually one of the three special cases, or so-called "exceptions" come into force.

If one of the conditions set out in para 2 of Art. 133 Directive is fulfilled, the negotiation model applies. Due to the fundamentally different participation schemes of the Member States, the Directive has not adopted a uniform solution, but instead imposes an obligation to negotiate. The employees establish an organ (called special negotiating body, in the following SNB) which represents all employees of the merging companies in the various countries. The SNB negotiates with the management about how many employees' representatives should be in the supervisory board and what rights should they have. Either they agree and conclude an agreement or if

7 Recital Nr. 18 of the Directive 2001/86/EC on SE.

they cannot agree or one of the negotiating parties refuses to negotiate, then the standard rules apply by act of law as backup rules. Consequently, the negotiation takes place in the shadow of the standard rules, since the application of the standard rules — which guarantee the maintenance of the existing strict rules — puts the employer under pressure to achieve a compromise in the negotiation.

C. The Three Cases Triggering the Specific Rules

I. First Case: 500 Employees and Existing Employee Participation System

In my view, the first case of the specific rules (Art. 133 para 2 of the Directive 2017/1132) is a flawed and superfluous regulation, since it imposes a negotiation obligation on the parties without the ultimate goal, namely without the risk of losing or lowering the level of employee involvement. Even more, this rule can obstruct the automatic application of a system that is more favourable for the employees.[8] Let me demonstrate this statement through an example. A Romanian company merges with an Austrian company (PLC or LLC), which is the acquiring company. The Romanian company employs only a couple of employees or no employees and has no employee participation system. The Austrian company has a workforce of over 500 employees and the employees enjoy a one-third participation rate in the supervisory board. Without any special rule, the Austrian law of employee participation would apply in this case, meaning that the employees would enjoy the participation rights after the merger as a matter of course. This special rule, however, induces the negotiation procedure. The bottom line is that in such cases of Art. 133 para 2 of the Directive 2017/1132, automatic application of the stricter employee participation system is invariably prevented from taking place.

The only benefit of this regulation could be the consideration of foreign employees, however, this expectation is not fulfilled either. To illustrate this statement, let us turn the former case around. In the second example, the Romanian company employs over 500 employees, but has no employee participation system, since in Romania there is no such obligation. The Austrian company has less than 300 employees and no participation sys-

8 Georg Eckert and Matthias Schimka, *Die Arbeitnehmermitbestimmung bei grenzüberschreitenden Verschmelzungen nach dem EU-VerschG*, wbl 2008, 201 (204-205).

tem. Here, Art. 133 para 2 of the Directive 2017/1132 does not apply, since, according to the seat principle, the Austrian general rules on employees' participation applies. The consequence is that the Romanian employees will go de jure wholly unrepresented in the acquiring company. In Austria, the principle of territoriality applies, which stipulates that only staff employed in the territory of Austria count for the employee participation system. Although this result complies with the idea that a merger alone should not create participation rights, the first case nevertheless fails to produce any advantages.

Another shortcoming of this rule is the unclear definition of the term "employee". The Directive does not provide any guidance on the question of when one has to be recognized as an employee for the application of this rule. The majority view is that only the employees of the merging (participating) company must be recognized, but not the employees of the subsidiaries. This view is supported by the wording of the directive ("merging companies"). Yet, an inconsistency exists within the Directive. For the calculation of the threshold of 500 employees, only the employees of the merging company count. To the contrary, for the composition of the special negotiating body, the employees of the subsidiaries and establishments of the merging companies likewise have to be figured in. It hardly makes sense for the employees of subsidiaries not to matter for reaching the threshold, whilst they are simultaneously represented in the special negotiating body.

II. Second Case: Reduction of the Level of Employee Participation

The second case set in Art. 133 para 2 lit. (a) of the Directive 2017/1132 is appropriate for realizing the goal, namely of preventing the lowering of the level of employee participation in a cross-border merger. For precipitating the application of this rule, it suffices if in one of the merging companies, a higher proportion of employee participation exists than in the company resulting from the merger.

The question thus arises as to how to assess the level of employee participation. The question in particular is which of the two matter regarding the proportion of the employees' representatives — the rights set in the law or the rights realised in the merging companies. The wording "operated" in the merging companies strongly suggests that the existing situation is decisive.[9] If the employees in a merging company have had the chance to elect or send representatives, but have not made use of this right, and this company did not have employees' representatives, then there is no need to negotiate on the participation. This interpretation is in line with the "before and after" principle, which requires maintaining at least the same level of employee participation that existed before the merger.

III. Third Case: Restriction of Participation Rights to Domestic Employees

According to Art. 133 para 2 lit. (b) of the Directive 2017/1132, the parties shall negotiate, "where the national law applicable to the company resulting from the cross-border merger does not provide for employees of establishments of the company resulting from the cross-border merger that are situated in other Member States the same entitlement to exercise participation rights as is enjoyed by those employees employed in the Member State where the company resulting from the cross-border merger has its registered office." In my view, this is the most controversial case, which, however, most frequently applies.

This case differs from the first and second cases, since its goal is less to prevent the reduction of employees' participation rights, but rather to guarantee that also the employees of the company outside the MS of the seat State have participation rights. This rule aims at prohibiting discrimination against foreign employees.[10] In my point of view, this rule is unrealistic and alien to the law system of most MS, since it violates the principle of territoriality. In Germany or Austria, like in most other MS, the scope of labour law and more specifically, the scope of the law on employee participation are both restricted to the territory of the state. That means that only employees employed permanently in the territory of the state have the right to elect the employees' representatives and be elected. There are only a few exceptions under this principle, for example, in case of personnel employed abroad in a dependent part of an Austrian establishment which still

9 Stefan Kühteubl and Elisabeth Wasinger in Thomas Talos and Martin Winner (eds), *EU-Verschmelzungsgesetz* (2016), § 258, mn. 29; Georg Eckert, in Susanne Kalss (ed.), *Verschmelzung – Spaltung – Umwandlung* (2010), Vor § 1 EU-VerschG, mn. 20.

10 Gregor Thüsing and Gerrit Forst, "MgVG" in Mathias Habersack and Florian Drinhausen, *SE-Recht* (2016), MgVG § 5 mn. 17.

falls under the scope of the Austrian rule.[11] As a general rule, employees employed in the territory of another MS are not represented in the supervisory board. In the EU, only in Sweden and Denmark does there exist a law that provides the opportunity for employees in foreign subsidiaries to vote and to be elected as board-level employee representatives.[12] Yet, even in these contexts, this does not constitute an automatic right on the part of the employees, but instead depends either on the shareholders' decision (in Denmark) or the trade union's requirement (in Sweden). Considering the few countries that extend the active and passive participation rights beyond their national border and the limited substantive scope of these rights, the third case is an exaggerated claim.

In this context, it is worth mentioning the Erzberger-judgment[13] of the Court of Justice of the EU (in the following CJEU). In this case, TUI, a German group of companies, employed 80% of its employees in subsidiaries in another MS and these employees lacked any representation in the German supervisory board. The main question here was, whether it is compatible with Arts. 18 and 45 AEUV to restrict the right to vote and to be elected as the employees' representative in the supervisory board of the company only to those employees who are employed in the territory of the country. The CJEU only scrutinized the compatibility of the restricted personal scope with the free movement of workers and the non-discrimination principle, but has not examined whether the rule complies with the freedom of establishment. According to the CJEU, it is a legitimate decision by German authorities to limit the scope of the application of participation mechanisms to employees employed by establishments located in its territory, "since such a delimitation is based on an objective and non-discriminatory criterion."[14]

The Directive requires the comparison of participation rights between the merging companies and the company resulting from the merger. Here, the main question is whether it should be an abstract or specific comparison. Shall we make the comparison based on rights to which the employees employed in foreign MS were entitled or on the rights they actually ex-

---

11 Georg Eckert and Matthias Schimka, *Die Arbeitnehmermitbestimmung bei grenzüberschreitenden Verschmelzungen nach dem EU-VerschG*, wbl 2008, 201 (204). Georg Eckert, in Susanne Kalss (ed.), *Verschmelzung – Spaltung – Umwandlung* (2010), Vor § 1 EU-VerschG, mn. 21.

12 Aline Conchon, *Board-Level Employee Representation Rights in Europe – Facts and Trends* (2011), 28-29.

13 C-566/15, 18.07.2017, *Erzberger*, ECLI:EU:C:2017:562.

14 C-566/15, 18.07.2017, *Erzberger*, ECLI:EU:C:2017:562. para 38.

ercised before the merger? If we focus on the rights the employees would have been entitled to, it means the comparison of the abstract national rules (like a competition of the national rules). The alternative is to compare the level of rights actually enjoyed in the merging companies and in the company resulting from the merger. In practise, the adoption of the abstract or specific approach can make a huge difference. In fact, the adoption of the abstract interpretation would entail that the negotiation procedure is set in motion in all cross-border mergers if the law of the country of the company resulting from the cross-border merger restricts the scope of the participation rules to its territory.

Let me illustrate the difference with the example of an English LLC without an employee participation system in place, merging into an Austrian LLC without employee participation system (less than 300 employees) and the company resulting from the merger has its seat in Austria.[15] If we interpret Art. 133 para 2 lit. (b) of the Directive in an abstract manner, then the third case is precipitated, since the English employees do not count according to the Austrian rules. The negotiation process must be initiated with the result that a supervisory board has to be created, despite the fact that none of the merging companies has a participation system in place. This rule applies even to companies with a small number of employees. However, if we take the participation rights actually exercised before the merger as a starting point of the comparison, we get another result. The conditions are not fulfilled, so the parties are not obliged to negotiate and the general rules apply. Hence, the third case should only be instigated if the application of the domestic rules on employee participation would put the employees in the other MS in a worse situation regarding the participation than they were before the merger.

The majority of the Austrian[16] and German[17] authors are in favour of the specific comparison and for the application of this rule, requiring the existing situation of the employees to become worse. There are some fur-

15 Beispiel von Thomas Müller-Bonanni and Michael Müntefering, Grenzüberschreitende Verschmelzung ohne Arbeitnehmerbeteiligung? NJW 2009, 2347 (2349).

16 Matthias Unterrieder and Franz Fazekas, Immer mitbestimmter Aufsichtsrat bei grenzüberschreitenden Verschmelzungen? RdW 2010, 227-230; Georg Eckert in Susanne Kalss (ed.), *Verschmelzung – Spaltung – Umwandlung* (2010), Vor § 1 EU-VerschG Rz 20; Kühteubl and Wasinger in Talos and Winner, § 258, mn. 33.

17 Gregor Thüsing and Gerrit Forst, "MgVG" in Mathias Habersack and Florian Drinhausen, *SE-Recht* (2016), 1223. et seq.; Thomas Müller-Bonanni and Michael Müntefering, Grenzüberschreitende Verschmelzung ohne Arbeitnehmerbeteiligung? NJW 2009, 2347 (2349).

ther rationales for this interpretation. First, in case of an abstract comparison, the first and second cases would be redundant, as the third case would always apply, and all incoming mergers would fall under this case. Second, the wording of the Directive speaks for the specific approach, as it requires the same entitlement to exercise participation rights as is enjoyed by the domestic employees. Third, the negotiation would have to be proceeded even in cases where none of the merging companies had an employee participation system before the merger. This cannot be the goal of the European legislator.

Overall, the specific situation of the merging companies should be decisive. Meanwhile, the situation of employee participation in each merging company has to be compared with the situation of the company resulting from the merger. In order to apply the rule, three conditions have to be met: (1) at least one of the merging companies had participation system prior to the merger; (2) the company resulting from the merger has an employee representation system; and (3) the company resulting from the merger has foreign employees, meaning employees employed in another MS. All three conditions have to be fulfilled cumulatively in order to make a comparison possible.

D. The Negotiation Procedure

I. The Background Regulation of SE

The rules on the negotiation procedure between the management or administrative organs of the participating companies and the special negotiating body are based on the respective regulation of the Societas Europaea. It is interesting to examine how the various law systems refer to this background regulation. The Directive and the Austrian regulation feature different regulatory techniques regarding the reference to the rules of the SE. The Directive explicitly lists the provisions of the SE, which are applicable to the negotiation in case of a cross-border merger. On the flipside, the Austrian rule[18] contains a general reference to the SE and imposes application of the rules of the SE to cross-border mergers provided that these address the right to employee participation. The consequences of this general reference are, first of all, the uncertainty attached to which rules actually

18 Art. 260 para 1 ArbVG (Arbeitsverfassungsgesetz, Labour Constitution Act).

apply and secondly, the application of redundant rules on cross-border merger designed specifically for the SE.

For example, the Austrian (and German) law[19] imposes the recomposition of the special negotiating body if, during its operation, the structure or the number of employees of the participating companies changes to such an extent that this would induce the change of its composition. This is a clear example of golden-plating, which could, in turn, raise concerns regarding the different levels of employee protection in the various MS and thus the risk of forum-shopping for companies.[20]

II. Lack of Employee Representation

The first step of the negotiation procedure is to create the so-called special negotiation body. The management or the administrative organs of the participating companies initiate the creation of this body by providing the necessary information for the employees' representatives to start the negotiation. The question arises as to what happens in companies without an employee representation system. What are the legal consequences of the missing employee representation system? Do the employees lose their participation rights or is the employer obliged to inform the employees directly? In my opinion, we should differentiate between two cases. In the first case, the employees have the right to create a representation body, but they do not make use of this opportunity. Art. 133 para 3 last sentence of the Directive 2017/1132/EU refers to Art. 3 para 2 lit. (b) of the Directive on SE, which sounds: "Member States shall provide that employees in undertakings or establishments in which there are no employees' representatives through no fault of their own have the right to elect or appoint members of the special negotiating body." Consequently, the Directive only requires employees to have the right to elect their representatives. If employees have had the chance to elect a works council, but they have not made use of this right, they cannot put in a claim for direct election or for receiving direct information. The second case of a lack of representation is if the employees have not had the right to elect one; in this case, they should have the right to elect their representatives directly. As in Austria, the election of a works

19 In Austria Art. 216 para 5 ArbVG (Arbeitsverfassungsgesetz, Labour Constitution Act), in Germany Art. 7 para 4 MgVG (Law on the Employees' Participation in case of Cross-Border Merger).

20 See Bech-Bruun and Lexidale, (eds.) *Study on the Application of the Cross-Border Mergers Directive* (2013), 95.

council is optional, and the employer is not obliged to directly contact the employees whilst the non-consideration of these employees is in line with the requirements of the Directive. However, some States went beyond accomplishing this rule. The German law created an opportunity for employees to participate even in establishments without works councils. According to § 10 Abs. 7 MgVG, employees elect the members of the special negotiation body in a secret and direct ballot if there is no works council in place. This goes beyond the requirements of the Directive, but is in line with it, if we consider the Directive as a minimum standard of harmonisation.

In the third case, the employees do not have a representation system, because they fail to reach the respective threshold. For example, in Austria, only employees in an establishment with at least five employees have the right to create a works council. Such a threshold for the election of a representative body complies with the Directive. Art. 3 para 2 lit. (b) last sentence of the SE Directive explicitly mentions that it is allowed to introduce and maintain thresholds for the establishing of a representative body.

Finally, the Directive does not provide any guidance on the question of what happens with the seats in the special negotiation body not occupied due to the lack of employee representation in some companies. Theoretically, the seats can be left free or they can be redistributed. If the seats are let out, the special negotiating body becomes smaller. Here, the MS have some leeway to make their own regulation.

E. Proposal by the European Commission to Amend the Rules

The Proposal of the European Commission amending Directive (EU) 2017/1132 from April 2018 affects employee participation in cross-border mergers on three points. First, it specifies the reporting obligation on the part of the management of the companies to the employees. Second, it suggests a specific obligation by the company to inform employees on the application of the standard rules or to enter into negotiations with the special negotiation body and on the outcome of the negotiations.[21] Third, it extends the existing protection in case of a subsequent domestic merger also to subsequent cross-border mergers, divisions and conversions. None of these rules brings about radical change in the existing participation regime.

21 Proposal for a Directive amending Directive (EU) 2017/1132, 69.

Two of the three amendments aim at providing more information to the employees. This goes back to the requirement of the European Parliament[22] and trade unions[23] about the establishment of minimum standards on information and consultation of employees in case of cross-border mergers. The Proposal mentions that this initiative is in line with the 8th principle of the European Pillar of Social Rights, which requires that employees or their representatives have the right to be informed and consulted in good time on "restructuring and merger of undertakings".[24] Although the Pillar also mentions consultation, the Proposal restricts itself rather to rights to information. Even if employees have the right to submit their opinions on the report received from management, real discussion on its content does not have to take place.

Art. 124a of the Proposal maintains and slightly changes the existing reporting obligation of the management set in Art. 124 of the Directive 2017/1132. The reason for this is first, that the Proposal indicates the change of Art 124 of the Directive 2017/1132. According to the new Art 124, the members of the merging companies can agree on waiving of the requirement to draw up a report on the legal and economic aspects of the cross-border merger. The new Art 124a has been inserted in order to guarantee that the employees are informed also in this case.

Moreover, Art 124a of the Proposal introduces more detailed rules on the content of the information obligation. The novelty is the enumeration of the issues, which is designed to explain the consequences of cross-border merger to employees. It covers four fields, namely the implications of the cross-border merger on future business and on the safeguarding of employment relationships.[25] Further, the report shall cover "any material changes in the conditions of employment and in the locations of the companies' places of business". Finally, it has to indicate whether the three mentioned factors relate to any subsidiaries of the merging companies. The subjects of the reporting obligation such as "future business" are loosely formulated, which leaves great leeway for the national implementation of these rules. The addressees of the reporting obligation are not only the representatives of the employees, but in lieu of them also the employees themselves. The Proposal likewise sets a deadline for the reporting obligation to occur one

22 European Parliament resolution of 13 June 2017 on cross-border mergers and divisions (2016/2065(INI)), point 10.

23 Proposal for a Directive amending Directive (EU) 2017/1132, 16.

24 C(2017) 2600 final. Commission recommendation establishing the European Pillar of Social Rights, 8.b.

25 Proposal for a Directive amending Directive (EU) 2017/1132, 64.

month before the date of the general meeting at the latest. The employees have the right to submit their opinion on the report, which has to be appended to the report. The Proposal does not specify the possible content of the opinion, so it can range from objections on the information received to suggestions on the improvement of the employees' situation. There is no real consultation obligation, since the management need not react to the employees' opinion. From the Proposal, it is not apparent whether the MS are expected to adopt any sanction for the case that the management fails to report to the employees.

This reporting obligation seems to be a duplication of the already existing obligations to report on the part of the employer. As I assume that a cross-border merger usually constitutes a transfer of undertaking, the Directive 2001/23/EC[26] applies to this restructuring. Art. 7 of the Directive 2001/23/EC sets the transferor's and the transferee's information obligations in matters of transfer of undertakings. The information obligation covers also "the legal, economic and social implications of the transfer for the employees". It further provides obligation of consultation on measures in relation to the employees. Where there are no representatives of the employees in an undertaking or business through no fault of their own, the employees concerned must be informed directly. Art. 124a para 6 of the Proposal stipulates that the submission of the report take place without prejudice to the applicable information and consultation rights arising from the Directives 2001/23/EC, 2002/14/EC or 2009/38/EC, and so as a result, these rules take priority over the obligation to inform by Directive 2017/1132. To sum up, the suggested reporting obligation in cross-border mergers does not seem to create additional protection for employees. However, if we consider the uncertainty of the question of whether a cross-border merger always constitutes a transfer of undertaking,[27] the more precise obligation to inform yields the benefit of clarity.

Secondly, the Proposal suggests inserting a para 8 into Art. 133 of the Directive 2017/1132 with a new obligation to inform.[28] The company is supposed to inform its employees whether it chooses to apply standard rules for participation or enters into negotiation with the special negotiating

---

26 Council Directive 2001/23/EC of 12 March 2001 on the approximation of the laws of the Member States relating to the safeguarding of employees' rights in the event of transfers of undertakings, businesses or parts of undertakings or businesses, OJ L 82, 22.3.2001, 16-20.

27 Bech-Bruun and Lexidale, (eds.) *Study on the Application of the Cross-Border Mergers Directive*, 2013, main findings, 67.

28 Proposal for a Directive amending Directive (EU) 2017/1132, 69.

body. In the latter case, the company is supposed to communicate the outcome of the negotiations to its employees. The formulation does not however clarify which company has to fulfil this obligation and thus which employees should be informed, but presumably, it was meant to cover all participating (merging) companies. This obligation to inform makes sense if it relates to a unilateral decision of the management of the companies. In other cases, if the employee representatives are involved in the decision-making process, it would be their task to inform the employees. Hence, the obligation to inform on the outcome of the negotiations is, in fact, redundant.

According to Art. 133 para 7 of the Directive 2017/1132, the company resulting from the cross-border merger is obliged to take measures to ensure that the employees' participation rights are protected in the event of any subsequent domestic merger. Taking measures refers to the application of the rules set in Art. 133 paras 1 to 6 of the Directive 2017/1132, namely new negotiation procedure or the use of the standard rules. The Proposal extends this protection to subsequent cross-border mergers, divisions or conversions. The duration of protection remains unchanged, set in three year intervals. It is beneficial for the Proposal to suggest a uniform regulation on this subsequent protection likewise in cases of cross-border division and conversion. The lack of the same rule on domestic merger is understandable, as it does not necessarily bring about any changes in the employees' participation rights. The coverage of cross-border mergers, divisions or conversions restricts the incentive to evade participation rights by subsequent restructuring of the company. This is particularly relevant for limiting seat transfer that is often motivated by the wish to escape employee participation.

To sum up, the amendments complement and partly duplicate the existing rights to information on the part of employees in case of a cross-border merger. The required pure unilateral flow of information seems to benefit the employees without placing inappropriate administrative burden on the companies.[29] The inclusion of cross-border merger, division and conversion under the protection of subsequent changes makes the regulation more coherent. However, these are not the most relevant options for evading the application of the rules on strict employee participation. The suggested amendments on cross-border mergers do not touch on the most controversial issues of the regulation.

29 This was also the result of the Impact Assessment prepared by the European Commission, see Proposal for a Directive amending Directive (EU) 2017/1132, 20.

F. The Options for Evading Employee Participation Rights

I. Introduction

There are various ways to evade the application of employee participation rules. This statement is equally true for strict national rules and the European rules on cross-border mergers. In the following, I am going to scrutinize the most significant risks to participation rights.[30] Under point II, I will highlight how cross-border mergers can be used to escape strict national participation rights. Section III focuses on the option to evade employee participation in case of a cross-border merger. As a cross-border merger is a time-consuming and complicated process, exploration of alternatives becomes attractive. Hence, under headings IV and V, I will give an outline on the company law alternatives of a cross-border merger and the fate of employee participation in such cases. I will particularly address the applicable law in seat transfer, as it is a highly topical method for evading strict employee participation regimes.

II. Cross-Border Merger Before Reaching the Threshold

The "before and after" principle can motivate companies to carry out a cross-border merger before the company has reached the threshold of the obligatory employee participation system or of the higher level of participation. For example, a German company approaching the margin of the parity participation system of 2,001 employees may decide for a cross-border merger before hiring the critical number of employees and evade the strict German participation system in this way. Here, a cross-border merger serves as a tool for escaping from a strict national employee participation system. In order to offset this possibility, the Proposal could have suggested the adoption of the same rule as it did for cross-border seat transfer (Art. 86l para 2 of the Proposal) and the division of companies (Art. 160n para 2 of the Proposal). According to this rule, the specific rules on employee participation could have applied, if at least one of the merging companies has an average number of employees equivalent to four-fifths of the

30 For a general overview on how to evade employee participation see e.g.: Gerlind Wisskirchen, Alexander Bissels and Martin Begiebing, Unternehmerische Mitbestimmung – unvermeindbar?, Zeitschrift für Familienunternehmen und Stiftungen, 6/2012, 209-214.

applicable national threshold, which prompts employee participation. However, the Proposal did not make use of this opportunity.

III. Use of Temporary Workers

Another option for evading a strict employee participation system (both in national context and in case of a cross-border merger) is to make use of temporary workers instead of one's own workforce. Art. 133 para 2 lit. (a) of the Directive 2017/1132 does not define the term "employee" for the threshold of 500 employees. Thus, the MS certainly have leeway to classify temporary workers and decide whether they qualify them as employees for the participation system.

IV. Relocation of the Corporate Growth Abroad

Most MS apply the principle of territoriality to their employee participation system and thus restrict the application of the national participation rules to the employees acting usually in the territory of their own MS. It is therefore an option to outsource the necessary expansion of the workforce abroad, namely into another MS with a looser participation system. Instead of hiring more employees and exceeding the threshold, it is easier for the company to establish a subsidiary, a branch or an establishment abroad and employ the necessary employees there.

Recitals 14 to 16 of the Preamble of the Directive 2017/1132 contain significant statements about branches. First, it states that in case of the opening of a branch — much like the creation of a subsidiary — this constitutes one of the companies' opportunities to exercise their right of establishment in other Member States. In addition, the CJEU confirmed that setting up a branch in another Member State by a company formed in one Member State falls under the protection of the freedom of establishment.[31] A branch — as an organizational unit of a foreign company — can often

31 C-212/97, CJEU 9.3.1999, *Centros*, ECLI:EU:C:1999:126, paras 17-22. Reference also in C-106/16, 25.10.2017, *Polbud*, ECLI:EU:C:2017:804, para 38.

be established and operated under very similar conditions such as a limited liability company, but without bringing up share capital.[32]

Recital 16 admits that "in certain respects, the economic and social influence of a branch can be comparable to that of a subsidiary company". It stresses that the similar situation would — in the absence of any coordination — lead to disparities regarding the protection of shareholders "between companies which operate in other Member States by opening branches and those, which operate there by creating subsidiaries." This is a significant finding, even if it refers specifically to disclosure. Hence, the Directive imposes obligations with respect to disclosure of the company at the branch.

Regarding cross-border mergers, the Directive contains no rules on branches. Dependent branches of foreign companies do not fall under the employee participation system of the foreign State based on the principle of territoriality. By setting up a branch in another MS, the company can evade the application of the strict employee participation rules. As the Directive 2017/1132 recognizes that subsidiaries and branches can have similar social implications, it could be conceivable to extend the rules on employee participation in case of a cross-border merger also to branches.

V. Seat Transfer

1. Applicable Company Law in the Light of the Case Law of the CJEU

According to the case law of the CJEU, the freedom of establishment includes that companies can freely transfer their seats (both registered and real) to another MS.[33] This means, on the one hand, that the company can transfer its real seat (meaning the headquarter or centre of administration) over to another MS without being forced to close up shop and form a new company. As a result, the company can maintain its original legal form. On the other hand, as the CJEU confirmed in the *Polbud* judgment, the freedom of establishment covers the transfer of the registered seat of a compa-

---

32 For example, in Hungary, see Section 2 lit. (b) of the Act CXXXII of 1997 on Hungarian Branch Offices and Commercial Representative Offices of Foreign-Registered Companies.

33 See the case law of the CJEU in Maximilian Fuchs and Franz Marhold, *Europäisches Arbeitsrecht* (2018), 484-498.

ny, even if the real head office and the entire operational business of that company remains in the territory of the state of origin.[34]

The law on seat transfer is strongly linked to the question of applicable company law. The Member States do not have a uniform solution for the law applicable to the company that transfers its seat, as EU law has not taken on harmonization measures in this field. There are two basic approaches for determining the applicable law, namely the incorporation versus real seat principle. According to the incorporation theory, the registered seat is the decisive connecting factor involved. Appreciation of the real seat theory proves to be rather varied, however. According to the real seat theory, either the place of the company's central administration and management or the place of its main operation determine the applicable law. The identification of these connecting factors can be difficult in practice, particularly in companies with decentralized structure. The MS meanwhile exhibit a very diverse picture regarding the determination of the applicable law.[35]

The freedom of establishment can easily be used to escape from a strict compulsory employee participation system by transferring only the registered seat to another MS without transferring the centre of administration or business activity.[36] This seems to constitute the greatest risk for employee participation.[37] In countries where the registered seat determines the applicable company law (and thus the law on the employee participation), this leads to the loss of the employee participation in the country of origin. For example, a German limited liability company (GmbH) can convert into a Dutch limited liability company (B.V.) or a British limited (LLC) with the result that the German employee participation system no longer applies to it anymore. The applicable company law changes, even if there was no change in the business activity and in the circumstances of the workforce.

34 C-106/16, 25.10.2017, *Polbud*, ECLI:EU:C:2017:804, paras 29-44.

35 For an overview of the connecting factors applied by the national laws of the MS see: Carsten Gerner-Beuerle, Federico M. Mucciarelli, Edmund-Philipp Schuster and Mathias M. Siems, *Study on the Law Applicable to Companies* (2016), 117-127.

36 Acknowledged in the Proposal for a Directive of the European Parliament and of the Council amending Directive (EU) 2017/1132 as regards cross-border conversions, mergers and divisions, COM(2018) 241 final, 3.

37 See the German experience: Sebastian Sick, Der deutschen Mitbestimmung entzogen: Unternehmen mit ausländischer Rechtsform nehmen zu, *Mitbestimmungsförderung Report Nr. 8.* (2015). On the German legal background and discussion see in detail: Marc-Philippe Weller, "Unternehmensmitbestimmung für Auslandsgesellschaften", in Bernd Erle, Wulf Goette and Detlef Kleindiek, (eds.) *FS Hommelhoff* (2012), 1275.

Due to the case law of the CJEU, several national authors and courts seem to believe that the real seat theory is no longer an alternative, as it would fail to comply with the freedom of establishment.[38] Several MS seem to have accepted that the incorporation theory determines the law applicable to companies transferring their seats within the EU. However, many countries maintained the real seat theory formally or even officially.[39] In fact, the CJEU's case law regarding the applicable law is not obvious. It made clear that in lieu of uniform European regulation, MS are free to define the connecting factor that determines the national law applicable to a company.[40] It further emphasized in several judgments including the *Polbud* judgment that Art. 54 TFEU uses the terms "registered office," "central administration" and "principal place of business" on an equal footing and these are therefore connecting factors of equal value. This clearly indicates that it is also in line with EU law, if the MS requires the company to have a certain physical presence in that state such as a headquarters in order to apply the national law to it.[41] However, the CJEU also limited this rule by stating that if a company governed by the law of one MS converts itself to a company under the law of the another MS and satisfies the conditions imposed by the latter MS, then the MS of origin is not allowed to prevent or deter the company from undertaking cross-border conversion. At least the rules are not allowed to be more restrictive than those applied to domestic restructuring.[42] Consequently, the selection of the most favourable legislation for the registered seat — so-called regime shopping — does not constitute an abuse of the law. The *Polbud* judgment says that at least in case of an outgoing seat transfer, a MS cannot make the transfer of the registered seat dependent on the relocation of the real seat. This means in the end that the MS can use various connecting factors for the determination of law on incoming cross-border conversion, but not on outgoing conversion. It further stated that the protection of workers can constitute overriding reasons in the public interest.[43] The *Polbud* case was

---

38 Carsten Gerner-Beuerle, Federico M. Mucciarelli, Edmund-Philipp Schuster and Mathias M. Siems, *Study on the Law Applicable to Companies* (2016), 292.

39 *Ibid.* 137.

40 C-210/06, 16.12.2008, *Cartesio*, ECLI:EU:C:2008:723, paras 109-110; C-106/16, 25.10.2017, *Polbud*, ECLI:EU:C:2017:804, para 34 with reference to C-81/87, 27.09.1988, *Daily Mail and General Trust*, ECLI:EU:C:1988:456, paras 19-21.

41 Carsten Gerner-Beuerle, Federico M. Mucciarelli, Edmund-Philipp Schuster and Mathias M. Siems, *Study on the Law Applicable to Companies* (2016), 293.

42 C-106/16, 25.10.2017, *Polbud*, ECLI:EU:C:2017:804, para 43.

43 C-106/16, 25.10.2017, *Polbud*, ECLI:EU:C:2017:804, para 54.

not suitable for discovering the legitimate limits of the freedom of establishment, since the mandatory liquidation of the company — as a condition of a seat transfer — was considered a disproportionate measure. Nevertheless, it hardly invariably implies that other, less strict and more individualized measures would not comply with the freedom of establishment.

The uncertainty along with the different national provisions regarding the transfer of a seat call for a harmonization of the seat transfer and the law applicable to employee participation. The Commission proposed the adoption of a regulation on cross-border seat transfer.[44] In the following section, I will give a short appraisal of the planned rules on employee participation. The focus is on the question of whether the rules are suitable for preventing the use of seat transfer for the evasion of a strict employee participation regime.

2. *Law Applicable to Employee Participation System*

Theoretically, a range of different options are in place for regulating seat transfer at the European level. The two extreme cases are the adoption of the incorporation or the real seat theory and determination of the applicable law on the participation system based on one of these theories. The pure determination of the applicable national law could have the advantage of avoiding the prevalence of the extremely complicated rules on SE and cross-border merger. Incorporation theory, moreover, would favour the mobility of companies, whereas the employees' associations such as the ETUC strongly speak for the real seat principle.[45] However, as both theories represent extreme approaches, it has always been very unlikely that a compromise could be reached at the European level in terms of the adoption of one of these theories.

The preliminary question is whether the law on employee participation system belongs to the category of company or labour law and thus follows the conflict of laws of company or labour law.[46] Usually, employee participation law is treated as part of company law and thus follows the company

44 See the definition of cross-border conversion in Art. 86b of the Proposal, 46.

45 The ETUC requires "genuine economic activity" for the relocation of the registered seat. ETUC position paper – ETUC demands in view of the upcoming company law package, adopted at the Executive Committee on 13-14 December 2017.

46 See on this: Marc-Philippe Weller, Unternehmensmitbestimmung für Auslandsgesellschaften, *FS Hommelhoff* (2012) 1275, (1285).

law statute, although the specific nature of this field is recognized.[47] This intermediate position justifies a specific regulation. Accordingly, another option would be to harmonize the law and introduce a new employee participation law based on the rules of the European company or the rules on cross-border mergers. The Proposal opted for this solution and recommended adoption of uniform rules on employee participation. The rules are modelled on the participation system of the European company and cross-border merger, but differ slightly from them. Due to lack of space, I will only briefly highlight some new rules which are of relevance for the evasion of strict national rules.

An important strong change compared with the model regulations is the definition of the first case for the application of the specific rules on employee participation. Instead of setting a sharp threshold of 500 employees, the Proposal links this case to the respective national threshold of the departure MS, which, in turn, triggers participation by employees. If the company carrying out the conversion has had an average number of employees equivalent to four-fifths of this threshold, the first case is applied. This novelty could efficiently prevent the use of seat transfer for evading a strict national participation regime shortly before the company reaches the number of employees set in the threshold. On the other hand, one could argue that this new rule only replaces the national threshold with a European threshold. In my view, making the precipitation of the first case dependent on a certain percentage of the respective national threshold is certainly a better solution than using a sharp uniform threshold, since it can more efficiently prevent exploitation of conversion for the evasion of strict participation regimes.

In addition, other rules seem to guarantee the maintenance of a strict employee participation system. Compared with Art. 133 of the Directive 2017/1132, the Proposal provides even stronger protection of existing participation rights. For example, the Proposal applies Art. 4 para 4 of the SE Directive to conversion. Furthermore, it stops short of adopting para 4(a) of Art. 133 of the Directive 2017/1132, which provides the relevant organs of the merging companies with the right to directly apply the standard rules for participation.

All in all, the Proposal on the employee participation in case of a seat transfer meets the main criterion. The adoption of this regulation would contribute to prevention of the phenomenon of companies transferring their seats to other MS when their only or main motivation is the evasion

47 Mathias Habersack and Dirk A. Verse, *Europäisches Gesellschaftsrecht* (2011), 32.

of the strict rules on employee participation in the state of origin. The rules protect the participation system even slightly stronger than is the case in cross-border mergers.

G. Conclusion

The adoption of the "before and after" principle in the European rules on employee participation in cross-border merger resulted in a complicated and partly unclear set of rules. In my view, the first and third cases of the application of the specific rules on employee participation are problematic, because they are partly redundant, and partly non-conformist with the principle of territoriality. The compulsory equal treatment of employees situated in other MS is alien to the participation regime of most MS. The rigid number of 500 employees does not consider the national features of participation regimes. The procedural approach of the regulation leaves the MS great leeway for implementing the rules, which can result in different levels of protection.

The Proposal of the European Commission did not contain any crucial novelty on cross-border merger. It provided some information rights to employees' representatives and directly to employees. However, similar rights have already been included in the Directive 2017/1132 and Directive 2001/23/EC on the transfer of undertakings (protection of employment). It further suggested some fine-tuning regarding the protection of employees' rights in case of subsequent restructuring. However, the Proposal has not touched on the unclear or inappropriate rules of employee participation. On the positive side, the Proposal placed a strong recommendation in favour of employee participation in case of a seat transfer forward. To sum up, the adoption of the Proposal would not solve major existing shortcomings in European regulation on cross-border, but could improve the situation regarding seat transfer overall.

Bibliography

Bech-Bruun and Lexidale, (eds.) *Study on the Application of the Cross-Border Mergers Directive*, 2013.

Aline Conchon, *Board-Level Employee Representation Rights in Europe – Facts and Trends*, ETUI report (Brussels, 2011).

Georg Eckert and Matthias Schimka, *Die Arbeitnehmermitbestimmung bei grenzüberschreitenden Verschmelzungen nach dem EU-VerschG*, wbl 2008, 201.

Georg Eckert, "EU-VerschG" in Susanne Kalss (ed.), *Verschmelzung – Spaltung – Umwandlung* (2nd ed. Manz Verlag, Wien, 2010), 533.

ETUC position paper – ETUC demands in view of the upcoming company law package, Adopted at the Executive Committee on 13-14 December 2017.

Maximilian Fuchs and Franz Marhold, *Europäisches Arbeitsrecht*, (5th ed. Verlag Österreich, Wien, 2018.

Carsten Gerner-Beuerle, Federico M. Mucciarelli, Edmund-Philipp Schuster and Mathias M. Siems, *Study on the Law Applicable to Companies*, Final Report to the European Commission GD Justice, (2016).

Mathias Habersack and Dirk A. Verse, *Europäisches Gesellschaftsrecht*, (4th ed. Verlag C.H. Beck, 2011).

Matthias Jacobs, SEBG, in *Münchener Kommentar zum Aktiengesetz*, 7th vol. (4th ed. Verlag C.H. Beck, München, 2017).

Stefan Kühteubl and Elisabeth Wasinger "Mitbestimmung der Arbeitnehmer bei einer grenzüberschreitenden Verschmelzung von Kapitalgesellschaften" in Thomas Talos and Martin Winner (eds.), *EU-Verschmelzungsgesetz* (2nd ed. Verlag Österreich, Wien, 2016), 505.

Thomas Müller-Bonanni and Michael Müntefering, Grenzüberschreitende Verschmelzung ohne Arbeitnehmerbeteiligung? NJW 2009, 2347.

Johanna Naderhirn and Anna Ritzberger-Moser, § 258 ArbVG, in Rudolf Strasser, Peter Jabornegg and Reinhard Resch (eds.), *ArbVG Kommentar*, (Manz Verlag, Date: 1.9.2013, rdb.at).

Hartmut Oetker, Art. 16 RL 2005/56/EG, in Martin Franzen and Inken Gallner and Hartmut Oetker, *Kommentar zum europäischen Arbeitsrecht*, (2nd ed. C.H. Beck, München, 2018).

Sebastian Sick and Lasse Pütz, Der deutschen Unternehmensmitbestimmung entzogen: Die Zahl der Unternehmen mit ausländischer Rechtsform wächst, *WSI Mitteilungen 2011*, 34-40.

Sebastian Sick, Der deutschen Mitbestimmung entzogen: Unternehmen mit ausländischer Rechtsform nehmen zu, *Mitbestimmungsförderung Report Nr. 8.* (Düsseldorf, 2015).

Gregor Thüsing and Gerrit Forst, "MgVG" in Mathias Habersack and Florian Drinhausen, *SE-Recht* (2nd ed. Verlag C.H. Beck, München, 2016), 1113.

Matthias Unterrieder and Franz Fazekas, Immer mitbestimmter Aufsichtsrat bei grenzüberschreitenden Verschmelzungen? RdW 2010, 227.

Marc-Philippe Weller, "Unternehmensmitbestimmung für Auslandsgesellschaften", in Bernd Erle, Wulf Goette and Detlef Kleindiek, (eds.) *Festschrift für Peter Hommelhoff zum 70. Geburtstag*, (Schmidt Verlag, Köln, 2012), 1275.

Gerlind Wisskirchen, Alexander Bissels and Martin Begiebing, Unternehmerische Mitbestimmung – unvermeindbar?, Zeitschrift für Familienunternehmen und Stiftungen, 6/2012, 209.

Regulations

Proposal for a Directive of the European Parliament and of the Council amending Directive (EU) 2017/1132 as regards cross-border conversions, mergers and divisions, COM(2018) 241 final.

Council Directive 2001/23/EC of 12 March 2001 on the approximation of the laws of the Member States relating to the safeguarding of employees' rights in the event of transfers of undertakings, businesses or parts of undertakings or businesses, OJ L 82, 22.3.2001, 16-20.

Council Directive 2001/86/EC of 8 October 2001 supplementing the Statute for a European company with regard to the involvement of employees, OJ L 294, 10.11.2001, 22-32.

Directive 2005/56/EC of the European Parliament and of the Council of 26 October 2005 on cross-border mergers of limited liability companies, OJ L 310, 25.11.2005, 1-9 (no longer in force).

Directive (EU) 2017/1132 of the European Parliament and of the Council of 14 June 2017 relating to certain aspects of company law, OJ L 169, 30.6.2017, 46-127.

Impact Assessment – Accompanying the document – Proposal for a Directive of the European Parliament and of the Council amending Directive (EU) 2017/1132 as regards the use of digital tools and processes in company law and Proposal for a Directive of the European Parliament and of the Council amending Directive (EU) 2017/1132 as regards cross-border conversions, mergers and divisions, Brussels, 25.4.2018 – SWD(2018) 141 final.

Act CXXXII of 1997 on Hungarian Branch Offices and Commercial Representative Offices of Foreign-Registered Companies.

Bundesgesetz vom 14 Dezember 1973 betreffend die Arbeitsverfassung, BGBl. Nr. 22/1974 Arbeitsverfassungsgesetz (ArbVG, Labour Constitution Act in Austria).

Gesetz über die Mitbestimmung der Arbeitnehmer bei einer grenzüberschreitenden Verschmelzung (MgVG) Vom 21. Dezember 2006 (BGBl. I S 3332) (Law on the Employees' Participation in Case of Cross-Border Merger in Germany).

The Transfer of Undertaking Directive: A Puzzling Piece of Legislation

Edoardo Ales[*]

Summary

A. Introduction – The substantive normative core of the directive

During its first thirty years of existence, Directive 77/187 (hereafter referred to as "the directive"), on the transfer of undertaking,[1] has been significantly modified. However, its *substantive normative core*[2] on the safeguarding of workers' rights has remained largely unchanged. As widely known, it is now contained in Articles 3, 4, 5 and 6 of Directive 2001/23.[3]

---

* Professor at the University of Naples "Parthenope", lecturer at the WU Vienna.

1 Council Directive 77/187/EEC of 14 February 1977 on the approximation of the laws of the Member States relating to the safeguarding of employees' rights in the event of transfers of undertakings, businesses or parts of businesses, OJ L 61, 5.3.1977, 26-28.

2 Emphasis always added.

3 Council Directive 2001/23/EC of 12 March 2001 on the approximation of the laws of the Member States relating to the safeguarding of employees' rights in the event

This essay looks at this *substantive normative core* from the perspective of the individual employment relationship, i.e. the conservation of the job and the working conditions that exist on the day of the transfer. To this end, it will analyse the imposing case law of the Court of Justice of the EU in detail (hereafter referred to as "the Court" and "the Court of Justice"), which has been called to answer several puzzling questions arising from the application of Articles 3 and 4 of the Directive. The latter only apparently is plain.

This is undoubtedly the case of Article 3, cornerstone of the *substantive normative core* that approaches the issue of safeguard of workers' rights from a simultaneously "static" (para 1) and "dynamic" (para 3) perspective. "Static" in the sense of the single employment relationship, as it is at the day of the transfer; "dynamic", as it is for regulation, after the transfer, also by collective agreement, if there are any.

Severe interpretative uncertainties in both paragraphs have urged national judges to request several preliminary rulings from the Court, with the consequence that the Court has had to clarify, to a reasonable extent, the *substantive normative core*, with reference both to its "static" and the "dynamic" aspects.

In logical sequence, the Court has emphasised the actual aim of the Directive itself, i.e.

> "to ensure, *as far as possible*, that the employment relationship continues unchanged with the transferee, in particular by obliging the transferee to continue to observe the terms and conditions of any collective agreement (Article 3 (2)) and by protecting workers against dismissals motivated solely by the fact of the transfer (Article 4 (1))."[4]

Shortly thereafter, the Court specified that the Directive "is intended to achieve only partial harmonization essentially by extending the protection guaranteed to workers independently by the laws of the individual Member States to cover the case where an undertaking is transferred. Its aim is therefore to ensure, as far as possible, that the contract of employment or the employment relationship continues unchanged with the transferee so that the employees affected by the transfer of the undertaking are not placed in a less favourable position solely as a result of the transfer. It is not

---

of transfers of undertakings, businesses or parts of undertakings or businesses, OJ L 82, 22.3.2001, 16-20.

4 CJEU, 7 February 1985, C-19/83, Wendelboe, ECLI:EU:C:1985:54, point 15.

however intended to establish a uniform level of protection throughout the Community on the basis of common criteria."[5]

These statements already highlight two interesting aspects: "possible" as a condition under which "the employment relationship continues unchanged with the transferee" and "partial harmonization" as an aim of the Directive.

B. *The balance between a static safeguard of working conditions and dynamic freedom of the employer*

"Possible" as condition seems to refer both to the continuation of employment relationship as such and to continuation without modifications, since the Court explicitly refers to Article 4 para 1 (dismissal due to the transfer) and to Article 3 para 2 (collective agreement as a source of regulation of working conditions). The Court, as highlighted in the following, further specified both references.

The clarification on the partial harmonisation is not redundant, as the Directive was adopted on the juridical basis of Article 100 ECT i.e. in the view of the approximation of national legislations. This was not with the view of defining minimum standards, as typical of Article 118a, added by the Single European Act in 1986.

Partial harmonisation means, above all, leaving a margin of manoeuvre to the Member States within the perspective of non-regression, as stated by Article 8 of the Directive, on the ground of what was already foreseen by Article 117 ECT, well before the introduction of Article 118a ECT. It means to avoid, as much as possible, the communitarisation of "undercard" provisions that do not belong to the *substantive normative core* of the Directive, the boundaries of which appear by consequence.

Within such a perspective, the decision in *Tellerup*[6] (better known as *Daddy's Dance Hall*) is instructive, in which the Court states that the protection offered by the Directive

> "is a matter of public policy, and therefore independent of the will of the parties to the contract of employment. The rules of the directive, in particular those concerning the protection of workers against dismissal by reason of the transfer, must be considered to be mandatory, so that

5 CJEU, 11 July 1985, C-105/84, Danmols Inventar, ECLI:EU:C:1985:331, point 26.

6 CJEU, 10 February 1988, C-324/86, Tellerup (Daddy's Dance Hall), ECLI:EU:C:1988:72, points 12-18.

it is not possible to derogate from them in a manner unfavourable to employees."

However, by combining this statement with the principle of partial harmonisation, the Court derived that "in so far as national law allows the employment relationship to be altered in a manner unfavourable to employees in situations other than the transfer of an undertaking, in particular as regards their protection against dismissal, such an alternative is not precluded merely because the undertaking has been transferred in the meantime and the agreement has therefore been made with the new employer". According to the Court, in fact, "since by virtue of Article 3 (1) ... the transferee is subrogated to the transferor's rights and obligations under the employment relationship, that relationship may be altered with regard to the transferee to the same extent as it could have been with regard to the transferor, provided that the transfer of the undertaking itself may never constitute the reason for that amendment" (point 17).

This is a first example of the "balancing act" that the Court is obliged to perform in order to hold together the "static" and the "dynamic" perspective described above. Although not spelt out, it anticipates the principle of balancing between a static safeguard of working conditions and the dynamic freedom of the employer to rearrange their regulation after the transfer, a principle that will dramatically emerge in the Court's case law of the new century.

Further balancing acts are performed, for instance, with reference to the right of the worker to oppose the transfer, a right that, in the light of the mandatory nature of the Directive's provisions, seems to be put into question. In *Katsikas*, the Court clarified the point, with the rather obvious statement that the duty to accept the transfer "would jeopardize the fundamental rights of the employee, who must be free to choose his employer and cannot be obliged to work for an employer whom he has not freely chosen."[7]

However, by consequence, "in the event of the employee deciding of his own accord not to continue with the contract of employment or employment relationship with the transferee, the directive does not require the Member States to provide that the contract or relationship is to be maintained with the transferor. In such a case, it is for the Member States to de-

7 CJEU, 16 December 1992, C-132/91, C-138/91 and C-139/91, Katsikas, Skreb and Schroll, ECLI:EU:C:1992:517, point 32.

termine what the fate of the contract of employment or employment relationship should be."[8]

Therefore, if the Member States do not foresee the continuation of the employment relationship by the transferor, in the case that a worker refuses to keep on working for the transferee, the transferee will be free to dismiss this worker, being affected by the consequences defined by each national legal order in case of unlawful dismissal, which fall outside EU Law. According to the latter, in fact, "the transfer of the undertaking, business or part of the undertaking or business shall not in itself constitute grounds for dismissal by the transferor or the transferee" (Article 4 para 1).

The refusal of the worker to follow the fate of the transferred undertaking is just one of the critical points deriving from the "dynamisation" of the static perspective of the maintenance of rights within the transfer.

In fact, in *Delahaye*,[9] the Court affirmed that the Directive "must be interpreted as not precluding in principle, in the event of a transfer of an undertaking from a legal person governed by private law to the State, the latter, as new employer, from reducing the amount of the remuneration of the employees concerned for the purpose of complying with the national rules in force for public employees. However, the competent authorities responsible for applying and interpreting those rules are obliged to do so as far as possible in the light of the purpose of that directive, taking into account in particular the employee's length of service, in so far as the national rules governing the position of State employees take a State employee's length of service into consideration for calculating his remuneration."

> However, "if such a calculation leads to a substantial reduction in the employee's remuneration, such a reduction constitutes a substantial change in working conditions to the detriment of the employees concerned by the transfer, so that the termination of their contracts of employment for that reason must be regarded as resulting from the action of the employer, in accordance with Article 4(2) (..)".

Therefore, according to EU Law, the only consequence of the worsening of working conditions to the point of convincing a worker to resign, seems to be the liability of the transferee for the termination of the employment relationship, which will be for just cause.

As the Court clarified, Article 4 para 2 must be interpreted as meaning that, in cases where the termination of a contract of employment or an em-

8 Ibid., point 35.
9 CJEU, 11 November 2004, C-425/02, Delahaye, ECLI:EU:C:2004:706, point 35.

ployment relationship is brought about because the conditions for the applicability of that provision have been met, independently of any failure on the part of the transferee employer to fulfil their obligations under that directive, *the Member States are not required to guarantee the employee a right to financial compensation, for which the transferee employer is liable, in accordance with the same conditions as the right upon which an employee can rely where the contract of employment or the employment relationship is unlawfully terminated by his employer*.

> "However, the national court is required, in a case within its jurisdiction, to ensure that, at the very least, the transferee employer in such a case bears the consequences that the applicable national law attaches to termination by an employer of the contract of employment or the employment relationship, such as the payment of the salary and other benefits relating, under that law, to the notice period with which an employer must comply."[10]

Concluding on this point, if, on the one hand, the Directive strongly affirms the right to the maintenance of the working conditions enjoyed at the moment of the transfer, on the other hand, it does not adequately guarantee its application within the dynamic phase of transfer. In actuality, it leaves the decision to the national legislator as to whether or not a more effective instrument can be foreseen than that of resignation for just cause, which in my view cannot be deemed an adequate instrument in the view of realising the aim of the Directive.

However, the lack of a "creative" approach should not be misinterpreted in terms of the absence of the Court's strategy with regards to the maintenance of working conditions. Rather, it is a less striking, sometimes oblique tactic made from specific interventions that, insisting on the definition of maintenance, put more or less definite limits on unacceptable applications of this ambiguous legal framework.

For instance, in *Collino and Chiappero*, the Court had already pointed out the substantive limits to transferee discretionary power by stating that,

> "in calculating the rights of a financial nature attached, in the transferee's business, to employees' length of service, such as a termination payment or salary increases, the transferee must take into account the entire length of service of the employees transferred, both in his employment and that of the transferor, in so far as his obligation to do so

10 CJEU, 27 November 2008, C-396/07, Juuri, ECLI:EU:C:2008:656, point 35.

> derives from the employment relationship between those employees and the transferor, and in accordance with the terms agreed in that relationship."[11]

By allowing the transferee to modify working conditions in the case of national law permitting it outside a transfer of undertaking, the partial harmonisation approach is therein confirmed and a non-EU Law zone of sorts is created given the situation of national legislations not being in line with the aim of the Directive. Case law of the Court risks being therein eroded from the outside, along with the same *substantive normative core* of the Directive at risk, therein jeopardising its capacity to reach its aims.

The same effect can be found in *Martin*,[12] in which the Court, after having affirmed that the protection guaranteed by the Directive is of public policy, stated that "the rules of the directive must be considered to be mandatory, so that it is not possible to derogate from them in a manner unfavourable to employees" (point 39). Having derived that employees are not entitled to waive the rights conferred on them by the directive and that those rights cannot be restricted even with their consent" (point 40), once again in the name of partial harmonization (point 41), the Court limits its application to the extent "to ensure that the employee is protected in his relations with the transferee to the same extent as he was in his relations with the transferor under the legal rules of the Member State concerned" (point 41). With the consequence that

> "in so far as national law allows the employment relationship to be altered in a manner unfavourable to employees in situations other than the transfer of an undertaking, such an alternative is not precluded merely because the undertaking has been transferred in the meantime and the agreement has therefore been made with the new employer" (point 42).

In actuality,

> "being the transferee subrogated to the transferor's rights and obligations under the employment relationship, that relationship may be altered with regard to the transferee to the same extent as it could have been with regard to the transferor, provided that the transfer of the un-

11 CJEU, 14 September 2000, C-343/98, Collino e Chiappero, ECLI:EU:C:2000:441, point 53.

12 CJEU, 6 November 2003, C-4/01, Martin, ECLI:EU:C:2003:594.

dertaking itself may never constitute the reason for that amendment" (point 42).

In *Martin*, the worsening of working conditions (retirement age) derives from the same transfer, i.e., from the necessity to equalise treatments between incoming and already employed workers. Consequently, such a worsening should be regarded as prohibited under the Directive. However, if at the time some incoming employees accept early retirement on terms other than those laid down by the originally applicable collective agreement delineating more favourable conditions of service, and the collective agreement giving rise to that provision has, as a matter of national law, ceased to apply to them, these employees lose the right laid down by that collective agreement (point 47).

This last reference enables decisive reasoning on the collective agreement as a source of production and regulation of workers' rights once the transfer has taken place.

That this comes into play highlights and detonates the contradiction, inherent in the same wording of Article 3, between "static" protection of rights[13] and the survivor of rights recognised by the collective agreement, once the transfer has taken place.[14] This above all, in light of the refusal by the Court of the theory of incorporation of the working conditions foreseen by the collective agreement within the individual employment contract.

Indeed, precisely in light of this refusal, the collective agreement and the collective bargaining from which it could stem again are the only instruments that, with their ongoing effect after the transfer, maintain the working conditions applied at the time of transfer itself in a dynamic perspective. However, as already highlighted by the Court in *Martin*, and as we will see shortly, the refusal of the theory of incorporation does not follow the adoption of the theory of the dynamic referral as such. The application of the latter will, in fact, delineate that the collective agreement applied at the time of the transfer should keep on producing its effects, within the internally contradictory condition, for both parties of the employ-

---

13 "The transferor's rights and obligations arising from a contract of employment or from an employment relationship existing on the date of a transfer shall, by reason of such transfer, be transferred to the transferee" (para 1).

14 "Following the transfer, the transferee shall continue to observe the terms and conditions agreed in any collective agreement on the same terms applicable to the transferor under that agreement, until the date of termination or expiry of the collective agreement or the entry into force or application of another collective agreement" (para 3).

ment relationship, despite the subjective subrogation that has taken place. Anticipating one of the conclusions to be drawn, one could speak of "dynamic-static referral" to collective agreement, but not to collective bargaining.

Of course, this conclusion needs to be supported by specific arguments. This will be achieved using the case law of the Court, with the additional aim of highlighting the practical open issues at stake, generated by the contradiction inherent to Article 3.

C. Three open issues

From such a perspective, one can argue that there are three open issues: (i) that of the limits to the dynamic referral; (ii) that of the automatic substitution of the working conditions in case the transferee applies a different collective agreement; and (iii) that of the continuing effect of a rescinded collective agreement.

I. Limits to the dynamic referral

(i) The issue of the dynamic referral singled out by *Alemo-Herron*[15] already surfaced in *Martin* and, above all, has already been addressed exhaustively in *Werhof*.[16] However, with the latter being a German case, notwithstanding the remarkable echo it has created in that legal order,[17] it did not raise as much of a stir as *Alemo-Herron*, the latter being favoured by the competitive advantage granted by English being the dominant language of international literature.[18]

---

15 CJEU, 18 July 2013, C-426/11, Alemo-Herron, ECLI:EU:C:2013:521.

16 CJEU, 9 March 2006, C-499/04, Werhof, ECLI:EU:C:2006:168.

17 BAG, 23 September 2009, 4 AZR 331/08; BAG, 24 February 2010, 4 AZR 691/08; BAG, 19 October 2011, 4 AZR 811/09.

18 Jeremias Prassl, Freedom of Contract as a General Principle of EU Law? Transfers of Undertakings and the Protection of Employer Rights in EU Labour Law, ILJ, 2013, 434; Rebecca Zahn, The Court of Justice of the European Union and Transfers of Undertakings. Implications for Collective Labour Rights, ELLJ, 2015, 72. On that issue, only partly follow-up of Alemo-Herron, see John McMullen, TUPE: Ringing the (Wrong) Changes. The Collective Redundancies and Transfer of Undertakings (Protection of Employment) (Amendment) Regulations 2014, ILJ, 2014, 149.

Be that as it may, in *Werhof*,[19] the Court stated the cornerstones of its doctrine on the effect of collective agreement and collective bargaining in the transfer of undertaking. It can be summarised as follows:

a) "the terms and conditions under that collective agreement are to continue to be observed only until the date of its termination or expiry, or the entry into force or application of another collective agreement";
b) "the wording of the Directive does not in any way indicate that the Community legislature intended that the transferee be bound by collective agreements other than the one in force at the time of the transfer and, consequently, that the terms and conditions be subsequently amended through the application of a new collective agreement concluded after the transfer. Such an assessment is, moreover, consistent with the objective of the Directive, which is merely to safeguard the rights and obligations of employees in force on the day of the transfer";
c) "the Directive was not intended to protect mere expectations to rights and, therefore, hypothetical advantages flowing from future changes to collective agreements";
d) "Member States may limit the period for observing the terms and conditions arising from a collective agreement, provided that that period is not less than one year. In a way, this limitation is subsidiary, since it is applicable if none of the abovementioned situations, that is, termination or expiry of the existing collective agreement, or entry into force or application of a new collective agreement, arises within a period of one year after the transfer";
e) "in addition, although in accordance with the objective of the Directive the interests of the employees concerned by the transfer must be protected, those of the transferee, who must be in a position to make the adjustments and changes necessary to carry on his operations, cannot be disregarded";
f) "if the 'dynamic' interpretation of the contractual reference clause were applied, that would mean that future collective agreements apply to a transferee who is not party to a collective agreement and that his fundamental right not to join an association could be affected"; and
g) "on the other hand, the 'static' interpretation makes it possible to avoid a situation in which the transferee of a business who is not party to a collective agreement is bound by future changes to that agreement."

---

19 CJEU, 9 March 2006, C-499/04, Werhof, ECLI:EU:C:2006:168, points 29-35.

In this way, the Court, with good reason in my opinion, grants negative freedom of association of the transferee that, in the case of dynamic referral to *collective bargaining*, would be irreparably compromised by forcing the transferee, along with others, to open a dispute with the transferred worker. In the case of modification of working conditions, the referral clause was included, a modification that seems to be excluded by Article 3 para 1.

This is a matter of necessary interpretation, aimed at guaranteeing the internal coherence of the provisions of Article 3, which is destined to clash irretrievably.

The statement that has given rise to deep indignation in the literature has to be framed in such a perspective;[20] according to this statement, "although in accordance with the objective of the Directive the interests of the employees concerned by the transfer must be protected, those of the transferee, who must be in a position to make the adjustments and changes necessary to carry on his operations, cannot be disregarded."[21] In my view, what is at stake is not the unlawful introduction of a further aim of the Directive unforeseen by the Community legislator, as argued by the literature quoted above;[22] rather, it is an essay of the Court to make the Directive work.

On the other hand, by issuing such a statement, the Court has only made explicit a concept that, as we have seen before, was already present in its earliest case law,[23] i.e., the "possible" as a condition under which "the employment relationship continues unchanged with the transferee".

In such a perspective, *Alemo-Herron* adds very little to the *Werhof* doctrine, by operationalising it as far as some contextual elements are concerned. Therefore, for statements such as:

> "Article 3 (..), *read in conjunction with Article 8* of that directive, cannot be interpreted as entitling the Member States to take measures which,

---

20 Jeremias Prassl, Freedom of Contract as a General Principle of EU Law? Transfers of Undertakings and the Protection of Employer Rights in EU Labour Law, ILJ, 2013, 434; but also Nicola Countouris, Wanjiru Njoya, 2011/23/EC Transfer of Undertaking, in Monika Schlachter (ed.), EU Labour Law. A Commentary, (2015) 421.

21 CJEU, 9 March 2006, C-499/04, Werhof, ECLI:EU:C:2006:168, point 31.

22 Jeremias Prassl, Freedom of Contract as a General Principle of EU Law? Transfers of Undertakings and the Protection of Employer Rights in EU Labour Law, ILJ, 2013, 434.

23 CJEU, 7 February 1985, C-19/83, Wendelboe, ECLI:EU:C:1985:54, point 15 and CJEU, 11 July 1985, C-105/84, Danmols Inventar, ECLI:EU:C:1985:331, point 26.

> while being more favourable to employees, are liable to adversely affect the very essence of the transferee's freedom to conduct a business"

(point 36), and

> "(..) Article 3 (..) must be interpreted as precluding a Member State from providing, in the event of a transfer of an undertaking, that dynamic clauses referring to collective agreements negotiated and adopted after the date of transfer are enforceable against the transferee, where that transferee does not have the possibility of participating in the negotiation process of such collective agreements concluded after the date of the transfer" (point 37).

In actuality, it seems to me that, with this last statement, the Court has considerably safeguarded the role of collective bargaining, allowing national legislators to foresee a dynamic referral to it if the transferee is able, even potentially, to influence this bargaining.

The same reference to the Article 8 Directive, emphasised above, does not seem to justify the concerns about the configuration of the Directive's provisions as maximum instead of minimum requirements,[24] since the Court (also recently) has continued admitting the compatibility of national legislations more favourable than the Directive with EU Law.[25]

Therefore, to conclude on this point, *Werhof* and *Alemo-Herron* do confirm the impression, already brought up by *Martin*, of a "dynamic-static referral" to the collective agreement as the sole instrument capable of providing Article 3 with some sense, as it is excluded from para 2 on the adoption of the incorporation theory. The referral is *dynamic* since it refers to the collective agreement and to its capacity to take into account, better than any

---

24 Jeremias Prassl, Freedom of Contract as a General Principle of EU Law? Transfers of Undertakings and the Protection of Employer Rights in EU Labour Law, ILJ, 2013, 434; but also Nicola Countouris, Wanjiru Njoya, 2011/23/EC Transfer of Undertaking, in Monika Schlachter (ed.), EU Labour Law: A Commentary, (2015) 421.

25 CJEU, 6 March 2014, C-458/12, Amatori, ECLI:EU:C:2014:124, in which the Court states that the Directive does not preclude a national legislation, which, (a) on the transfer of part of the undertaking, permits the transferee to take over the employment relationship from the transferor if that part of the undertaking does not constitute a functionally autonomous economic entity existing before the transfer; and (b) enables the transferee to take over the employment relationships from the transferor if, after the transfer of part of an undertaking concerned exercises extensive, overriding powers over the transferee. See on it Massimo Pallini, La rilevanza del consenso del lavoratore nelle operazioni di esternalizzazione, RGL, 2014, II, 427.

individual contract, the events of each employment relationship, and it is *static* because it does not open to the application of collective bargaining carried out after the transfer has taken place, unless the transferee can influence its outcome.

II. The automatic substitution of the transferor's collective agreement

(ii) Some of the issues linked to the "dynamic-static referral" echo also in the second question: the one related to the automatic substitution of the transferor collective agreement with the one applied by the transferee.

In this case, it seems to me that a true *aporia* is at stake, accentuated by the refusal of the theory on dynamic referral to *collective bargaining* and by the adoption of the theory of the "dynamic-static referral" to *collective agreement*. Being an *aporia*, it can be solved only by granting prevalence to one exigence over the other: either maintenance (in the case of maintenance through a collective agreement) or change (not necessarily under the logic of maintenance) through collective bargaining.

Even if the Court cannot approach such an *aporia* systemically, being obliged to decide as it is on specific cases, it has drawn a line to the worsening of working conditions deriving from the automatic substitution of collective agreements, which are to be taken for granted according to Article 3 para 2 of the Directive.

A paramount example of this approach can be found in *Scattolon*,[26] in which the Court stated that the "implementation of the option to replace, with immediate effect, the conditions which the transferred workers enjoy under the collective agreement with the transferor with those laid down by the collective agreement in force with the transferee cannot therefore have the aim or effect of imposing on those workers conditions which are, overall, less favourable than those applicable before the transfer. If it were otherwise, achievement of the objective pursued by Directive 77/187 could easily be called into question in any sector governed by collective agreements, which would undermine the effectiveness of that directive" (point 76).

The Court seems to lean towards a solution to the *aporia* in which the principle of maintenance will prevail on the one of change (even through collective bargaining), assigning to the national judge the task of assessing the overall extent of the worsening conditions brought about by the new collective agreement. By doing this, the Court denies the absoluteness of

26 CJEU, 6 September 2011, C-108/10, Scattolon, ECLI:EU:C:2011:542.

the principle of automatic substitution of the collective agreement applied by the transferor.

III. The continuing effect of the rescinded collective agreement

(iii) The solution adopted on the last issues at stake, that of the continuing effect of the rescinded collective agreement, is highly influenced by the stance taken by the Court on two just analysed issues.

In actuality, it seems to me that the Court closed the loop in *Österreichischer Gewerkschaftsbund*[27] by stating that Article 3 para 3 of the Directive "is intended to maintain not the application of a collective agreement as such but the 'terms and conditions' put into place by such an agreement".[28] In this way, the Court confirms, beyond any reasonable doubt, the theory of the "dynamic-static referral" and the prevalence of the maintenance of workers' rights on the reasons of collective bargaining and on the multiple situations attached to it (as, in the case at stake, the continuing effect of the rescinded collective agreement). On the other hand, the Court also opened up new EU Law scenarios for national judges in the view of the maintenance of working conditions in the case of their unilateral modification in absence of a collective agreement applied by the transferee, a modification which a worker can oppose more easily in court without being obliged to resign.

Bibliography

Elisabeth Brameshuber, Balancing vs. Preservation of Rights under the Acquired Rights Directive, *ILJ*, 2016, 443.

Nicola Countouris, Wanjiru Njoya, 2011/23/EC Transfer of Undertaking, in Monika Schlachter (ed.), *EU Labour Law: A Commentary*, (Kluwer Law International, 2015), 421.

John McMullen, TUPE: Ringing the (Wrong) Changes. The Collective Redundancies and Transfer of Undertakings (Protection of Employment) (Amendment) Regulations 2014, *ILJ*, 2014, 149.

27 CJEU, 11 September 2014, C-328/13, Österreichischer Gewerkschaftsbund, ECLI:EU:C:2014:2197. See on it, Elisabeth Brameshuber, Balancing vs. Preservation of Rights under the Acquired Rights Directive, ILJ, 2016, 443.

28 CJEU, 11 September 2014, C-328/13, Österreichischer Gewerkschaftsbund, ECLI:EU:C:2014:2197, point 23.

Massimo Pallini, La rilevanza del consenso del lavoratore nelle operazioni di esternalizzazione, *RGL*, 2014, II, 427.

Jeremias Prassl, Freedom of Contract as a General Principle of EU Law? Transfers of Undertakings and the Protection of Employer Rights in EU Labour Law, *ILJ*, 2013, 434.

Rebecca Zahn, The Court of Justice of the European Union and Transfers of Undertakings. Implications for Collective Labour Rights, *ELLJ*, 2015, 72.

Regulations and case law

Council Directive 77/187/EEC of 14 February 1977 on the approximation of the laws of the Member States relating to the safeguarding of employees' rights in the event of transfers of undertakings, businesses or parts of businesses, OJ L 61, 5.3.1977, 26-28.

Council Directive 2001/23/EC of 12 March 2001 on the approximation of the laws of the Member States relating to the safeguarding of employees' rights in the event of transfers of undertakings, businesses or parts of undertakings or businesses, OJ L 82, 22.3.2001, 16-20.

CJEU, 7 February 1985, C-19/83, *Wendelboe*, ECLI:EU:C:1985:54.

CJEU, 11 July 1985, C-105/84, *Danmols Inventar*, ECLI:EU:C:1985:331.

CJEU, 10 February 1988, C-324/86, *Tellerup (Daddy's Dance Hall)*, ECLI:EU:C:1988:72.

CJEU, 16 December 1992, C-132/91, C-138/91 and C-139/91, *Katsikas, Skreb and Schroll*, ECLI:EU:C:1992:517.

CJEU, 14 September 2000, C-343/98, *Collino and Chiappero*, ECLI:EU:C:2000:441.

CJEU, 6 November 2003, C-4/01, *Martin*, ECLI:EU:C:2003:594.

CJEU, 11 November 2004, C-425/02, *Delahaye*, ECLI:EU:C:2004:706.

CJEU, 9 March 2006, C-499/04, *Werhof*, ECLI:EU:C:2006:168.

CJEU, 27 November 2008, C-396/07, *Juuri*, ECLI:EU:C:2008:656.

CJEU, 6 September 2011, C-108/10, *Scattolon*, ECLI:EU:C:2011:542.

CJEU, 18 July 2013, C-426/11, *Alemo-Herron*, ECLI:EU:C:2013:521.

CJEU, 6 March 2014, C-458/12, *Amatori*, ECLI:EU:C:2014:124.

CJEU, 11 September 2014, C-328/13, *Österreichischer Gewerkschaftsbund*, ECLI:EU:C:2014:2197.

BAG, 23 September 2009, 4 AZR 331/08.

BAG, 24 February 2010, 4 AZR 691/08.

BAG, 19 October 2011, 4 AZR 811/09.

Cross-Border Transfers of Undertakings

Diana Niksova[*]

Summary

* 'Post-doc' Research and Teaching Associate at the University of Vienna.

A. Introduction

Economic trends, such as consolidation and globalisation, are urging business leaders to rethink their organisations' structures, including the choice of geographical location. Many economic operators relocate their businesses abroad to benefit from the competitive advantages offered by foreign countries. In their search for an attractive business location, they are not only influenced by economic factors, but also by regulatory frameworks. From the perspective of labour law, such restructuring may result in a cross-border transfer of undertakings within the meaning of the Transfer of Undertakings Directive 2001/23/EC.[1] Even though there are only few cases relating to cross-border transfers currently before the national courts and none before the ECJ, this does not mean that cross-border transfers of undertakings do not occur in business practice. According to data from the European Restructuring Monitor of the European Foundation for the Improvement of Living and Working Conditions, the number of restructuring operations where the activity is relocated or outsourced outside the country's borders has been increasing steadily and the European Commission expects it to continue increasing in the future.[2]

In the event of a cross-border transfer of undertakings that is connected with a relocation and change of the employees' place of work, in which the transferor and the transferee are governed by the laws of different Member States, many labour law problems arise. However, Directive 2001/23/EC itself does not contain any express legal provisions concerning cross-border situations since it was enacted at a time when there was relatively little cross-border merger activity.[3] Even though that situation has changed dramatically, Directive 2001/23/EC has not been adjusted to suit the new developments and does not provide solutions in the event of the cross-border transfer of undertakings. Therefore, the problems that arise in cross-border

1 Council Directive 2001/23/EC of 12 March 2001 on the approximation of the laws of the Member States relating to the safeguarding of employees' rights in the event of transfers of undertakings, businesses or parts of undertakings or businesses, L 82/16, 22.3.2001.

2 Commission of the European Communities, First phase consultation of social partners under Article 138(2) of the EC Treaty concerning cross-border transfers of undertakings, businesses or parts of undertakings or businesses, http://ec.europa.eu/social/main.jsp?catId=706&langId=de&intPageId=208 (accessed on 2.6.2018).

3 Bob Hepple, *The legal consequences of cross-border transfers of undertakings within the EU* (1998) 38, http://ec.europa.eu/social/main.jsp?catId=706&langId=de&intPageId=208 (accessed on 2.6.2018).

scenarios create legal uncertainty for both employers as well as employees.[4] In this context, this paper deals with labour law aspects of cross-border relocation transfers. The labour law problems that arise in cross-border transfers of undertakings will be examined on the basis of the following case:[5]

An Austrian company situated in Vienna, which produces mechanical products for cars, is sold and relocated to a Slovak company based in Bratislava that is within the same group. Consequently, the Slovak company takes over all the material assets of the production plant. The department's equipment, machinery and inventory are transferred from Vienna to Bratislava. The distance from the old to the new location is 60 kilometers. The Slovak company also takes over the production methods and customer lists and continues the production of existing orders in Slovakia. The customers are informed of the new address in Slovakia. The managing director of the production plant informs the employees that the department in Vienna has been "closed" and the employees' contracts are therefore going to be terminated. On the same day, the employees receive an offer to enter into an employment contract with the Slovak company. However, the employees who were employed in the production plant in Vienna refuse to work in Slovakia and reject the offer. They contest the dismissal with the argument that the production plant has not been closed, but was subject to a transfer of undertakings within the meaning of Directive 2001/23/EC. Article 4(1) of Directive 2001/23 prohibits any dismissals grounds of which is the transfer of undertakings.

In this context, the following questions arise: Firstly, does the Transfer of Undertakings Directive 2001/23/EC apply in cross-border situations? Since the Directive does not explicitly cover cross-border transfers of undertakings, it is not clear whether it is applicable in the event of a cross-border relocation from one Member State to another, or — even more challenging — from a Member State to a Non-Member State. If this question was to be answered in the affirmative, the next question would be whether a relocation can ever constitute a transfer of an undertaking within the

4 Commission of the European Communities, First phase consultation of social partners under Article 138(2) of the EC Treaty concerning cross-border transfers of undertakings, businesses or parts of undertakings or businesses, http://ec.europa.eu/social/main.jsp?catId=706&langId=de&intPageId=208 (accessed on 2.6.2018).

5 In 2011, the German Federal Labour Court was confronted with a similar case between Germany and Switzerland: 26.5.2011 – 8 AZR 37/10, NZA 2011, 1143 = AP Nr. 409 zu § 613a BGB (Deinert) = Arbeit und Arbeitsrecht 2011, 695 (Schröder/Abraham) = EELC 2012/1, 4 (Schreiner) = ZESAR 2012, 411 (Leuchten).

meaning of Directive 2001/23/EC. A transfer of an undertaking requires that the economic entity retains its identity. However, in a cross-border scenario, where the business is relocated from one country to another, differences do occur in the legal, economic and social environment. Therefore, it is not clear whether an economic entity can retain its identity in a cross-border situation or whether the relocation constitutes a closure of the establishment rather than a transfer of an undertaking. Finally, the consequences of cross-border transfers of undertakings must be analysed. In this paper, special emphasis will be put on individual labour law aspects. Since cross-border relocation transfers are connected to a change in the place of work, it is important to investigate whether the employees are obliged to work at the new location in Slovakia. Can they be fairly dismissed if they refuse to work at the new location or does the transfer constitute the grounds for dismissal and is the dismissal therefore unjustified pursuant to Article 4 of Directive 2001/23/EC? To answer these questions, it is also crucial to determine which law is applicable — the Austrian or the Slovak law? Since the transferor and the transferee are governed by the laws of different Member States, the conflict of laws rules need to be thoroughly investigated.

B. *Application of Directive 2001/23/EC in Cross-Border Scenarios*

Since cross-border transfers of undertakings are not explicitly covered by Directive 2001/23/EC, it is at present legally uncertain whether the Directive is applicable in cross-border scenarios where the business is transferred to a foreign owner and relocated from one Member State to another. According to Article 1(2) of Directive 2001/23/EC it "*shall apply where and in so far as the undertaking, business or part of the undertaking or business to be transferred is situated within the territorial scope of the Treaty*". According to Article 52 TEU in connection with Article 355 TFEU the Treaty shall apply to the Member States. Therefore, pursuant to Article 1(2) of Directive 2001/23/EC the business to be transferred must be situated in a Member State. However, the Directive is not restricted to domestic situations only, where the business to be transferred is situated in one and the same Member State before and after the transfer. If a business situated in a Member State is transferred to another Member State, in my view, the cross-border transfer will also be subject to Directive 2001/23/EC. Since the Directive is applicable in all Member States in domestic situations, it also applies in cross-border situations between two or more Member States.[6]

The objective of Directive 2001/23/EC also requires its applicability in cross-border situations, since the rights of the employees must also be safeguarded in cross-border restructuring.[7] Furthermore, according to Recital 2 of Directive 2001/23/EC, economic trends are bringing, at both the national and *Community level*, changes in the structure of undertakings through transfers of undertakings. Recital 2 of the Directive, therefore, also indicates that cross-border situations are covered by Directive 2001/23/EC.[8]

To conclude, Directive 2001/23/EC is applicable in the event of a relocation transfer from one Member State to another Member State (for relocation transfers from a Member State to a Non-Member State see Chapter D.). However, the next question that arises is whether a relocation between Member States constitutes a transfer of an undertaking within the meaning of Directive 2001/23/EC or whether it results in a closure of the establishment rather than in a transfer of an undertaking.

C. Requirements

I. Change of Ownership

As in domestic situations, two requirements must be met to conclude that a transfer of an undertaking within the meaning of Directive 2001/23/EC has occurred: First, a change of ownership is required, and second, the economic entity must retain its identity. If an Austrian company is sold to a Slovak company and the assets are transferred to the foreign company, as in the case introduced at the start of this paper, a change of ownership within the meaning of Article 1(1)(a) of Directive 2001/23/EC has taken place. A cross-border merger or spin-off may also result in a cross-border transfer of undertakings. On the other hand, the mere change in the ownership of a company through a share deal does not constitute a transfer of undertak-

6 Sebastian Krebber, "Die volle Wirksamkeit von Richtlinien in länderübergreifenden Sachverhalten", ZVglRWiss 1998, 124 (148).

7 Constantin von Alvensleben, Die Rechte der Arbeitnehmer bei Betriebsübergang im Europäischen Gemeinschaftsrecht (1992) 156 et seqq.

8 Wolfgang Däubler, "Der Erwerb deutscher Betriebe durch ausländische Unternehmen" in Meinhard Heinze and Alfred Söllner (eds.), *Arbeitsrecht in der Bewährung: Festschrift for Otto Kissel* (1994) 119 (126).

ings, even if the new shareholder is a foreigner.[9] Special emphasis in this paper will be put on the second requirement: Can the economic entity retain its identity in the event of a relocation to another country?

II. Identity of the Economic Entity in Cross-Border Scenarios

Since cross-border relocations of operations are connected to substantial changes in the environment, particularly in the legal, economic, linguistic and social context, the question arises of whether the differences prevent the economic entity from retaining its identity. Some legal commentators find that in international transactions, business relocations to a far away location constitute a closure rather than a transfer of an undertaking. The main argument is that many employees do not wish to move abroad to carry out their work far from their previous location. For this reason, some authors conclude that long distance cross-border relocations are more likely to be classified as the closing down rather than the transfer of an undertaking.[10]

So far, there is no judgment on cross-border transfers of undertakings from the ECJ. The Austrian Supreme Court of Justice has not had to decide on the matter of cross-border transfers of undertakings either. However, the German Federal Labour Court has already decided several cases related to relocation transfers.[11]

In 2011, the German Federal Labour Court was confronted with a case very similar to the initial case outlined above: A German employer sold his business to a Swiss company and transferred the equipment, machinery and inventory to Switzerland. The distance between the transferor's loca-

---

9 Björn Gaul, Simon Jeffreys, Andreas Tinhofer and Stanislas van Wassenhove (CMS Employment Practice Area Group), *Study on the application of Directive 2001/23/EC to cross-border transfers of undertakings*, Study nº VT/2005/101 (September 2006) 13 et seqq.

10 E.g. Hermann Reichold, "Neues zum grenzüberschreitenden Betriebsübergang" in Horst Konzen, Sebastian Krebber, Thomas Raab, Barbara Veit and Bernd Waas (eds.), *Festschrift for Rolf Birk* (2008), 687 (700 et seqq.).

11 E.g. German Federal Labour Court (BAG) 20.4.1989 – 2 AZR 431/88, AP Nr. 81 zu § 613a BGB (Kreitner); German Federal Labour Court (BAG) 29.10.1992 – 2 AZR 267/92, IPRax 1994, 123 (Mankowski 88 et seqq.); German Federal Labour Court (BAG) 26.5.2011 – 8 AZR 37/10, AP Nr. 409 zu § 613a BGB (Deinert) = ecolex 2012, 80 (Niksova) = Arbeit und Arbeitsrecht 2011, 695 (Schröder/Abraham) = European Employment Law Cases (EELC) 2012/1, 4 (Schreiner) = ZESAR 2012, 411 (Leuchten).

tion and that of the transferee was 59 kilometers. The Swiss company also took over the customer relations as well as the production methods and continued the production at the new location. The German Federal Labour Court held that the establishment had not been closed since the closure of an establishment is defined as the termination of the productive collaboration between the employee and the employer by reason of a final decision by the employer to give up the economic activity. A decision to cease an activity, however, has not occurred if the employer sells the economic activity to another company that continues the production at a new location. Such a situation is considered to constitute a transfer of an undertaking within the meaning of Directive 2001/23/EC.[12]

As the German Federal Labour Court has stated, since the German employer did not take a final decision to give up the economic activity, but instead chose to sell the assets to another company that continued the same activity, the establishment was not closed. The question of whether or not the economic entity retains its identity must be answered by considering the seven criteria established by the ECJ in the judgement *Spijkers*, which relate to:

- the type of the undertaking or business in question,
- whether or not the business's tangible assets are transferred,
- the value of its intangible assets at the time of the transfer,
- whether or not the majority of its employees are taken over by the new employer,
- whether or not its customers are transferred,
- the degree of similarity between the activities carried on before and after the transfer, and
- the period, if any, for which those activities were suspended.[13]

In my view, the set of criteria established by the ECJ in the judgement *Spijkers* is also sufficient for cross-border scenarios to determine whether a cross-border relocation constitutes a transfer of an undertaking. In other words, as in domestic situations, the same criteria must be used to determine whether a cross-border transfer of an undertaking has occurred and the cross-border issues do not need to be defined further in Directive 2001/23/EC. Therefore, in the event of a cross-border relocation of a production plant, if the main tangible (premises, equipment, inventory,

12 German Federal Labour Court (BAG) 26.5.2011 – 8 AZR 37/10, European Employment Law Cases (EELC) 2012/1, 4-6 (Schreiner).

13 ECJ C-24/85, 18.3.1986, *Spijkers*, ECLI:EU:C:1986:127 para 13.

tools etc.) and intangible (goodwill, licence, commercial lease) assets are sold to the new employer who takes over the customer relations and production methods and continues to carry out the same operations without substantial interruption, the situation constitutes a transfer of an undertaking and does not result in a closure of the establishment.[14] The relocation is not in itself an obstacle to the transfer of an undertaking within the meaning of Directive 2001/23/EC and does not render the Directive automatically inapplicable.[15]

However, it is disputable whether the distance between the transferor's location and that of the transferee constitutes an additional criterion in order to determine whether or not the economic entity retains its identity. The German Federal Labour Court has found that 60 kilometers is a relatively short distance since the employees are able to reach the new location by car within an hour. Therefore, according to the German Federal Labour Court, this relatively short distance does not preclude there being a cross-border transfer of an undertaking.[16] However, the German Federal Labour Court seems to hold the view, that if the distance between the transferor's place of business and that of the transferee exceeds a certain number of kilometers, no transfer of undertakings has taken place. In another (domestic) case, in which the distance between the transferor's location and that of the transferee was 300 kilometers, the German Federal Labour Court did not assume there to be a transfer of an undertaking even though the type of undertaking in question stayed the same and the same activity continued to be carried out at the new location. The court held that the economic entity was not maintained since the personnel refused to work at the new location and a newly structured group of employees had to be built up at the new location to pursue the same economic activity as before the relocation.[17]

However, in this context, it is important to distinguish between labour-intensive and non-labour-intensive sectors. In certain labour-intensive sec-

14 German Federal Labour Court (BAG) 26.5.2011 – 8 AZR 37/10, European Employment Law Cases (EELC) 2012/1, 4-6 (Schreiner). See also Marcus Kania, "Betriebsverlagerungen ins Ausland als Weg aus der Krise?" ZESAR 2010, 112 (114).

15 Björn Gaul, Simon Jeffreys, Andreas Tinhofer and Stanislas van Wassenhove (CMS Employment Practice Area Group), *Study on the application of Directive 2001/23/EC to cross-border transfers of undertakings*, Study n° VT/2005/101 (September 2006) 6 et seqq.

16 German Federal Labour Court (BAG), 26.5.2011 – 8 AZR 37/10, European Employment Law Cases (EELC) 2012/1, 4-6 (Schreiner).

17 German Federal Labour Court (BAG), 12.02.1987 – 2 AZR 247/86, EWiR § 613a BGB 12/87, 1177 (Willemsen).

tors, in which the activities are based essentially on manpower, the distance may play a significant role, since such an entity is only capable of maintaining its identity if the essential personnel in terms of number and skills is transferred to the transferee.[18] In cross-border scenarios, however, the majority of employees will usually not be prepared to move to the new location, except when the relocation is near a border. Therefore, the relocation of a business in a labour-intensive sector, where the activity in question is not determined by material or tangible assets, to a country which is far away is more likely to constitute a closure rather than a transfer of an undertaking.

In non-labour-intensive sectors, such as production plants, by contrast, the economic entity can retain its identity if the new employer takes over the significant material assets, even if many employees refuse to work at the new location. Since the economic entity requires a significant amount of equipment, the decisive factor is whether the transferee takes over the tangible assets needed for the activity in question.[19] The transfer of the employees is then a legal consequence, but not a selection criterion. Consequently, in these sectors, the fact that many employees do not wish to move to a distant location has no bearing on whether there would be a transfer of an undertaking.[20] A transfer of an undertaking may even occur if the business is transferred to a Non-Member State far away, for example a relocation of a production plant from Austria to China. This then raises the next question: Is Directive 2001/23/EC also applicable if the business is transferred and relocated from a Member State to a Non-Member State?

---

18 See ECJ C-13/95, 11.3.1997, *Ayse Süzen*, ECLI:EU:C:1997:141 para 21.

19 Björn Gaul, Simon Jeffreys, Andreas Tinhofer and Stanislas van Wassenhove (CMS Employment Practice Area Group), *Study on the application of Directive 2001/23/EC to cross-border transfers of undertakings*, Study n° VT/2005/101 (September 2006) 6.

20 Diana Niksova, *Grenzüberschreitender Betriebsübergang* (2014) 10 et seqq. See also Björn Gaul, Simon Jeffreys, Andreas Tinhofer and Stanislas van Wassenhove (CMS Employment Practice Area Group), *Study on the application of Directive 2001/23/EC to cross-border transfers of undertakings*, Study n° VT/2005/101 (September 2006) 17.

D. *Cross-Border Transfers of Undertakings from a Member State to a Non-Member State*

I. *Scope of Directive 2001/23/EC*

Legal commentators have diverging views on the question whether Directive 2001/23/EC applies to cross-border relocation transfers from a Member State to a Non-Member State. Article 1(2) of Directive 2001/23/EC only refers to the place of origin of the business unit "to be transferred", meaning the country where the transferor is situated. However, it does not give any regard to the destination of the transfer. Therefore, some legal commentators find that according to its wording, the location of the transferee is not relevant at all. Consequently, they deduce that relocation transfers of undertakings outside and inside the EU shall be subject to the same rules and that Directive 2001/23/EC shall also be applicable to transfers outside the territory of the EU.[21] Other legal commentators, however, hold that Directive 2001/23/EC is not applicable to transfers outside the territory of the EU, since Non-Member States are not bound by the provisions of the Directive. EU legislation is limited to the Member States (and EEA countries) in terms of territorial coverage. Consequently, the Transfer of Undertakings Directive 2001/23/EC only shall apply to a transfer within the EU (or EEA).[22]

In this context, the timing of the transfer of an undertaking plays a crucial role. Depending on the chronological order of relocation and transfer, two scenarios can be distinguished: Either the business is transferred to the transferee first, and then, in a second step, relocated by the transferee to another country, or the transferor relocates his business to another country first, and then, in a second step, transfers the business to the transferee. Usually, however, the relocation and the transfer of business assets are not concluded simultaneously, since the legal effectiveness of the transfer and

21 Sebastian Krebber, ZVglRWiss 1988, 124 (139 et seq and 161); Norbert Wimmer, IPRax 1995, 207 (209); European Trade Union Conferedation (ETUC), *First phase consultation concerning cross-border transfers of undertakings, businesses or parts of undertakings or businesses*, https://www.etuc.org/sites/www.etuc.org/files/ARD_ETUC_answer_final2007_1.pdf (accessed on 7.5.2018).

22 Constantin von Alvensleben, *Die Rechte der Arbeitnehmer bei Betriebsübergang im Europäischen Gemeinschaftsrecht* (1992) 157; Karl-Georg Loritz, RdA 1987, 65 (84); European Association of craft, small and medium-sized enterprises (UEAPME), Reply to the first phase of consultation concerning cross-border transfers of undertakings, https://ueapme.com/docs/pos_papers/2007/070801_pp_1st_consult_transfer.pdf (accessed on 7.5.2018).

the operational commencement of the business at the new location will not take place at the same time.[23] The timing makes a significant difference regarding the conflict of laws rules that determine whether the transfer of an undertaking is governed by the law of a Member State or by the law of a Non-Member State that has not implemented the Transfer of Undertakings Directive 2001/23/EC.[24]

II. Conflict of Laws Rules: The Law Governing the Transfer of Undertakings

1. Introduction

Directive 2001/23/EC does not contain any provisions for the conflict of laws. Therefore, the transfer of an undertaking is governed by the law that is applicable under the relevant conflict of laws rules.[25] The instrument of Private International Law is the Rome I Regulation No. 593/2008[26] of which Article 8 lays down special conflict rules relating to individual contracts of employment. The essential feature of the system established by the Rome I Regulation is the principle of freedom of choice, which means that the parties are free to make a choice of law. This is also the case for individual employment contracts (Article 8(1) of the Rome I Regulation). In default of any choice of law, the employment contract will be governed by the law of the country "*in which, or failing that, from which the employee habitually carries out his work in performance of the contract*" (Article 8(2) of the Rome I Regulation). This regular place of work of the employee is interpreted broadly by the ECJ.[27] If the employee does not habitually carry out

23 Marcus Kania, *Grenzüberschreitende Betriebsübergänge aus europarechtlicher Sicht* (2012) 68 et seqq. See also Björn Gaul, Simon Jeffreys, Andreas Tinhofer and Stanislas van Wassenhove (CMS Employment Practice Area Group), *Study on the application of Directive 2001/23/EC to cross-border transfers of undertakings*, Study n° VT/2005/101 (September 2006) 17 et seqq.

24 Martin Franzen, *Der Betriebsinhaberwechsel nach § 613a BGB im internationalen Arbeitsrecht* (1994) 110.

25 Björn Gaul, Simon Jeffreys, Andreas Tinhofer and Stanislas van Wassenhove (CMS Employment Practice Area Group), *Study on the application of Directive 2001/23/EC to cross-border transfers of undertakings*, Study n° VT/2005/101 (September 2006) 1 et seqq.

26 Regulation (EC) No. 593/2008 of the European Parliament and of the Council of 17 June 2008 on the law applicable to contractual obligations (Rome I), L 177/6, 4.7.2008.

27 ECJ C-29/10, 15.3.2011, *Koelzsch*, ECLI:EU:C:2011:151, para 43 et seqq.

his or her work in any one country or from any one country, his or her employment contract is deemed to be subject to the law of the country where the place of business through which he or she was engaged is situated (Article 8(3) of the Rome I Regulation). However, whereas the factor of the country in which the employee habitually carries out his or her work must be given a broad interpretation, the factor of the place of business through which the employee was engaged must be interpreted strictly and as a subsidiary factor, it can apply only if the court is not in a position to determine the country in which the work is habitually carried out.[28] Finally, Article 8(4) of the Rome I Regulation regulates an "escape clause". If it appears from the circumstances as a whole that the employment contract is more closely connected with another country, it shall be governed by the law of that country.

Furthermore, Article 9 of the Rome I Regulation No. 593/2008 regulates the "overriding mandatory provisions", also called *lois de police*, that are applicable to any situation falling within their scope, irrespective of the law otherwise applicable to the contract under the Rome I Regulation. Therefore, in the first step it is crucial to investigate whether the transfer of undertakings rules fall within the scope of Article 9 of the Rome I Regulation.

2. *Article 9 of the Rome I Regulation No. 593/2008: Transfer of Undertakings Rules as "Overriding Mandatory Provisions"?*

> *"Overriding mandatory provisions are provisions the respect for which is regarded as crucial by a country for safeguarding its public interests, such as its political, social or economic organisation, to such an extent that they are applicable to any situation falling within their scope, irrespective of the law otherwise applicable to the contract under this Regulation."*

Article 9 of the Rome I Regulation has the purpose of enabling the court of the forum to take account of the public interest in exceptional circumstances. However, Recital 37 of the Rome I Regulation states that the overriding mandatory provisions must be construed restrictively. In the judgement *Nikiforidis*, the ECJ also held that as a derogating measure, the overriding mandatory provisions must be interpreted strictly.[29]

28 ECJ C-384/10, 15.12.2011, *Voogsgeerd*, ECLI:EU:C:2011:842, paras 35, 47.
29 ECJ C-135/15, 18.10.2016, *Nikiforidis*, ECLI:EU:C:2016:774, para 44.

The German Federal Labour Court[30] as well as most legal commentators in Germany[31] find that the transfer of undertakings rules do not fall within the scope of Article 9 of the Rome I Regulation since they pursue private interests of the parties rather than public interests within the meaning of Article 9 of the Rome I Regulation. As the German Federal Labour Court has stated, the objective of the transfer of undertakings rules is primarily the protection of the employees whose rights must be safeguarded in the event of a change of ownership.[32] It is true that in the judgement *Alemo-Herron* the ECJ has ruled that Directive 2001/23/EC

> *"does not aim solely to safeguard the interests of employees in the event of transfer of an undertaking, but seeks to ensure a fair balance between the interests of those employees, on the one hand, and those of the transferee, on the other".*[33]

Still, the fair balance between the interests of the employees and those of the transferee relates to private interests of the parties and not to public interests within the meaning of Article 9 of the Rome I Regulation. According to the German Federal Labour Court, the international character of a provision is not necessarily an indication for an "overriding mandatory provision" either. Provisions are not to be qualified as "overriding mandatory provisions" only because other Member States have the same or similar provisions.[34] Hence, transfer of undertakings provisions are not "overriding mandatory provisions" within the meaning of Article 9 of the Rome I Regulation. Which law is applicable must, therefore, be answered with regard to Article 8 of the Rome I Regulation.[35]

---

30 German Federal Labour Court (BAG), 29.10.1992 – 2 AZR 267/92.

31 Martiny in: MüKo BGB[7] (2018) Article 8 Rom I-VO para 132; Schlachter in: ErfK[18] (2018) Articles 3, 8 und 9 Rom I-VO para 23; Peter Mankowski, IPRax 1994, 88 (94 et seqq.); Wolfgang Däubler, "Der Erwerb deutscher Betriebe durch ausländische Unternehmen" in Meinhard Heinze and Alfred Söllner (eds.), *Arbeitsrecht in der Bewährung, Festschrift for Otto Kissel* (1994), 119 (126); Hermann Reichold, "Neues zum grenzüberschreitenden Betriebsübergang" in Horst Konzen, Sebastian Krebber, Thomas Raab, Barbara Veit and Bernd Waas (eds.), *Festschrift for Rolf Birk* (2008), 687 (693); Ulrich Drobnig and Hans-Jürgen Puttfarken, *Arbeitskampf auf Schiffen fremder Flagge* (1989) 85; Anna Caroline Gravenhorst, RdA 2007, 283 (285). Different view Marcus Kania, *Grenzüberschreitende Betriebsübergänge aus europarechtlicher Sicht* (2012) 138 et seqq.

32 German Federal Labour Court (BAG) 29.10.1992 – 2 AZR 267/92.

33 ECJ C-426/11, 18.7.2013, *Alemo Herron*, ECLI:EU:C:2013:521, para 25.

34 German Federal Labour Court (BAG) 29.10.1992 – 2 AZR 267/92.

35 Martin Franzen, *Der Betriebsinhaberwechsel nach § 613a BGB im internationalen Arbeitsrecht* (1994) 74 et seqq; German Federal Labour Court (BAG) 26.5.2011 – 8

3. *Article 8(2) of the Rome I Regulation No. 593/2008: Relocation Transfers and Change of the Applicable Law*

Article 8 of the Rome I Regulation provides special protection to employees. If no choice of law has been made, the employment contract will be governed by the law of the country in which or from which the employee habitually carries out his or her work (Article 8(2) of the Rome I Regulation). However, the regular place of work can change if the business is relocated to another country and the employee carries out his or her work at the new location and is not only temporarily employed in that other country.[36] If the employee and the transferee agree that after the relocation the employee shall habitually work in the transferee's country, a change of the applicable law will follow. However, the applicable law does not change at the date of the agreement that the obligations arising out of the employment contract will be performed at the new location, but at the date when the employee actually starts to work at his or her new workplace. Since the relevant factor is, pursuant to Article 8(2) of the Rome I Regulation, the place in which or from which the employee habitually carries out his or her work, the applicable law does not change if the employee refuses to work at the new location and does not start to carry out his or her work there. However, if he or she is willing to work at the new location, the employment contract will be governed by the law of the country where the transferee's premises are situated at the date when the employee starts to carry out his or her work at the new location.[37]

To sum up, in a cross-border scenario, first of all the law where the transferor is situated is applicable (if the habitual place of work of the employees is also in that country). The applicable law, however, changes if the employee's workplace is moved to the transferee's location, since the decisive factor for the governing law is that of the place of work. If the trans-

---

AZR 37/10, AP Nr. 409 zu § 613a BGB (*Deinert*); Diana Niksova, *Grenzüberschreitender Betriebsübergang* (2014) 87 et seqq.

36 Martiny in: MüKo BGB[7] (2018) Article 8 Rom I-VO para 81; Abbo Junker, "Gewöhnlicher Arbeitsort und vorübergehende Entsendung im Internationalen Privatrecht" in: Stephan Lorenz, Alexander Trunk, Horst Eidenmüller, Christiane Wendehorst and Johannes Adolff (eds.), *Festschrift for Andreas Heldrich* (2005) 719 (736); Peter Mankowski, IPRax 2003, 21 (23 f); Gregor Thüsing, NZA 2003, 1303 (1307 f); Olaf Deinert, RdA 2009, 144 (145); Olaf Deinert, *Internationales Arbeitsrecht* (2013) § 9 para 148; Marcus Kania, *Grenzüberschreitende Betriebsübergänge aus europarechtlicher Sicht* (2012) 101.

37 Marcus Kania, *Grenzüberschreitende Betriebsübergänge aus europarechtlicher Sicht* (2012) 103.

fer of an undertaking takes place in Austria and the business is relocated to a Non-Member State in a second step, the transfer will be governed by the Austrian transfer of undertakings rules since the place of work of the employees is in Austria and has not changed yet. If the business is relocated to another country in a second step and consequently, the place of work of the employees changes because they start to work at the new location, the applicable law will change.[38] If the Non-Member State the law of which is applicable after the relocation has not implemented Directive 2001/23/EC, as is the case, for example for the US, the rights and obligations provided in Directive 2001/23/EC, will not be preserved after the relocation. This means that if an Austrian employer sells his business to an US company, any dismissals are prohibited and the US company must take over the employment contracts. However, if in a second step, the business is relocated to the US and the employees move to the new location and start to work there, the Austrian law will not be applicable anymore unless a choice of law has been made. If the US law does not prohibit any dismissals in this situation, the employees can be dismissed after the relocation. Moreover, all the other rights and obligations of Directive 2001/23/EC get lost after the change of the applicable law. Therefore, the takeover of the employment contracts and the prohibition of any dismissals connected to the transfer of an undertaking can only be guaranteed if the laws of each of the countries in which the transferor and the transferee are situated contain the transfer of undertakings rules.[39]

Some of the Non-Member States do have the same or at least comparable transfer of undertakings rules, like for example Switzerland. According to Swiss law, the transferee must also take over the employment contracts and any dismissals due to the transfer of undertakings are prohibited.[40] Therefore, in the German case in which a German employer sold his business to a Swiss company, the rights and obligations of Directive 2001/23/EC were preserved also after the relocation. The same would be the case for Serbia. Under Serbian law, the employment contracts do transfer to the transferee and any dismissals by reason of the transfer of under-

38 Björn Gaul, Simon Jeffreys, Andreas Tinhofer and Stanislas van Wassenhove (CMS Employment Practice Area Group), *Study on the application of Directive 2001/23/EC to cross-border transfers of undertakings*, Study n° VT/2005/101 (2006) 2.

39 Abbo Junker, *Internationales Arbeitsrecht im Konzern* (1992) 231 et seqq. See also Diana Niksova, *Grenzüberschreitender Betriebsübergang* (2014) 97 et seqq.

40 Portmann in Basler Komm[5] Article 333, Obligationenrecht para 2.

takings are prohibited.[41] However, if the law in the country of the transferee does not contain transfer of undertakings rules, the takeover of the employment contracts and the prohibition of any dismissals connected with the transfer of undertakings cannot be guaranteed after the change of the applicable law.

4. *Article 8(4) of the Rome I Regulation No. 593/2008: Escape Clause*

In my view, a change of the applicable law cannot be prevented by the "escape clause" within the meaning of Article 8(4) of the Rome I Regulation. Article 8(4) of the Rome I Regulation states that

> "*where it appears from the circumstances as a whole that the contract is more closely connected with a country other than that indicated in paragraphs 2 or 3, the law of that other country shall apply*".

In such a case, the employee's regular place of work is irrelevant, as is the location of the business through which he or she was engaged. In a cross-border scenario, the question arises whether the employees are more closely connected with the country of the transferor even after the relocation to the transferee's country.

The ECJ has ruled that account must be taken of the whole circumstances when determining whether the contract is more closely connected with another country. Relevant factors are, for example, the country in which the employee pays taxes on the income from his or her activity, the country in which he or she is covered by a social security scheme and pension, sickness insurance or invalidity schemes, parameters relating to salary determination and other working conditions.[42] However, where a business has been relocated to another country and the employees have started to carry out their work at the new location (and have not been employed there only temporarily), the contract will usually not be connected with the transferor's country anymore, even if the employees still live in the transferor's country or have the nationality of that country. Still, the circumstances as a whole must be examined in each individual case to determine whether the contract is more closely connected with the transferor's country.

41 See Ljubinka Kovačević, "Individual Rights of Employees in Transfers of Undertakings in Serbia", 227 et seqq. (in this book).

42 ECJ C-64/12, 12.9.2013, *Schlecker*, ECLI:EU:C:2013:551, para 41.

5. *Objective of Directive 2001/23/EC and Preservation of Statutory Rights?*

Some legal commentators argue that safeguarding the employees' rights, which is the primary objective of Directive 2001/23/EC, should also include statutory rights of the employees.[43] The change of the applicable law would not only cause problems in the event of a cross-border transfer from a Member State to a Non-Member State, but even within the EU, since the standard of employee protection differs among the Member States.

It is true that the purpose of Directive 2001/23/EC is to prevent transferred employees from being placed in a less favourable position than they were in before the transfer, solely due to the transfer.[44] Therefore, the employment contract or the employment relationship shall continue unchanged with the transferee. However, it is not intended by the Directive to establish a uniform level of protection throughout the EU on the basis of common criteria.[45] Since the statutory rights differ among the Member States, they are, in my view, not preserved if an employment relationship with a high level of statutory employee protection is transferred into the scope of a national law offering minor protection, not even for the period of one year.[46] Since Directive 2001/23/EC does not contain conflict of laws rules, the general conflict rules do apply. The relevant factor is the habitual place of work of the employees (Article 8(2) of the Rome I Regulation). If the regular workplace changes, the applicable law changes as well. Consequently, the mandatory rules applicable to the employment relationship before the transfer are not preserved unless there is a choice of law within the meaning of Article 8(1) of the Rome I Regulation.

---

43 Björn Gaul, Simon Jeffreys, Andreas Tinhofer and Stanislas van Wassenhove (CMS Employment Practice Area Group), *Study on the application of Directive 2001/23/EC to cross-border transfers of undertakings*, Study n° VT/2005/101 (2006) 23.

44 ECJ C-108/10, 6.9.2011, *Scattolon*, ECLI:EU:C:2011:542, para 59.

45 ECJ C-343/98, 14.9.2000, *Collino and Chiappero*, ECLI:EU:C:2000:441, para 37; ECJ C-209/91, 12.11.1992, *Watson*, ECLI:EU:C:1992:436, para 27 et seq.

46 For a different view see Wolfgang Däubler, "Der Erwerb deutscher Betriebe durch ausländische Unternehmen" in Meinhard Heinze and Alfred Söllner (eds.), *Arbeitsrecht in der Bewährung, Festschrift for Otto Kissel* (1994) 119 (137); Hermann Reichold, "Neues zum grenzüberschreitenden Betriebsübergang" in: Horst Konzen, Sebastian Krebber, Thomas Raab, Barbara Veit and Bernd Waas (eds.), *Festschrift for Rolf Birk* (2008) 687 (700 et seqq). Däubler and Reichold argue that the change of the law governing the employment contract shall occur after the period of one year.

The same problem arises with regard to continuity of terms and conditions agreed in collective agreements. Article 3(3) of Directive 2001/23/EC provides that the transferee shall continue to observe the terms and conditions agreed in any collective agreement on the same terms applicable to the transferor under that agreement, until the date of termination or expiry of the collective agreement or the entry into force or application of another collective agreement. Consequently, collective agreements can change where the transferee is bound by another collective agreement and the working conditions provided for in the transferor's collective agreement are not maintained. The same is true for works agreements between the employer and the works council. In such cases, where the transfer involves a substantial change in working conditions to the detriment of the employee and the employment contract is consequently terminated, according to Article 4(2) of Directive 2001/23/EC, the employer shall be regarded as having been responsible for the termination of the contract. Since collective agreements as well as works agreements can be altered in a manner that is unfavourable to employees, the same is, in my view, true for statutory provisions unless there is a choice of law within the meaning of Article 8(1) of the Rome I Regulation.[47]

As a result, relocation transfers are treated differently from cross-border transfers without relocation. Where the place of work does not change after the transfer of an undertaking to a foreign employer, the law of the Member State, in which the business is located and where the workplace is situated, will apply also after the transfer. A mere change in the position of the employer will not lead to a change in the applicable law. Due to this fact, a business takeover by a new foreign owner that does not affect the place of business, does not cause any labour law problems. A conflict of laws only occurs if a foreign company takes over a national business and subsequently there is a relocation of the business abroad.[48] The reason why relocation transfers are treated differently from cross-border transfers without relocation is that Article 8 of the Rome I Regulation refers to the habitual place of work of the employees, which changes in a relocation transfer, but does not change in a transfer without relocation. Since Directive 2001/23/EC does not contain any conflict of laws rules, the general conflict of laws rule of Article 8 of the Rome I Regulation does apply.

---

47 See also Diana Niksova, *Grenzüberschreitender Betriebsübergang* (2014) 68 et seqq.

48 Björn Gaul, Simon Jeffreys, Andreas Tinhofer and Stanislas van Wassenhove (CMS Employment Practice Area Group), *Study on the application of Directive 2001/23/EC to cross-border transfers of undertakings*, Study n° VT/2005/101 (2006) 16 et seqq.

However, given that the main problems arising from the application of the Directive on cross-border transfers stem from determining which national law applies to the transfer, de lege ferenda, Directive 2001/23/EC shall introduce rules that determine the law applicable to employment contracts in situations where there may be a conflict between the laws of different countries.

III. De Lege Ferenda

Even though the Commission initiated the first phase consultation of social partners under Article 154(2) of the TFEU concerning cross-border transfers of undertakings in 2007,[49] the social partners did not see the need for any changes in Directive 2001/23/EC concerning cross-border transfers. Therefore, the wording of the Directive has not been changed and adapted to cross-border situations. However, in my view, it is recommendable to change the wording of the Directive regarding relocation transfers that involve the physical relocation of the business transferred from one Member State to another. Many labour law problems do arise in cross-border situations and Directive 2001/23/EC does not provide solutions for these problems since it does not contain any legal provisions concerning cross-border transfers at all. In a context of increasing corporate mobility, it is advisable to clarify that cross-border transfers of undertakings within the EU are also covered by Directive 2001/23/EC and to introduce a provision on the conflict of laws into the Directive. The Directive shall either refer to the Rome I Regulation or explicitly rule which law shall apply in cross-border situations.[50] As stated in Article 23 of the Rome I Regulation, the Rome I Regulation shall not prejudice the application of provisions of EU law which, in relation to particular matters, lay down conflict of laws rules relating to contractual obligations.

---

49 Commission of the European Communities, First phase consultation of social partners under Article 138(2) of the EC Treaty concerning cross-border transfers of undertakings, businesses or parts of undertakings or businesses, http://ec.europa.eu/social/main.jsp?catId=706&langId=de&intPageId=208 (accessed on 2.5.2018).

50 See also Diana Niksova, *Grenzüberschreitender Betriebsübergang* (2014) 106 et seq.

E. Legal Consequences: Individual Labour Law Aspects

I. Automatic Transfer of the Employment Contract and Change of the Place of Work

Article 3(1) of Directive 2001/23/EC provides for the transfer of the transferor's rights and obligations arising from a contract of employment or from an employment relationship existing on the date of the transfer. Consequently, the transferee steps into the shoes of the transferor and takes over the employment relationship with the employees affected. As in domestic situations, in the event of a cross-border transfer, the transfer of the employment relationship to the transferee does not change the contents of the employment contract and the employee's individual contractual rights are also safeguarded.[51]

However, in cross-border scenarios, this general concept of automatic transfer of the employment contract to the transferee raises some problems. Where the cross-border transfer is connected to a relocation of the business to another country, special consideration must be given to the place of work since this employment condition necessarily has to be modified in a relocation transfer. Where the transfer of an undertaking is linked to its relocation, the new employer will generally need to change the workplace of the transferred employees. However, it is doubtful if the contents of the employment contract regarding the place of work may be modified due to the transfer.[52]

Generally, the mere fact of the transfer of undertakings does not allow the transferee to modify the employment contract or employment relationship, since the objective of Directive 2001/23/EC is the safeguarding of employees' rights in the event of a transfer. The place of work is also considered as a substantial part of an employment relationship. Therefore, an employer cannot decide to change the place of work solely for the reason of the transfer. However, employment conditions

---

51 Björn Gaul, Simon Jeffreys, Andreas Tinhofer and Stanislas van Wassenhove (CMS Employment Practice Area Group), *Study on the application of Directive 2001/23/EC to cross-border transfers of undertakings*, Study n° VT/2005/101 (2006) 75.

52 Björn Gaul, Simon Jeffreys, Andreas Tinhofer and Stanislas van Wassenhove (CMS Employment Practice Area Group), *Study on the application of Directive 2001/23/EC to cross-border transfers of undertakings*, Study n° VT/2005/101 (2006) 32.

> "*may be altered with regard to the transferee to the same extent as [they] could have been with regard to the transferor, provided that the transfer of the undertaking itself may never constitute the reason for that amendment*".[53]

The question of whether a modification of the place of work after a transfer of an undertaking is admissible, depends on the relevant national rules of law that are applicable. In the event of a transfer and relocation from Austria to Slovakia, as in the initial case outlined above, it will be the law of the transferor's country — meaning Austrian law — that governs this question since at this time, the applicable law has not yet changed, as the employee has not started to carry out his or her work in Slovakia yet. Therefore, the habitual place of work of the employee is still Austria and Austrian law is applicable.

Under Austrian law, employees must accept a change of the workplace provided such a change is "reasonable". In relocations without a transfer of an undertaking, the Austrian Supreme Court of Justice has developed a so-called "reasonability test", which is based on different factors, such as

- the distance between the employee's home address and the previous or new workplace,
- time of travel before and after the relocation,
- travel expenses before and after the relocation,
- the public transport system and traffic jams,
- relation between the time of travel and working time,
- whether the employer offers reimbursement of additional travel costs,
- personal circumstances, such as if the employee has to bring his or her child to the kindergarten on his or her way to work.[54]

If these factors are "reasonable", the place of work can be changed without the employee's consent. In my view, the same criteria must be applied in cross-border situations. Particularly in cases where the former and the new workplace are just across the border, there shall be no difference with re-

---

53 ECJ C-324/86, 10.2.1988, *Daddy's Dance Hall*, ECLI:EU:C:1988:72, para 17; ECJ C-343/98, 14.9.2000, *Collino and Chiappero*, ECLI:EU:C:2000:441, para 52. See also Martin Franzen, *Der Betriebsinhaberwechsel nach § 613a BGB im internationalen Arbeitsrecht* (1994) 147 et seqq.

54 Austrian Supreme Court of Justice (OGH) 14.6.2000 – 9 ObA 48/00z, DRdA 2001/17, 244 (Pfeil) = wbl 2001, 106 (Goricnik). See also Björn Gaul, Simon Jeffreys, Andreas Tinhofer and Stanislas van Wassenhove (CMS Employment Practice Area Group), *Study on the application of Directive 2001/23/EC to cross-border transfers of undertakings*, Study n° VT/2005/101 (2006) 32.

gards to the "reasonability test" between a relocation within the territory of Austria (e.g. relocation from Vienna to St. Pölten where the distance is ca. 60 kilometers) and a relocation from Austria to another country (e.g. relocation from Vienna to Bratislava where the distance is also 60 kilometers). The mere fact that the new workplace is situated in another country, does not automatically mean that the employee's consent is required with regards to the criteria of the "reasonability test".

However, in my view, under Austrian law, in a cross-border scenario the employee's consent will still be required if the relocation results in the change of the law governing the employment relationship according to Article 8 of the Rome I Regulation and the law applicable after the relocation is less favourable for the employee. Since the applicable law will change pursuant to Article 8(2) of the Rome I Regulation in default of any choice of law, and relocations often take place to countries where the applicable law is less favourable for the employees, in cross-border scenarios a change of the place of work will usually only be admissible with the employee's consent.[55]

If the employee refuses to agree on the change to his or her place of work, the foreign transferee takes over the employment contract and must employ the employee at his or her previous workplace. Consequently, in the initial case of this paper, the employee becomes an employee of the Slovak employer, but retains his or her place of work in Austria. However, if the whole business has been "closed" in Austria and the Slovak employer has no use for the employee in Austria and if the employee refuses to work at the new location where he or she has been offered to work, then there is only one possibility: dismissal of the employee. In my view, such a dismissal is not in breach of Article 4(1) of Directive 2001/23/EC (and its implementing national law).[56]

55 For German law see Diana Niksova, "Grenzüberschreitende Umstrukturierungen zwischen Theorie und Praxis – Zeit für eine Neuausrichtung?" in Tim Husemann and Anne Christin Wietfeld (eds.), *Zwischen Theorie und Praxis – Herausforderungen des Arbeitsrechts* (2015) 175 (190 et seqq.).

56 See also Martin Franzen, *Der Betriebsinhaberwechsel nach § 613a BGB im internationalen Arbeitsrecht* (1994) 147 et seqq.; Michael Wollenschläger and Armin Frölich, AuR 1990, 314 (320).

II. Relocation Transfers and Dismissal of the Transferred Employees

Article 4(1) of Directive 2001/23/EC provides for the protection of the employees concerned against dismissal by the transferor or the transferee solely by reason of the transfer. The objective of the Directive is to ensure the continuity of the employment relationships, irrespective of any change of ownership. In Austria, Article 4(1) of the Directive has not been implemented on a statutory basis, but the Austrian Supreme Court of Justice has indicated in its judgements that any dismissal grounds of which is a transfer of an undertaking will be void.[57]

However, according to Article 4(1) of Directive 2001/23/EC, economic, technical or organisational reasons entailing change in the workforce may justify a dismissal. In my view, in the event of a relocation transfer where the new employer is unable to offer a suitable position to the employee at the old location, the dismissal of the employee who refuses to work at the new location, may be justified by economic reasons. In this case, it is not the transfer of undertakings that constitutes grounds for dismissal, but the relocation. If the business had not been transferred to a foreign employer, but if it had been relocated by the same company without change of ownership, the employer would also be able to dismiss those employees who do not wish to work at the new location if he or she no longer had use for them at the old location. Therefore, the dismissal can be justified by economic reasons independent from the transfer of undertakings. Still, the employer will have to establish that the need to terminate the employment relationship is not connected to the transfer of undertakings, but the dismissal was motivated by a reason other than the transfer, namely, the relocation.

If it was not possible to justify the dismissal through economic reasons and consequently, economic operators were not able to relocate their businesses to other countries and were forced to quit their restructuring plans indefinitely, the measure would be liable to impede the exercise of freedom of establishment or render it less attractive and would therefore be incompatible with Article 49 TFEU. In the judgement *AGET Iraklis*, the ECJ has ruled that economic operators must have the freedom to bring the activity of their establishment to an end:

> *"Such exercise also entails, in principle, the freedom to determine the nature and extent of the economic activity that will be carried out in the host Mem-*

57 Austrian Supreme Court of Justice (OGH), 11.11.1998 – 9 ObA 240/98d; 22.10.1997 – 9 ObA 274/97b.

> *ber State, in particular the size of the fixed establishments and the number of workers required for that purpose, and also […] the freedom subsequently to scale down that activity or even the freedom to give up, should it so decide, its activity and establishment.*"[58]

Advocate General *Wahl* has stated this even more clearly:

> "*For this freedom to be truly effective, it must also give a cross-border economic group the right to scale down and, ultimately, dissolve an establishment in a Member State. In other words, to leave a Member State — even if this is simply in order to pursue an economic activity in a Member State where it is more gainful.*"[59]

This means that not only measures that render access to a market less attractive constitute an obstacle to the exercise of freedom of establishment within the meaning of Article 49 TFEU, but also measures that reduce or even eliminate the ability of economic operators to leave a Member State and set up in a new market.[60] In the light of this case law as regards the interpretation of freedom of establishment, in the event of a relocation of the business to another country, a provision that prohibits terminating employment contracts due to economic reasons with those employees who refuse to work at the new location, would be liable to constitute an obstacle to the exercise of freedom of establishment, since economic operators would not be able to relocate their businesses to other countries. According to settled case law, a restriction on freedom of establishment is permissible only if it is justified by overriding reasons in the public interest. The restriction must be appropriate for ensuring attainment of the objective in the public interest which it pursues and must not go beyond what is necessary to attain it.[61] As the ECJ has pointed out in *AGET Iraklis*, justification is only possible if it complies with fundamental rights, concretely the freedom to conduct a business enshrined in Article 16 of the Charter of Fundamental Rights of the EU.[62] Article 52(1) of the Charter accepts that limitations may be imposed on the exercise of rights enshrined by the Charter

58 ECJ C-201/15, 21.12.2016, *AGET Iraklis*, ECLI:EU:C:2016:972, para 53.

59 Opinion of Advocate General Wahl in C-201/15, 9.6.2016, *AGET Iraklis*, ECLI:EU:C:2016:429, para 65.

60 Robert Rebhahn, "Griechischer Kündigungsschutz und Niederlassungsfreiheit", EuZA 2017, 385 (390). See ECJ C-201/15, 21.12.2016, *AGET Iraklis*, ECLI:EU:C:2016:972, para 55.

61 ECJ C-201/15, 21.12.2016, *AGET Iraklis*, ECLI:EU:C:2016:972, para 61 with further references.

62 ECJ C-201/15, 21.12.2016, *AGET Iraklis*, ECLI:EU:C:2016:972, para 65.

as long as the limitations are provided for by law, respect the essence of those rights and freedoms and in accordance with the principle of proportionality, they are necessary and genuinely meet recognized objectives of general interest or the need to protect the rights and freedoms of others. The overriding reasons in the public interest that are recognized by the ECJ include the protection of workers.[63] This is also reflected in Article 30 of the Charter according to which every worker has the right to protection against unjustified dismissal. Therefore, protection against unjustified dismissal constitutes a legitimate aim for restricting the freedom of establishment as guaranteed by Article 49 TFEU and the freedom to conduct a business enshrined in Article 16 of the Charter. However, if no dismissals were allowed in relocation transfers due to economic reasons even if the employees refused to work at the new location and the employer had no further use for them at the old location, this would have the consequence of entirely preventing economic operators from effecting dismissals due to economic reasons and consequently relocating their business to other countries. Therefore, in my view, such a measure would not satisfy the requirements of the principle of proportionality.

III. Right of Objection

In many countries, the employees concerned can make use of their right of objection, which has special significance in cross-border scenarios. Some countries, for example Germany, have a general right of objection in the event of transfers of undertakings. Austrian law, however, does not contain a general right of objection, but restricts the right to two special cases, in which the transfer of an undertaking may be detrimental to the employees. § 3(4) of the Austrian implementing law (Law to adapt employment contract legislation, Arbeitsvertragsrechts-Anpassungsgesetz, AVRAG) states that the right of the employees to object to the transfer is given where (1) the transferee refuses to take over the transferor's obligations in relation to an occupational pension scheme arising from individual employment contracts, or (2) the collective agreement which applies to the transferee provides for a weaker level of protection against dismissal and the transferee refuses to incorporate the provision concerning the protection against dismissal of the collective agreement which applies to the

63 ECJ C-201/15, 21.12.2016, *AGET Iraklis*, ECLI:EU:C:2016:972, para 70 et seqq. with further references.

transferor into the individual employment contracts of the transferring employees.[64]

However, the Austrian Supreme Court of Justice has held that the right of employees to object to a transfer of an undertaking may not be restricted to the two situations covered by § 3(4) of the AVRAG if there is a reason equivalent to these two cases.[65] As the change of the place of work in connection with a cross-border transfer leads to a significant change in the employees' situation, in my view, they shall be granted a right of objection if they do not wish to work at the new location, according to § 3(4) of the AVRAG per analogiam. Pursuant to § 3(1) of the AVRAG, the rights and obligations of the employment contract are taken over by the transferee. There is an exception concerning the obligations in relation to an occupational pension scheme arising from individual employment contracts. For this reason, the Austrian legislator has granted the right of objection in this case. If in a cross-border situation the place of work must be changed after the relocation transfer, the employees who do not wish to work at the new location shall be granted a right of objection in this case since rights arising from the employment contract shall not change due to a transfer of an undertaking. The same is true where the law governing the employment contract would change and be less favourable for the employees after the relocation transfer.[66]

The consequence is that the employment relationship will not be transferred to the transferee. However, the employees concerned can only object to a transfer of an undertaking if the transferor continues to operate a business subsequently. Otherwise, the employment contract will be terminated anyway. However, if it is terminated, according to Article 4(2) of Directive 2001/23/EC, the employer shall be regarded as having been responsible for the termination if the transfer involves a substantial change in working conditions to the detriment of the employee.

64 Björn Gaul, Simon Jeffreys, Andreas Tinhofer and Stanislas van Wassenhove (CMS Employment Practice Area Group), *Study on the application of Directive 2001/23/EC to cross-border transfers of undertakings, Study nº VT/2005/101* (2006) 37 et seqq.

65 Austrian Supreme Court of Justice (OGH), 22.2.2011 – 8 ObA 41/10b, ZAS 2012, 269 (Schörghofer) = ZAS-Judikatur 2011/87 (Reiner) = RdW 2011/294, 288 (Hießl) = der Standard 2011/16/01 (Tinhofer).

66 As regards the favourability principle see Diana Niksova, *Grezüberschreitender Betriebsübergang* (2014) 172.

IV. Termination due to a Substantial Change of Working Conditions

Since cross-border transfers are often connected to a change of the place of work, which is regularly seen as a substantial change of working conditions, Article 4(2) of Directive 2001/23/EC is significant in cross-border situations. Under Austrian law, Article 4(2) of Directive 2001/23/EC has been implemented in § 3(5) of the AVRAG. According to this provision, the legal consequences of Article 4(2) of Directive 2001/23/EC are restricted to substantial changes resulting from another collective agreement or works agreement. However, in cross-border situations substantial changes may also arise from the change in the applicable law. Since the Austrian legislator did not consider cross-border situations, changes arising from the change of the law which governs the employment contract were not taken into account. However, in my view, these changes must also be considered, according to § 3(5) of the AVRAG per analogiam.

Moreover, § 3(5) of the AVRAG shall also apply where the place of work must be changed after the relocation transfer. § 3(5) of the AVRAG only considers changes arising from the collective agreements or works agreements, but not contractual changes. This is because contractual changes are prohibited according to § 3(1) of the AVRAG anyway.[67] However, where the place of work must be changed in a cross-border scenario, the employees who resign in this situation because they do not wish to work at the new location shall be treated as if the employer had dismissed them, according to § 3(5) of the AVRAG per analogiam.[68]

V. Solution: Choice of Law?

To avoid the situation of employees making use of their right of objection or terminating their employment contracts, the parties can make a choice of law providing that after the relocation transfer, the law of the transferor will still govern the employment contract. The choice of law between the employee and the transferor must be taken over by the foreign transferee who steps into the shoes of the transferor.[69] Therefore, in the initial case of

67 Sieglinde Gahleitner and Heinz Leitsmüller, *Umstrukturierung und AVRAG* (1996) 245.

68 See also Diana Niksova, *Grenzüberschreitender Betriebsübergang* (2014) 173 et seqq.

69 Martin Franzen, *Der Betriebsinhaberwechsel nach § 613a BGB im internationalen Arbeitsrecht* (1994) 112 et seqq.

this paper, the applicable law would not change if the parties agreed on the applicability of the Austrian law after the transfer and relocation to Slovakia. However, where the "mandatory rules" of the law applicable pursuant to Article 8 of the Rome I Regulation give the employee better protection, its provisions replace the corresponding provisions of the chosen law. Consequently, a choice of law made by the parties shall not deprive the employees of the protection of the "mandatory rules" of the law which would be applicable under Article 8 in the absence of choice.[70] Therefore, if the law after the relocation is more favourable for the employees, it will apply despite the choice of law. Usually, however, relocations take place to countries where the law is less favourable for the employees. Employers do not wish to transfer the Austrian law to the new location and apply it to the transferring employees. In case of a choice of law and the application of the Austrian law also after the transfer, the relocation will often not be attractive for employers.[71] If, however, no choice of law has been made, the applicable law does change, even if the relocation constitutes a transfer of an undertaking within the meaning of Directive 2001/23/EC.

F. *Summary*

1. Directive 2001/23/EC applies to cross-border relocation transfers from one Member State to another Member State. In the event of a relocation transfer from a Member State to a Non-Member State, the takeover of the employment contracts and the prohibition of any dismissals connected to the transfer of undertakings can only be guaranteed, if the law of the country of the transferee also contains comparable transfer of undertakings rules. This results from the relevant conflict of laws rules.
2. The economic entity can also retain its identity in cross-border relocation transfers. As in domestic situations, whether or not a cross-border relocation constitutes a transfer of an undertaking must be determined under the seven criteria set up by the ECJ in the judgment *Spijkers*. Where the foreign transferee takes over the relevant factors, the relocation results in a cross-border transfer of an undertaking. Even a long distance between the transferor's location and that of the transferee

70 These "mandatory rules" are, however, to be distinguished from the "overriding mandatory rules" within the meaning of Article 9 of the Rome I Regulation. In my view, transfer of undertakings rules do fall within the category of "mandatory rules" within the meaning of Article 8(1) of the Rome I Regulation.

71 See Michael Reiner, "Gedanken zur Standortverlagerung", ZAS 2010, 117 (123).

does not prevent there being a transfer of an undertaking if the significant business assets are taken over by the transferee.

3. The transferee steps into the shoes of the transferor and takes over the employment contracts. The contents of the employment contracts may not be changed solely for the reason of the transfer. This is also true for the place of work of the employees. If the change of the place of work is only possible with the employee's consent and the employee refuses to carry out his or her work at the new location after the relocation transfer, the transferee must employ the employee at his or her previous workplace. However, if the business has been closed and the transferee has no use for the employee at the old location, the employee concerned, who refuses to work at the new location can be dismissed. Such a dismissal may be justified by economic reasons and is not in breach of Article 4(1) of Directive 2001/23/EC.
4. The employees concerned can make use of their right of objection. Under Austrian law, the right of objection is restricted to two special cases, in which the transfer of undertakings may be detrimental to the employees (§ 3(4) of the AVRAG). In cross-border scenarios where the place of work must be changed even though the parties have agreed on a place of work in Austria in the employment contract, employees shall be granted a right of objection, per analogiam to § 3(4) of the AVRAG, if they do not wish to work at the new location. The same is true where the law governing the employment contract changes and is less favourable for the employees after the relocation transfer.
5. Where an employment relationship is terminated because the transfer involves a substantial change in working conditions to the detriment of the employee, the employer shall be regarded as having been responsible for the termination (Article 4(2) of Directive 2001/23/EC). Under Austrian law, the legal consequences of Article 4(2) of Directive 2001/23/EC are restricted to substantial changes resulting from another collective agreement or works agreement (§ 3(5) of the AVRAG). However, in cross-border scenarios, substantial changes may also arise from the change of the applicable law or from contractual changes regarding the place of work. In such cases, employees who resign shall also be treated as if the employer had dismissed them, because § 3(5) of the AVRAG is applicable per analogiam.

Bibliography

Constantin von Alvensleben, *Die Rechte der Arbeitnehmer bei Betriebsübergang im Europäischen Gemeinschaftsrecht* (Nomos Verlag, Baden-Baden 1992).

Wolfgang Däubler, "Der Erwerb deutscher Betriebe durch ausländische Unternehmen" in: Meinhard Heinze and Alfred Söllner (eds), *Arbeitsrecht in der Bewährung, Festschrift for Otto Kissel* (Beck Verlag, München 1994) 119.

Olaf Deinert, Neues Internationales Arbeitsvertragsrecht, RdA 2009, 144.

Olaf Deinert, *Internationales Arbeitsrecht* (Mohr Siebeck, Tübingen 2013).

Ulrich Drobnig and Hans-Jürgen Puttfarken, *Arbeitskampf auf Schiffen fremder Flagge* (Engel Verlag, Kehl am Rhein 1989).

Martin Franzen, *Der Betriebsinhaberwechsel nach § 613a BGB im internationalen Arbeitsrecht* (Decker & Müller, Heidelberg 1994).

Sieglinde Gahleitner and Heinz Leitsmüller, *Umstrukturierung und AVRAG* (Orac Verlag, Wien 1996).

Björn Gaul, Simon Jeffreys, Andreas Tinhofer and Stanislas van Wassenhove (CMS Employment Practice Area Group), *Study on the application of Directive 2001/23/EC to cross-border transfers of undertakings*, Study n° VT/2005/101 (September 2006).

Anna Caroline Gravenhorst, Kündigungsschutz bei Auslandsverhältnissen mit Auslandsbezug, RdA 2007, 283.

Bob Hepple, *The legal consequences of cross-border transfers of undertakings within the European Union*, A Report for the European Commission DG-V (1998).

Abbo Junker, *Internationales Arbeitsrecht im Konzern* (Mohr, Tübingen 1992).

Abbo Junker, "Gewöhnlicher Arbeitsort und vorübergehende Entsendung im Internationalen Privatrecht" in: Stephan Lorenz, Alexander Trunk, Horst Eidenmüller, Christiane Wendehorst and Johannes Adolff (eds), *Festschrift for Andreas Heldrich* (Beck Verlag, München 2005) 719.

Marcus Kania, Betriebsverlagerungen ins Ausland als Weg aus der Krise? ZESAR 2010, 112.

Marcus Kania, *Grenzüberschreitende Betriebsübergänge aus europarechtlicher Sicht* (Nomos Verlag, Baden-Baden 2012).

Sebastian Krebber, Die volle Wirksamkeit von Richtlinien in länderübergreifenden Sachverhalten, ZVglRWiss 1998, 124.

Karl-Georg Loritz, Aktuelle Rechtsprobleme des Betriebsübergangs nach § 613a BGB, RdA 1987, 65.

Diana Niksova, *Grenzüberschreitender Betriebsübergang* (Manz Verlag, Wien 2014).

Diana Niksova, "Grenzüberschreitende Umstrukturierungen zwischen Theorie und Praxis – Zeit für eine Neuausrichtung?" in Tim Husemann and Anne Christin Wietfeld (eds), *Zwischen Theorie und Praxis – Herausforderungen des Arbeitsrechts* (Nomos Verlag, Baden-Baden 2015) 175.

Peter Mankowski, Europäisches Internationales Arbeitsprozessrecht – Weiteres zum gewöhnlichen Arbeitsort – (zu EuGH, 27.2.2002 – Rs. C-37/00 – Herbert Weber/Universal Ogden Services Ltd.,), IPRax 2003, 21.

Robert Rebhahn, Griechischer Kündigungsschutz und Niederlassungsfreiheit, EuZA 2017, 385.

Hermann Reichold, "Neues zum grenzüberschreitenden Betriebsübergang" in: Horst Konzen, Sebastian Krebber, Thomas Raab, Barbara Veit and Bernd Waas (eds), *Festschrift for Rolf Birk* (Mohr Siebeck, Tübingen 2008) 687.

Michael Reiner, Gedanken zur Standortverlagerung, ZAS 2010, 117.

Gregor Thüsing, Rechtsfragen grenzüberschreitender Arbeitsverhältnisse – Grundlagen und Neuigkeiten im Internationalen Arbeitsrecht, NZA 2003, 1303.

Norbert Wimmer, Neuere Entwicklungen im internationalen Arbeitsrecht – Überlegungen zur Politik des Arbeitskollisionsrechts, IPRax 1995, 207.

Michael Wollenschläger and Armin Frölich, Kündigungsschutz nach § 613a BGB beim grenzüberschreitenden Betriebsübergang, AuR 1990, 314.

Individual Rights of Employees in Transfers of Undertakings in Serbia

Ljubinka Kovačević[*]

Summary

A. *Introduction*

Under Serbian law, the protection of employees in the event of a transfer of undertakings is regulated under the auspices of the institute that regulates the change of employer and includes three basic instruments: (a) preservation of employment, i.e. transfer of all employment contracts from the

* Associate Professor at the Faculty of Law of the University of Belgrade.

transferor to the transferee; (b) preservation (albeit temporary) of the collective agreement entered into with the transferor; and (c) informing and consulting employees about company restructuring. Protection is guaranteed for all employees in all cases of change of employer, regardless of whether the identity of the company is preserved or not, which is a different (and more favourable) solution than the European concept of transfer of undertakings. Nevertheless, some of the relevant provisions of the Serbian Labour Act (2005) remain unclear because it is difficult to identify cases that qualify as a change of employer in a reliable manner. Moreover, the Labour Act does not contain rules on liability for any unsettled and due employees' claims that arose before the change of employer, which opens up the possibility of machinations. Some limitations, however, are established by special acts that provide limited joint and several liability of transferor and transferee. On the other hand, the rule in Serbian legislation that the change of employer, in itself, shall not constitute justified ground for dismissal is not expressly laid down, but instead is inferred from other provisions of the Labour Act. Appropriate efforts have to be made in order to establish adequate limitations and sanction their violation, assuming that the dismissal comes shortly after or immediately before the change of employer. This paper will tackle the aforementioned and other unclear legal provisions and gaps in the context of European and comparative labour law.

Since it is hard to fully comprehend certain individual employee rights in the event of a transfer of undertakings without considering the meaning of the term "change of employer" in Serbian law, the first part of this paper will be dedicated to the analysis of this notion in comparison with the European concept of transfer of undertakings. Later, we will tackle the principle of preservation of employment, including the importance of employee consent for the transfer of employment contracts to the transferee. This paper will also pay special attention to the obligation of implementing the collective agreement entered into with the transferor, especially in the context of preservation (or, rather, a ban on deterioration) of working conditions, while the issue of liability for employees' claims will also be analysed. As the protection from transfer-related dismissal has not been directly regulated by the Serbian Labour Act, this paper will try to examine the effectiveness of different regimes of protection against dismissal (by the transferor as well as the transferee). The final chapter will deal with the collective rights of employees as a complement to and a guarantee of their individual rights.

These issues will be examined in the context of harmonisation with the EU law, since EU *acquis* has an important effect on the development of Serbian labour legislation. This is particularly true for directives, while the effects of the judgments rendered by the Court of Justice of the EU seem negligible or even non-existent.

B. The Serbian Concept of Transfer of Undertakings

I. No Requirement of the Preservation of the Economic Identity

For the first time in Serbian legislation, protection of employees in the event of change of employer was regulated by the Labour Act of 2005.[1] In every case of a change of employer, the employees are entitled to continue to perform the work stipulated in their employment contracts, under the same conditions and rights enjoyed before the change. This type of succession arises directly from the Labour Act, regardless of whether or not the economic identity of the undertaking is preserved, i.e., irrespective of the changes introduced by the transferee and regardless of the moment of occurrence of a particular change.[2] In contrast to Serbian law, EU law and the laws of Member States provide protection of employee rights in the event of a transfer of undertaking, in the context of the Council Directive 2001/23/EC,[3] only if both of these conditions have been met: *change of employer* and *preservation of identity of an undertaking*.[4]

The preservation of an undertaking's economic identity as a requirement for protection of the rights of employees is rightfully criticised in the literature as a solution that represents an obstacle to achieving full and proper protection of employees.[5] The employer who is continuing or renewing the activity of his predecessor is thus given an opportunity to evade

1 Labour Act (OJRS, no. 24/05, 61/05, 54/09, 32/13, 75/14, 13/17, 113/17, 95/18), Arts. 147-152.

2 Labour Act (OJRS, no. 24/05, 61/05, 54/09, 32/13, 75/14, 13/17, 113/17, 95/18), Art. 147.

3 Council Directive 2001/23/EC of 12 March 2001 on the approximation of the laws of the Member States relating to the safeguarding of employees' rights in the event of transfers of undertakings, businesses or parts of undertakings or businesses (*Official Journal* L 82, 22.03.2001, 16-20).

4 For comments see: Nicola Countouris and Wanjiru Njoya, "2001/23/EC: Transfer of Undertakings", in Monika Schlachter (ed.), *EU Labour Law: A Commentary* (2014), 425-432.

5 Jean Pélissier, "Les restructurations d'entreprises et leur effets sur l'emploi" (1990) 1 RIDC, 154.

his obligations.[6] The transferee only needs to organise certain activities differently for the principle of preservation of employment to be considered non-applicable. Obligations of the transferee from the Council Directive 2001/23/EC will be considered fulfilled if the activities of the transferor have been preserved at the moment of the transfer (and only at this moment). If transferee were to decide to change the organization of activities after the transfer, his decision would not have any effect on the transfer of contracts and preservation of employment, but could have an effect on the termination of employment due to the needs of the employer.[7] It is rightfully pointed out in the literature that appropriate protection of employees could be provided only if the scope of the employment preservation principle included all variations of the transfer of undertakings, regardless of the changes introduced by the transferee and the moment these changes took place.[8] This exact solution has been included in the Serbian Labour Act. Its provisions do not specify the requirements for protection of employees' rights, as the guarantee is attached to all cases of a change of employer, regardless of whether or not the economic identity of an undertaking has been preserved.

II. Cases of Change of Employer in Serbian Legislation

1. Status Changes of Employer

Although the Labour Act does not define the term "change of employer", it does contain a blanket norm which refers to "*the status change of an employer, or change of an employer in accordance with the act*".[9] It is not simple, in practice, to identify cases of change of employer, especially if one takes into account a fairly broad legal definition of the term "employer"[10] and the lack of a definition of the term "employment relationship" from the

6 Jeff Kenner, *EU Employment Law: From Rome to Amsterdam and Beyond* (2003), 34-35.

7 J. Pélissier, 154.

8 *Ibid.*

9 Labour Act (OJRS, no. 24/05, 61/05, 54/09, 32/13, 75/14, 13/17, 113/17, 95/18), Art. 147.

10 "Employer is domestic or foreign legal or natural person who employs or commissions one person or more". Labour Act (OJRS, no. 24/05, 61/05, 54/09, 32/13, 75/14, 13/17, 113/17, 95/18), Art. 5, para 2.

Labour Act.[11] Elements of the definition of the term "employer" can be derived indirectly from legal provisions regulating essential rights of employers and obligations of employees. In relation thereto, one should bear in mind that an employer, as a person organizing an activity, needs to commission another person to carry out those activities for his account.

This means that the change of employer includes all situations in which the transfer of employment relationship rights and obligations occurs, due to the change of the economically stronger and legally superior party (*potentior persona*). In terms of the provisions of the Labour Act, a change of employer occurs after the death of an *employer natural person*, as his heirs enter into all rights and obligations at the moment of his death, unless the employer capacities are considered to be an essential term of the contract (e.g. if an employer is a person with disabilities and his employee is his assistant or if an employer is an elderly or sick person who is being taken care of by an employee on the basis of the household employment contract). On the other hand, in the case of a *legal person*, a change of employer most often occurs through status changes. It follows then, that if an employer is a company, operations such as merger by acquisition, merger by formation of new companies and division, are carried out by transfer of all rights and obligations from the transferor to the transferee, whereupon the merged company shall be dissolved without being liquidated.[12] Apart from this step, change of employer can occur if one company continues to exist, but transfers a part of its assets and obligations to one or several existing and/or newly founded companies (a so-called separation).[13] This is a situation when one company with several organizational parts transfers one of its parts (operational or business unit, sector, plant, factory etc.) to another company, thereby causing the change of employer for employees working in the organizational part being transferred, while the employees in other

11 In Yugoslav case law, subordination was not validated as an element of employment relationship, and other elements were qualified as such, primarily the exclusivity of work for the employer, personal work for the employer and full time work (Vlajko Brajić/ed./, *Radno pravo u praksi: Priručnik sudske prakse*/1974/, 1/54/). An almost unanimous view is represented in recent Serbian jurisprudence, which states that besides voluntariness, personal work and pay, subordination is a basic element of an employment relationship. For more on the development of the modern concept of employment relationship in Serbian law see: Ljubinka Kovačević, *Pravna subordinacija u radnom odnosu i njene granice* (2013), 208-209.

12 Act on Companies (OJRS, no. 36/11, 99/11, 5/15, 44/18, 95/18), Arts. 485-488. The provisions of this Act shall apply to the status changes of the public companies (Act on Public Companies, OJRS, no. 15/16, Art. 76).

13 Act on Companies (OJRS, no. 36/11, 99/11, 5/15, 44/18, 95/18), Art. 489.

organizational parts remain employed by the same company.[14] In this case, the transfer of a portion of the assets and liabilities from one company to another produces equal labour law consequences for the transfer of all the assets and liabilities of the company.

Change of employer also occurs with the status changes of associations,[15] endowments and funds,[16] cooperatives,[17] sports organizations,[18] scientific research institutes[19] and other legal entities. It can also occur in *all other cases of change of employer provided that they are prescribed by the act*. This instructive provision of the Labour Act refers, in other words, to any other act that regulates situations in which employees get a new employer, since the term "change of employer" is broader than the term "status change".[20] On the other hand, Serbian labour legislation does not regulate the legal (contractual) transfer of specific business activities from the transferor to the transferee, if there is no status change or another type of change of employer as established by the act.[21]

Furthermore, the Labour Act does not regulate change of employer in bankruptcy proceedings, while bankruptcy legislation, meanwhile, however, prescribes the possibility of reducing the rights transferred to the new employer. Bankruptcy procedure through reorganisation - which can include status changes or a transfer of (a part or the entire) assets of one or several existing or newly established entities - is recognized by the bankruptcy legislation.[22] The reorganisation plan may prescribe the dismissal of employees, but the mere fact that the bankruptcy procedure has been initiated represents a justified reason for termination of employment. This finally means that the provisions of the Bankruptcy Act derogate the

---

14 Jean Pélissier, Alain Supiot and Antoine Jeammaud, *Droit du travail* (2002), 421.

15 Act on Associations (OJRS, no. 51/09, 99/11), Arts. 45-48.

16 Act on Endowments and Funds (OJRS, no. 88/10, 99/11), Art. 54.

17 Act on Cooperatives (OJRS, no. 112/15), Art. 65.

18 Act on Sports (OJRS, no. 24/11, 99/11), Arts. 78-85.

19 Act on Scientific Research Activities (OJRS, no. 110/05, 50/06, 18/10, 112/15), Art. 37.

20 This is evidenced by the Opinion of the Ministry of Labour and Social Policy, no. 001-00-787/2010-02, of 29 October 2010.

21 Such direct transfers of undertakings, i.e., an asset deal, are, however, allowed and possible under Serbian law. Liability of the transferee for obligations in relation to the transferred company is regulated under the Obligation Relations Act as assumption of debt (Art. 452). See: Mirjana Radović, "Odgovornost sticaoca za obaveze prenosioca u slučaju prenosa preduzeća" (2017), 4-6 PIP, 95-117.

22 Act on Bankruptcy (OJRS, no. 104/09, 99/11, 71/12, 83/14, 113/27), Art. 157, para 1, subparas 12 and 15.

provisions of the Labour Act on protection of employees in the event of a change of employer, in the sense that the idea of taking over the employment contracts exists only as an option (if prescribed by the reorganization plan), which is in accordance with EU law.

2. *Change of Ownership of a Capital of a Legal Entity*

The change of ownership of a company is an issue also worth considering, although it does not entail changing the subjectivity of the company whose capital (assets) is the subject of privatization.[23] In this case, there is no change of employer, regardless of the possible change of the person authorized to represent the employer or exercise the employer's authority.[24] It is therefore interesting to note that the scope of application of the rules on the protection of employees in the event of a change of an employer was extended in Serbia's Labour Act to include "*the change of ownership of a capital of a company or another legal entity*".[25] The legislature thereby intended to emphasize the protective function of the employment preservation rule, i.e., to ensure that the continuity of employment and working conditions of an employee working for an employer, whose owner has changed, is not called into question. This was a significant decision, as a company restructuring plan from the majority owner can significantly affect the status of employees.[26] Namely, the privatization process can be preceded by the restructuring of the subject of privatization, if the competent body estimates that its capital or assets cannot be sold *via* public tender or public auction. In this situation, provisions on the protection of employees in the event of a change of employer will be applied to employees, and their rights will be further guaranteed by the obligation to enact a restructuring program, which has to include a *social program*.[27] On the one hand, the restructuring

23 Labour Act (OJRS, no. 24/05, 61/05, 54/09, 32/13, 75/14, 13/17, 113/17, 95/18), Art. 63.

24 A-C. Hartzén, N. Hős, F. Lecomte, C. Marzo, B. Mestre, H. Olbrich, S. Fuller, *The Right of the Employee to Refuse to be Transferred: A Comparative and Theoretical Analysis*, EUI Working Paper LAW No. 2008/20, 28.

25 Labour Act (OJRS, no. 24/05, 61/05, 54/09, 32/13, 75/14, 13/17, 113/17, 95/18), Art. 152.

26 Marija Dragićević, "Odgovornost za dospela potraživanja iz radnog odnosa u slučaju promene poslodavca", in Olga Jović-Prlainović (ed.), *Nacionalno i međunarodno pravo – aktuelna pitanja i teme* (2017), 335 (343).

27 In addition, the state-allocated funds from the budget for the implementation of the redundancy programs, in accordance with Decision on Establishing the Pro-

program was aimed at the business reorganization of the subject of privatization, in order to make it more competitive on the market and more attractive for potential buyers in the privatization process. On the other hand, the social program includes measures for the protection of employees, which, in addition to measures for preserving employment, cover the measures for protection in the event of dismissal, in the case that dismissals are necessary.

We should make a distinction between a social program enacted as part of the restructuring of the subject of privatization before the sale of the state-owned capital, and a social program enacted in the process of the sale. The social program in the second case represents a part of the agreement on the sale of capital or assets and is aimed at preserving the working conditions and rights of employees who will be continuing their employment. It is also aimed at ensuring certain rights in case of termination of employment due to reorganization of the business process. Finally, we should note that the mechanism for termination of the contract on the sale of capital or assets provides a certain guarantee that the rights of employees employed by the entities that are being privatized will be observed. The mechanism is triggered if, within the extended deadline, the buyer fails to fulfil his employment relationship-related obligations, as well as if he fails to pay the minimum wages and the corresponding social contributions in full.[28]

Although the aforementioned legal provisions formally provided a solid framework for the protection of employees, in reality the position of employees was extremely unfavourable. New owners exerted a much greater influence over their employees than what they were formally granted by the law. This is especially true for collective redundancies that were implemented without respecting the relevant protective (substantive and procedural) norms: from 2001 to 2008 more than 400,000 employees were dismissed in the privatization process, and another 300,000 during the following eight years.[29] Today, employees in privatized companies make up only

gram for Dealing with Redundancies in the Process of Privatization for 2015, 2016, 2017, 2018 and 2019, OJRS, no. 9/15, 84/15, 109/15, 16/16, 82/16, 5/17, 92/17, 29/18, 59/18, 3/19.

28 Act on Privatization (OJRS, no. 38/01, 18/03, 45/05, 123/07, 123/07, 30/10, 93/12, 119/12, 51/14, 52/14), Art. 41a.

29 Čedanka Andrić, "Protection of Employees' Rights in the Processes of Companies Restructuring in Serbia: Views from the Trade Unions", in Ljubinka Kovačević, Mirjana Radović (eds.), *Restructuring of Companies and Protection of Employees' Rights: Views from the EU, Austria, Serbia and Macedonia* (2017), 66 (67).

7% of the total number of employees in the Serbian economy,[30] many of them working in unbearable working conditions, not having been paid from the moment of privatization or, unjustifiably, having been paid only the minimum wage.[31]

The provision on the protection of employees in the case of an ownership change has, unfortunately, been deleted from the Labour Act as per the Amendment to the Labour Act of 2014. One of the reasons for this is that the deadline for compulsory privatization of social capital expired on December 31, 2015. However, this does not apply to privatization in general, as the privatization of public capital (capital of the Republic of Serbia, autonomous provinces and units of local self-government) and assets of the subjects that operate public capital is still ongoing.[32] Therefore, there is concern that the privatization of public capital will be accompanied by abuses similar to those that occurred during the previous period.[33] This is despite the fact that the current legislation ensures certain measures for the protection of employees' rights, such as the rule that the social program has to represent an integral part of the program of the sale of assets of the subject of privatization, or that the contract on the sale of assets may prohibit the downsizing of employees with open-ended employment contracts in the next two (or, in an exceptional case, three) years.[34]

---

30 *Ibid.*, 66.

31 Stalno radno telo Socijalno-ekonomskog saveta za ekonomska pitanja, *Efekti privatizacije u Srbiji* (2011), 84.

32 Act on Privatization (OJRS, no. 83/14, 46/15, 112/15, 20/16), Art. 6, paras 2 and 5.

33 Public companies founded by the Republic of Serbia have approximately 93,000 employees, while the companies founded by the local self-government units have more than 69,000 employees. The latest action plan for restructuring companies allowed for the initiation of bankruptcy proceedings against 188 enterprises with poor prospects of privatization where the majority owner is the state, as well as for the privatization of 512 enterprises. In addition, it provided for the restructuring of some of the largest enterprises, such as "Electric Power Industry of Serbia" (reducing the number of sectors from 65 to 35, in order to eliminate the need for state aid), "Serbiagas" (separation of transport and transport system management as well as distribution and distribution system management, to ensure secure natural gas supply), "Roads of Serbia" (merging the roads company with the company "Corridors of Serbia" into a single enterprise for road construction and maintenance) and "Serbian Railways" (forming separate companies for infrastructure, passenger transport and transport of goods).

34 Act on Privatization (OJRS, no. 83/14, 46/15, 112/15 i 20/16), Arts. 37, 50 and 52.

C. The Principle of the Preservation of Employment

Job security represents an important segment of employee protection in the case of transfer of undertakings in EU law. This is ensured through a rule which states that all employment contracts that were in effect on the day of the transfer of undertakings will automatically be carried over from the transferor to the transferee. This type of succession does not depend on the will of the respective entities, but originates *ex lege*. This principle is regulated by the Serbian Labour Act via the following rule: "*In the event of a status change, and/or change of employer, in conformity with the act, the successor employer shall take over from the predecessor employer the general act and all employment contracts that are valid on the day of the change of employer*."[35] Employment contracts, therefore, continue to produce effects between the employees and the new employer, which is why the people who were employed at the time of the change have the same contractual rights and obligations towards the transferee as before the change took place. This means furthermore that the employees automatically become creditors to the person being substituted to the employer, regardless of the type of employment, i.e. regardless of whether or not an employee has established a standard or flexible form of employment.[36]

However, employees are not obligated to work for the transferee. Any other solution would be contrary to the principle of the freedom of contract, the principle that labour is not a commodity, as well as the guarantee of the right to work, the right of everyone to earn a living from a freely chosen occupation and employment.[37] The consent of an employee to work includes his ability to stop working or continue working for some-

35 Labour Act (OJRS, no. 24/05, 61/05, 54/09, 32/13, 75/14, 13/17, 113/17, 95/18), Art. 147. The provisions of the Act on Companies take the same tone: "The employees of the transferring company who are assigned to the receiving company under the status change agreement or division plan shall continue working for the receiving company in accordance with labour legislation" (Art. 505, para 1, subpara 6). On the other hand, the Act on Sports (OJRS, no. 24/2011, 99/2011) directly regulates the issue of the status of employees in the case of a merger of sports associations (but not another type of status change): "by recording the merger the employees [...] become the employees of the acquiring company" (Art. 81, para 5).

36 Branko Lubarda, *Evropsko radno pravo* (2004), 286.

37 There is no freedom of work if people are working against their will, including cases in which they were hired of their own free will but no longer wish to continue working (in general or for a particular employer). Lenia Samuel, *Droits sociaux fondamentaux: Jurisprudence de la Charte sociale européenne* (2002), 19.

one else if he so chooses, which is why preventing an employee from leaving work with the risk of being punished can be qualified as forced labour.

The transferor is bound to notify the employees, in writing, of the transfer of their contracts to the transferee.[38] If an employee refuses the transfer of his employment contract to a third party, the transferor may initiate the termination of the employment relationship. Dismissal is based on a valid reason if an employee categorically refuses the transfer or if he fails to respond within five working days from the day of receipt of the employer's notification of the transfer.[39] This rule raises a question regarding *the status of employees who were not fired by the transferor, even though they did not accept the transfer of contract to a third party*. To be more precise, it remains unclear what their status will be if their employer does not terminate their contracts before the realisation of the status change. A possible solution to this legal vacuum is the use of legal fiction by entering into an open-ended employment contract on the day when the person, who has not previously entered into an employment contract with said employer, comes to work. In other words, just coming to work after refusing to continue working for the new employer would be enough to continue employment with the transferee.[40] A more acceptable interpretation would be that the refusal of an employee, in the case that he was not dismissed by the transferor, means that his contract is transferred to the transferee, since all employment contracts are transferred *ex lege*.[41]

When a change of employer occurs, the content of the employment contract binds both the employee and the transferee in the same way that it bound the employee and the transferor. The transferee is, therefore, able to exercise all the rights from the employment contracts related to the basic and secondary obligations of employees, such as the right to require employees to respect the non-compete clause, if such a clause exists in the

---

38 Labour Act (OJRS, no. 24/05, 61/05, 54/09, 32/13, 75/14, 13/17, 113/17, 95/18), Art. 149, para 1.

39 Labour Act (OJRS, no. 24/05, 61/05, 54/09, 32/13, 75/14, 13/17, 113/17, 95/18), Art. 149, para 2.

40 Zoran M. Ivošević and Milan Z. Ivošević, *Komentar Zakona o radu* (2006), 277.

41 Guiseppe Santoro-Passarelli, "The Transfer of Undertaking: Striking a Balance Between Individual Workers' Rights and Business Needs" (2007) 3 IJCLLIR, 325-326. One should bear in mind that Council Directive 2001/23/EC does not regulate the consequences of an employee's refusal to work for the transferee; the Member States do. This further means that, unless national laws say otherwise, an employee who decides not to continue his employment with the transferee may still be bound by his employment contract with the transferor. Roger Blanpain, *European Labour Law* (2012), 788.

contract. Moreover, the transferee may impose a disciplinary sanction if an employee violated work discipline before the change of employer took place, provided that, in the meantime, the statute of limitations has not expired.

On the other hand, employees can exercise all the rights and privileges deriving from their employment contracts, including *the ones whose exercise is dependent on the length of service*. This is recognized under Serbian law in terms of the right to severance pay and the right to a notice period, which is in line with the jurisprudence of the Court of Justice of the EU.[42] Continuity of work by an employee plays a role in calculating the severance pay, as well as in determining the length of the notice period. In this respect, a proposal can be made to ensure that continuity of employment is also recognized in respect to other rights, the exercise of which is dependent on the length of service.

D. *Preservation of Working Conditions of the Collective Agreement*

The rights and obligations of employees are not only regulated by the employment contract but also by the normative part of the collective agreement (or labour rulebook, if the collective agreement cannot be concluded),[43] and since this is the case, the protection of employees in the case of a change of employer includes (albeit only temporary) preservation of employees' rights arising from these legal acts. Consequently, all rights and

42 The European Court of Justice constructed a rule stating that, when establishing the rights of a financial nature related to the employee's length of service, the transferee is obliged to take into account the entire period of service the employee spent working in the company, both for him and for the transferor. Case C-343/98 14.09.2000, *Renato Collino and Luisella Chiappero v. Telecom Italia SpA*, *Reports of Cases*, 2000, I-06659, para 51.

43 Labour rulebook represents a unilateral general legal act that an employer can adopt in order to regulate rights, obligations and responsibilities resulting from the employment relationship, only if the conditions to conclude a collective agreement have not been met. It shall become invalid on the day the collective agreement is concluded. Bearing in mind the nature and the purpose of employers' normative prerogatives, the obligation to apply the transferor's labour rulebook by the transferee represents a unique solution. However, in French law there is a similar rule regarding certain general unilateral acts of employers (unilateral acts that provide certain benefits to employees) and company customs (the generic term *engagements unilatéraux* is used to label these acts and customs) which are also transferred to the transferee in case of a change of employer. Jean Pélissier, Gilles Auzero, Emmanuel Dockès, *Droit du travail* (2013), 750.

obligations established by the collective agreement or labour rulebook are transferred to the transferee as well. The Labour Act specifies the obligation of the transferee to apply the collective agreement entered into between the transferor and the representative trade union(s), as well as the labour rulebook enacted by the transferor. The aforesaid obligation exists for at least one year from the date of the change of employer, unless the collective agreement entered into with the transferor expires before that, or the transferee does not enter into a new collective agreement with the representative trade union(s).[44] This further means that Serbian legislation *favours the substitution of the collective agreement entered into with the transferor with a new collective agreement*, in order to adapt the "old" contractual provisions to the new circumstances or to create new provisions, in accordance with the needs of each specific case.

The obligation of the transferee to apply the collective agreement or labour rulebook enacted by the transferor for at least one year represents a guarantee for preservation of working conditions. The aforementioned autonomous sources of labour law then become the basis for regulation of employment relationships between the employees and the transferee, which is why working conditions cannot deteriorate for one year after the change of employer. Moreover, some segments of this ban may last longer, if one takes into account that a collective agreement entered into with the transferor produces indirect effects even after expiration, if (more favourable) working conditions and rights have been incorporated into the employment contract; in this case, the collective agreement with the transferor permanently modifies the employment contracts.[45]

There is no option of terminating the collective agreement concluded at the company level before the expiry of one year, although it is possible that the transferee enters an employers' organization that is bound by the branch collective agreement and, in this way, to apply a new collective agreement to the employees covered by the transfer. Related to this, we should bear in mind that the number of collective agreements concluded at the company level is extremely low. This is prompted by high unemployment rates and weakness of the trade unions, primarily due to the falling rates of unionization (less than 30% of employees in Serbia are members of

44 Labour Act (OJRS, no. 24/05, 61/05, 54/09, 32/13, 75/14, 13/17, 113/17, 95/18), Art. 150.

45 Roger Blanpain, *Belgium* (2012), 400.

trade unions)[46] and the lack of agility of the trade unions in terms of ensuring effective implementation of labour legislation. In contrast, there are attempts by the Serbian legislator to encourage social partners to regulate working conditions as a result of their compromise instead of unilateral regulation of rights and obligations deriving from individual employment relationships. In that sense, labour rulebook is enacted as a "substitute" for a collective agreement at the company level. In order to avoid the employers misusing this instrument, in case they do not accept the initiative of the representative trade unions to enter into negotiations for the collective agreement, employers are not allowed to use the labour rulebook to regulate the rights and obligations arising from an individual employment relationship. We should bear in mind that the transferee who is participating in the negotiations with the representative trade union cannot enact the labour rulebook if the negotiations take too long (i.e., more than 60 days) and that he is, furthermore, obligated to apply the collective agreement for at least one year after the change of employer.[47]

Finally, it should be noted that the obligation to apply a collective agreement concluded by the transferor exists even if the transferee is bound by a collective agreement entered into with the representative trade union from his company. In this case, there is a "*competition*" *between collective agreements*, which, as some authors warn, could jeopardize the protection of employees from discrimination.[48] This is due to the fact that the application of two different agreements to two different categories of employees working for the transferee may result in the employees of the same employer having different working conditions, including different pay for the same work or work of the same value.[49] However, it seems that such varying treatment is justified by the legal obligation of the transferee to preserve the working conditions of the employees covered by the transfer of

---

46 Branko Lubarda, *Radno pravo. Rasprava o dostojanstvu na radu i socijanom dijalogu* (2012), 819. This is significant if one takes into account the demanding quantitative conditions for obtaining the status of the representative trade union in Serbia (membership of at least 15% of the total number of company employees), which the International Labour Organization's Committee on Freedom of Association considered to be too high. This negatively influences the development of social dialogue and collective bargaining in Serbia.

47 This was confirmed in the Opinion of the Ministry of Labour no. 011-00-2283/2006-02. The same goes for the Decision of the Constitutional Court of the Republic of Serbia IU number 44/2008, of 18 December 2008 (OJRS, no. 9/09).

48 Ivana Grgurev, *Croatia* (2013), 106.

49 *Ibid.*

undertaking. There is also an issue with the position of employees if the collective agreement entered into with the transferee includes more rights and better working conditions than the rights and working conditions included in the collective agreement entered into with the transferor. This issue is not regulated by the Labour Act, which is why it is possible, with regards to a future act, to propose a solution, according to which the provisions of the collective agreement with better working conditions or more rights are applied to the employees covered by the transfer of undertaking.[50] Any other solution would be contrary to the principle *in favor laborem*.

E. The Liability for Claims of Employees Due Before the Change of Employer

The liability for obligations arising from the employment relationship refers primarily to the new obligations, i.e. obligations that arose after the change of employer took place. This is also true for the obligations that arose after the change of employer but are related to the period of employment with the transferor, such as an obligation to pay the thirteenth salary.[51] In addition to the liability for settling new claims of the employees, the change of employer raises another important issue — the liability for obligations incurred towards employees before the change of employer that were not settled by the transferor. This raises an issue as to who is liable for obligations that were due before the transfer of employment contracts to the transferee, as well as what is the basis and type of that liability.

Pursuant to the provisions of the Council Directive 2001/23/EC, the transferor is, as a result of the transfer of undertaking, completely relieved from obligations towards his employees, although this legal consequence is not dependent on the consent of employees.[52] The transfer of obligations is automatic and carried out *ex lege*, differing from the general rule of law on contracts and torts, which states that no one may assume the debt of a third party without the creditor's consent. However, there is a possibility (not obligation) for EU Member States to establish joint and several liabili-

50 Darja Senčur Peček, Sprememba delodajalca, in: Nataša Belopavlovič, Barbara Kresal, Katarina Kresal Šoltes and Darja Senčur Peček (eds), *Zakon o delovnih razmerjih s komentarjem* (2016), 427 (437).

51 J. Pélissier, G. Auzero, E. Dockès, 355-356.

52 R. Blanpain, *European labour law*, 787. Judgment in joined cases 144 and 145/87, 05.05.1988, *Harry Berg and Johannes Theodorus Maria Busschers v. Ivo Martin Besselsen*, ECR 1988, 02559, para 14.

ty of the transferor and the transferee for the aforementioned obligations, from the date of realization of a transfer of undertaking.[53] Joint and several liability refers only to the claims of persons who were employed at the moment of the change of employer and not to the claims of persons who already left the company (e.g. holiday pay and compensation for termination of employment for persons whose employment ended before the change of employer).[54] Also, the Directive does not provide protection for employees who worked for the transferor on the day of the transfer of undertakings but did not continue their employment with the transferee.[55]

EU Member States have regulated the issue of liability differently. The labour legislation of the Czech Republic, Cyprus, Denmark, Ireland, Latvia, Lithuania, Malta and Slovakia stipulate the *exclusive liability of the transferee* for contractual obligations that arose before a change in status occurred, while the legislation of Austria, Finland, Greece, Iceland, Italy, Liechtenstein, Luxembourg and Sweden stipulate the rule on *joint and several liability of the transferor and the transferee*.[56] From the perspective of the employees, unlimited joint and several liability is the best solution, since the risk of insolvency of the debtor is minimized, and the position of the creditor is safer in terms of greater prospects for the settlement of claims.

Other European countries have the rule on joint and several liability, but exclude it in certain cases, e.g., in the event of a change of employer in the bankruptcy procedure (France).[57] On the other hand, certain countries limit the application of the rules on joint and several liability. This aims to strike a balance between, on the one hand, the freedom of debtors to reorganize and, on the other hand, the protection of employees as creditors. *The limitation* can primarily refer to applying the rule only to certain cases of change of employer (transfer of a part of an undertaking in Poland),[58] or only to certain employees' claims, e.g. damages for violating the obligation to inform and consult employees (Great Britain).[59] In addition, it is possi-

53 Council Directive 2001/23/EC, Art. 3, para 1.

54 Case 19/83 07.02.1985, *Knud Wendelboe and others v. L.J. Music ApS, in liquidation*, ECR 1985, 00457, para 17.

55 R. Blanpain, *European labour law*, 787.

56 Commission Report on Council Directive 2001/23/EC of 12 March 2001 on the approximation of the laws of the Member States relating to the safeguarding of employees' rights in the event of transfers of undertakings, businesses or parts of undertakings or businesses [SEC(2007) 812], COM/2007/0334 fin, annex, question 2.1.

57 *Ibid.*

58 Zbigniew Hajn and Leszek Mitrus, *Poland* (2016), 88.

59 Commission Report on Council Directive 2001/23/EC ..., annex, question 2.1.

ble to introduce time limitation for applying the rule on joint and several liability, e.g. for a period of one year (Estonia, Germany, the Netherlands, Portugal) or three years (Spain) from the date of the change of employer, so that, after this period, the rule on exclusive liability of the transferee is in force.[60]

The Serbian Labour Act does not regulate the issue of liability, but the possibility of abuse in case of status changes is restricted by special acts that provide limited joint and several liability.

Due to the absence of rules on liability from the Labour Act, it can be concluded that the transferee is solely responsible for claims that were due before the transfer of the employment contracts to the transferee.[61] This goes for status changes in which the company ceases to exist without being liquidated, therein creating a new company or companies (merger by acquisition, merger by formation of new companies and division). In the case of separation, however, the protection of claims appears to be a particularly sensitive issue, since the transferor continues to exist. In accordance with the Act on Companies, there is a possibility for the transferor and the transferee to regulate their mutual rights and obligations differently in the event of a change in status of a company. They can place the liability on the transferor for all or some of the obligations, through the status change agreement or a division plan. For obligations that were not transferred to the transferee by the status change agreement or division plan — the transferee becomes jointly and severally liable with the transferor, but only up to the amount of the difference in the value of assets of the company that was transferred and the liabilities of the company that he took over, unless it was agreed otherwise by specific creditors.[62] If the status change results in the liquidation of the transferor, its obligations shall be transferred to

60 *Ibid.*

61 It is therefore important to mention the legal obligation of the transferor to fully and truthfully inform the transferee about the rights and obligations stemming from the employment contract, the collective agreement or labour rulebook. The aforementioned provision of Serbian Labour Act was inspired by Council Directive 2001/23/EC (Art. 3, para 2), although it would be more acceptable if the Labour Act required that this information be made in writing, as well as if it regulated the issue of the consequences of the failure of the transferor to fulfil this obligation. Therefore, the optimal solution seems to be the rule confirmed by the Council Directive 2001/23/EC that the failure of the transferor to inform the transferee of due obligations does not affect the exercise of the rights of employees.

62 Act on Companies (OJRS, no. 36/11, 99/11, 5/15, 44/18, 95/18), Art. 505, para 1, subpara 2.

the transferee in accordance with the status change agreement or the division plan, and the transferee becomes the new debtor in respect to these obligations. In the event that there are several transferees, each of them will have subsidiary liability for the obligations that were transferred to other transferees, up to the amount of the difference in the value of assets of the company that was transferred and the liabilities of the company that he took over, unless agreed otherwise with specific creditors.[63]

The Act on Endowments and Funds states that the provisions from the Act on Companies shall be applied to the status changes of endowments and funds.[64] On the other hand, the Law on Associations provides a rule on joint and several liability only in the case of division of associations,[65] while the Law on Sports foresees the joint and several liability of all sports associations that exist after the enrolment of the division or separation of the sports association.[66]

As the implementation of rules on joint and several liability cannot be assumed, it follows that in other cases (for example, status changes of cooperatives and scientific research organizations), the general rule of law on contracts and torts will be applied for the obligations that occurred before the change of employer. The same is true for other cases of change of employer, since this concept is broader than the notion of a status change of an employer. In this regard, one can notice the need for the Serbian legislator to consider and "weigh" all the advantages and disadvantages of the rule on exclusive and (unlimited and limited) joint and several liability for claims that were due before the change of employer,[67] and, in the name of the principle of legal certainty, to regulate this issue within the Labour Act.[68]

---

63 Act on Companies (OJRS, no. 36/11, 99/11, 5/15, 44/18, 95/18), Art. 505, para 3, subpara 4.

64 Act on Endowments and Funds (OJRS, no. 88/10, 99/11), Art. 54, para 7.

65 Act on Associations (OJRS, no. 51/09, 99/11), Art. 48, para 5.

66 Act on Sports (OJRS, no. 24/11, 99/11), Art. 84, para 6.

67 This creates the need to protect, through appropriate rules, both the claims of employees and the interest of employers, because rules that are too strict will make certain status changes as a way to restructure the company less appealing. Mirjana Radović, "Odgovornost društva sticaoca za obaveze društva prenosioca kod statusnih promena podele i izdvajanja", in Vuk Radović (ed.), *Usklađivanje poslovnog prava Srbije sa pravom Evropske unije* (2017), 145 (151).

68 All the more so because there does not seem to be a uniform judicial practice regarding this issue. This is evidenced by the different verdicts of the appellate courts regarding the protection of employees who sued "Serbian Railways" a.d. Belgrade, after the status change of this undertaking (separation accompanied by

F. Right to Protection Against Transfer-Related Dismissal

I. The Relationship between Dismissal and Change of Employer

Implementation of the principle of employment preservation in the event of change of employer presumes that this change, in itself, shall not constitute valid reason for dismissal. The prohibition of dismissal by the transferor or the transferee does not mean the prohibition of dismissal due to (otherwise) legitimate reasons relating to the abilities and conduct of employees or technological, economic or organizational changes that lead to termination of the need for a particular job or to reduction of work volume. And *vice versa*, the transfer of undertakings shall not be considered valid reason for dismissal by the transferor or the transferee,[69] although each Member State has the right to exclude certain specific categories of employees who are not covered by the laws or practices of the Member States in respect to protection against dismissal.[70] This, however, does not include the possibility for Member States to take away, by opting for this flexible solution, the protection against dismissal from the categories of employees

formation of new companies), for payment of outstanding remuneration for shift work performed before the status change (ruling of the Court of Appeal in Novi Sad Gž1.2372/16, 01.08. 2016, rulings of the Court of Appeal in Niš - 25Gž1.3206/15, 12.01.2016; 19Gž1. 2640/16, 07.10.2016; 19Gž1. 1763/16, 14.10.2016; 19Gž1. 3452/16, 10.11.2016 and 19Gž1. 3436/16, 10.11. 2016). The separation of four technological and business units from one of the largest enterprises in Serbia – "Serbian Railways" a.d. Belgrade included the formation of three companies from these units ("Serbian Railways Infrastructure", "Serbia Train" and "Serbia Cargo"), while the existing enterprise "Serbian Railways" a.d. Belgrade retained the fourth unit. The employees in the fourth unit retained their employment with the enterprise, while the issue of responsibility for payment of outstanding remuneration for shift work before the status change was raised before the courts. See: Borivoje Gajić, "Solidarna odgovornost i statusna promena privrednog društva" (2016) 3 BVKS, 153-174.

69 Council Directive 2001/23/EC, Art. 4, para 1.

70 Several countries used this option with regard to workers who do not need protection from dismissal due to the nature of their work or the level of their income (e.g. senior managers in Spain and Sweden), or the nature of their undertaking (such as relatives of the employer or employees who perform paid work in the household of the employer in Sweden). Same goes for the persons who enjoy special support or employment protection (also in Sweden). Acc. to: Commission Report on Council Directive 2001/23/EC ..., annex, question 2.4.

who, in accordance with their national legislation, enjoy even limited protection against dismissal.[71]

In accordance with the provisions of the International Labour Organization Convention No. 158 (ratified by Serbia),[72] one of the basic rules of Serbian labour law reads: the employer may not terminate the contract of an employee, unless there is a valid reason relating to the ability or conduct of the employee or the needs of the employer.[73] The requirement for valid reasons for dismissal was met by establishing a list of permissible reasons for dismissal in accordance with the Labour Act. On the other hand, the rule on protection against dismissal due to change of employer as such has not been directly confirmed. Still, this rule is derived from the provisions of the Labour Act on change of employer as well as termination of employment, but this cannot be enough for effective implementation of the principle of legal certainty and protection of employees against unfair dismissal.

II. Protection Against Dismissal by the Transferor

The rule on the transfer of employment contracts that are in force on the day of the change of employer would not make much sense if the employer could easily terminate said contracts a few days, or even weeks, before company restructuring. The absence of valid reason for dismissal will, in turn, be *quaestio facti* for each case individually, meaning that the courts will examine whether the transferor initiated termination of employment without the plan for transfer of undertakings and, if that is not the case, they will examine if personally or business motivated reasons for termination of employment existed or not. The circumstances of each individual case will determine the length of period after which the dismissal can no longer be considered related to the transfer of undertakings, i.e. after which it will be safe to assume that (direct or indirect) links between the transfer of undertakings and the employer's decision on dismissal have been broken.[74]

---

71 See: Case 237/84, 15.04.1986, *Commission of the European Communities v. Kingdom of Belgium*, ECR 1986, 1247.

72 The ratification act was published in the "Official Gazette of the SFRY – International Agreements", no. 4/84.

73 Labour Act (OJRS, no. 24/05, 61/05, 54/09, 32/13, 75/14, 13/17, 113/17, 95/18), Art. 179.

74 John McMullen, "Re-structuring and TUPE" (2012) 3 ILJ, 358.

Serbian lawmakers did not devise mechanisms for employers to be dissuaded in their intention to use termination of employment as a means of avoiding the rules on protection of employees in the event of a change of employer. On the other hand, there are (more or less successful) efforts in the laws of some European countries to limit the right of the transferor to initiate termination of employment in the period immediately preceding the restructuring. These efforts, however, are accompanied by the problem of determining the fair scope of restrictions, as well as the way in which the violations will be sanctioned.[75] In addition, the prevailing solution is not to institute a general ban on dismissing employees prior to restructuring; instead, it is emphasized that restructuring does not constitute a valid reason for dismissal. Therefore, an employer who plans to transfer assets and liabilities to a third party can dismiss an employee for economic reasons, as long as those reasons are not related to the restructuring.[76] This, more specifically, means that termination for future restructuring (in order to facilitate the restructuring) would be wrongful. Oftentimes in practice, an employer will dismiss a number of his employees right before a certain status change of the company takes place; the transferee will then, after the transfer of the undertaking, hire the same people, only under worse conditions (or he will not hire them at all).[77] This risk is also recognized in the Court of Justice of the EU case law, which took the view that employees who had been wrongfully dismissed by the transferor, just before the transfer of the company (and whose employment contracts were not taken over by the transferee) can ask for protection against wrongful dismissal against the transferee as well.[78] This is because their employment contracts should be considered in force, for at least two reasons. The first is that the person whom the employer dismissed just before the transfer of undertaking should be considered an employee of the company on the day of the transfer, while the other reason concerns the obligatory nature of protection of employees from dismissal due to the change of employer, making the provision of the Directive confirming such protection unacceptable for derogation at the expense of the employee.[79]

75 J. Pélissier, 157.

76 *Ibid.*

77 Darja Senčur Peček, "Aktualna vprašanja spremembe delodalajca" (2010) 2-3 DID, 312.

78 Ruth Nielsen, *European Labour Law* (2000), 338.

79 Case C/319-94, 12.03.1998, *Jules Déthier Équipement SA v. Jules Dassy and Sovam SPRL*, ECR 1998, I-1061, paras 39-40.

III. Protection Against Dismissal by the Transferee

The transfer of undertaking as such cannot justify the initiative of the transferee for termination of employment, although the assessment whether the dismissal was (exclusively or predominantly) motivated by the transfer will be a major issue in each case. This further means that an employer can be relieved of responsibility for wrongful dismissal only if his decision is proven to have been motivated by the abilities or conduct of an employee.[80] The same applies if there is evidence to prove the existence of reasons concerning the needs of the employer, in the so-called economic dismissal, where it can be considered, for example, that the employer had justifiable grounds for dismissal if the termination of employment was not only a result of the transfer of the undertaking, but an integral part of the broad set of activities undertaken in order to avoid insolvency and reduce current costs that are jeopardizing the survival of the company. The same would be true if the transfer of undertaking created an operational need for the company, making the dismissal justified.[81] These estimates are, however, extremely delicate, since there is a thin and fragile line of demarcation between the right to a *bona fide* termination for economic and other related company changes and the abuse of this right to facilitate company restructuring.

The rule on the transfer of employment contracts does not, however, presuppose that the transferee, after a certain status change, cannot introduce the amendment or even initiate termination of the employment contract. The principle of preservation of employment will no longer protect employees after a certain time.[82] Their status will be the same as any other employees' status and the transferee will retain all the rights of an employer, as recognized by law. This further means that the transferee can offer an employee to sign an amendment to the employment contract or even terminate his employment contract if he refuses to sign it. The new employer can also terminate employment due to poor performance or lack of knowledge and skills. Still, the aforementioned cases have certain characteristics, reflected in the fact that the transferee has to respect the benefits and limi-

80 Nicola Smit, "A Chronicle of Issues Raised in the Course of Dismissals by the Transferor and/or Transferee in Circumstances Involving the Transfer of an Undertaking" (2005) ILJJ, 1873-1874.

81 Bradley Workman-Davies, "The Right of Employers to Dismiss Employees in the Context of Business Transfers – An Analysis of the Automatically Unfair Dismissal Provisions of the Labour Relations Act" (2007) ILJSA, 2137.

82 J. Pélissier, 154.

tations of the right to terminate employment as related to the facts that occurred before the change of employer, as is the case with severance pay[83] and the length of the notice period in Serbian law, because they depend on the period of employment for the transferor.

The need for protection of employees against dismissal immediately following the transfer of undertaking has not been recognized in Serbian law. This includes protection against dismissal by the transferee when an employee fails to accept the amendment to the employment contract, offered immediately upon completion of the transfer (e.g. an offer to move to a lower position). In some legal systems, the employee has the right to reject such an offer and this cannot be qualified as a valid reason for dismissal.[84] Also, EU law has affirmed the stance that the employer is considered responsible for termination of employment if it occurred due to the fact that the transfer of undertaking was accompanied by a substantial change in the working conditions to the detriment of an employee.[85]

G. Collective Rights of Employees in the Event of a Transfer of Undertaking

Protection of employees in the event of a transfer of undertaking is also ensured by recognizing their collective rights, or, more precisely, by recognizing their right to participate in the decision making on issues relevant to their position in the event of company restructuring. The informing and consulting of employees' representatives are aimed at mitigating the negative consequences of restructuring and making fair decisions — decisions that are legitimate enough to be accepted by the employees and their representatives.

In the Serbian Labour Act, the question of employees' participation is regulated through general provisions on the right of employees to be informed, consulted and to express their views on important issues in the field of work. The provision on the establishment of the works council as well as the provision on the right of the trade union to be informed on

83 Labour Act (OJRS, no. 24/05, 61/05, 54/09, 32/13, 75/14, 13/17, 113/17, 95/18), Art. 158, para 3.

84 This can also be a case of *constructive dismissal* if the employee initiated the termination of employment because the transferee worsened the working conditions (in comparison with the working conditions of the transferor) to such an extent that staying employed would have been unbearable for the employee. Bob Hepple, "European Rules on Dismissal Law" (1996-1997) CLLJ, 208.

85 Council Directive 2001/23/EC, Art. 4, para 2.

"economic and social issues that affect the position of the employees or members of the trade union" also bear mentioning.[86] However, the aforementioned legal provisions seem insufficient to regulate key aspects of participation, especially if one takes into account the delicate position of employees in the so-called transition period, as well as the intention and effort of the domestic legislator to harmonise labour legislation with EU law.[87]

When it comes to change of employer, the Labour Act has confirmed the obligation of the transferor and the transferee to inform, before the transfer of undertaking, the representative trade union or, if one does not exist, to inform the employees (directly) on dates, reasons and legal, economic and social consequences of the change.[88] The same is true for measures to mitigate these consequences, only the employers are obliged, in cooperation with a representative trade union, to take measures to mitigate the consequences of the situation for the employees before the change takes place.[89]

The information process has to start on time in order to enable the representatives to make constructive suggestions, while the goal of timely consultations is to reach an agreement with representatives of the employees. Therefore, the issue of determining the moment of initiation of consultations appears to be a particularly sensitive issue, which is why some countries determine a precise earliest date when the consultations have to begin (e.g., by specifying the minimum number of days that must precede the date from which the decision on measures concerning employees will take effect).[90] In Serbian legislation as well as case law, this issue has remained open, while the ideal solution would be the one in which the time coordi-

86 Labour Act (OJRS, no. 24/05, 61/05, 54/09, 32/13, 75/14, 13/17, 113/17, 95/18), Arts. 13, 209.

87 This especially applies to regulation of mandates and operation of the works council, to which only one article was devoted from the entire Serbian labour legislation. For more on this topic see: Predrag Jovanović, "Putevi i stranputice industrijske demokratije u Srbiji", in Etelka Korpič Horvat and Darja Senčur Peček (eds.), *Tendence v. razvoju delovnega prava* (2009), 18 (32); Senad Jašarević, "Harmonizacija prava i prakse u oblasti participacije zaposlenih – Srbija i EU" (2011) 3 ZRPFNS, 379-395.

88 Labour Act (OJRS, no. 24/05, 61/05, 54/09, 32/13, 75/14, 13/17, 113/17, 95/18), Art. 151, paras 1 and 3.

89 Labour Act (OJRS, no. 24/05, 61/05, 54/09, 32/13, 75/14, 13/17, 113/17, 95/18), Art. 151, para 2.

90 For example, in Italian law both the transferor and the transferee have the obligation to inform employees' representatives, 25 days before the decision on the

nates of the consultations move, up to the moment when the employer is considering introducing major changes in the company structure.[91]

In addition, there is a need to create conditions for effective exercising of the right to information and consultation, which requires that employees have adequate administrative or judicial protection in the event that their right is violated. There is also a need to establish sufficiently effective and deterrent penalties that will be applied against the employer who violates the obligation to inform and consult employees (e.g., compensation for damages). Also, it is possible to amend the Labour Act with a provision that would regulate (or stimulate social partners to regulate) the election of representatives of employees in companies that do not have a representative trade union.[92]

H. Conclusion

Protection of employees in the event of a change of employer in Serbia was first regulated under the auspices of the Labour Act of 2005 as a result of a voluntary and partial harmonisation of Serbian legislation with EU law. Council Directive 2001/23/EC served as a model for the Serbian legislature in regulating the issues related to change of employer, while the effect of the European Court of Justice jurisprudence was negligible. Protection was guaranteed to all employees in all cases of change of employer, regardless of whether company identity has been preserved or not, thereby making it more favourable than the European concept of transfer of undertakings. Nevertheless, the relevant provisions of the Labour Act have often been evaded in practice, especially when it comes to the application of the principle of preserving employment. A large number of employees were dismissed shortly before or soon after the transfer of undertaking in order to make the restructuring easier. This was a particularly serious problem be-

---

transfer of undertaking, on the effects that the change of employer will have on employees. Employers must review the relevant issues with the trade union in case the employees ask them to. The violation of the information procedure may result in compensation for damages, or in decisions that are unfavourable to the employees remaining without effect, and, exceptionally, in the transfer of undertakings remaining without effect. Tiziano Treu, *Italy* (2016), 122.

91 Brian Napier, "Dismissal – The New I. L. O. Standards" (1983) 1 ILJ, 25.

92 For example, this could include confirmation of the employer's obligation to notify all employees of the change at a meeting, in which they could elect representatives to participate in consultations. Sandra Laleta, *Prestanak ugovora o radu* (2011), 254.

cause company restructuring was established as one of the "basic leverages of transition" due to the tendency towards higher profitability, better use of the means of production, more rational management and so forth.

Abuses of prerogatives by employers in the event of a transfer of undertakings were facilitated due to the content of certain legal provisions on changes of employer, which have not been upgraded since. This primarily stands for the inability to reliably identify the cases that may qualify as a change of employer, as well as for the absence of clear rules on the status of employees who do not want to continue working for the new employer. For some of these issues, the case law could, even before any intervention by the legislature, offer answers in terms of shaping the term "change of employer" and reviewing the status of employees who were not dismissed by the transferor, although they (explicitly or tacitly) expressed their desire not to continue working for the new employer.

When it comes to the ban on deterioration of the working conditions, there is a need in Serbian law to regulate the issue of the "competition" of the collective agreements, which exists due to the obligation of the transferee to implement the collective agreement concluded by the transferor. Special attention should be paid to the solution stating that the obligation to preserve working conditions exists even when the transferor did not enter into a collective agreement and instead established the rights of employees with a unilateral act (labour rulebook). Such a solution is almost unique in comparative law and represents a valuable contribution to the protection of individual rights of employees in the event of transfers of undertakings, despite the limited duration of that protection. This rule has limited effect due to the lack of influence on the creation of new labour norms. This is because the principle *in favor laborem* does not prevent employers and trade unions, when entering into a new collective agreement (which the legislator prefers), from adopting norms less favourable for employees than the norms contained in the collective agreement entered into with the transferor, or in the transferor's labour rulebook.

On the other hand, the Serbian Labour Act does not regulate the issue of liability for employees' claims due before the change of employer, nor is there consistent and uniform case law regarding this issue. This important issue should be regulated, after reviewing and weighing all the advantages and disadvantages of the rule on exclusive or (unlimited and limited) joint and several liability, from the perspective of the need to protect the weaker party in the employment relationship, and from the perspective of the need to make certain status changes disagreeable (unappealing) for companies, due to certain obligations. This also brings up the need to try and prevent abuse that occurs in practice when the transferor establishes a daughter company and transfers the undertaking to such a company, which then (as a transferee) dissolves due to bankruptcy, and the bankruptcy estate does not have sufficient funds for payment of employees' claims.

Employees' protection from transfer-related dismissal is a delicate issue in the system of protection of employees' rights in the event of a change of employer. The most powerful instruments for defending job security are the rules on termination of employment by the employer, which state that termination of employment represents a last resort, to be used only after having exhausted all other measures, as evidenced by the fact that one of the objectives of labour law is, in fact, the stability of open-ended employment contracts.[93] Therefore, employment security appears as an important segment of employees' protection in case of transfer of undertakings due to the need to prevent loss of jobs every time there is a change of employer. The rule on the transfer of employment contracts does not assume that the transferee cannot initiate, after certain status changes, the amendment or even termination of employment contracts. The principle of employment preservation will no longer protect the employees after the amendment has been made. In this regard, the need for further improvements to Serbian labour legislation in order to adopt clearer and more reliable rules on the protection of employees from dismissal can be noted, in order to enable the employees to continue to work for the transferee under the same conditions and to be protected from the dismissal exclusively or predominantly motivated by the transfer of undertakings, particularly when termination of employment is initiated shortly before or immediately after the transfer.

Finally, there is a need to supplement and strengthen the protection of individual employees' rights on the collective level. The rules on information and consultation of employees should be improved, through legal texts or case law, by establishing the moment of initiation of consultations, by determining the method of selecting representatives of employees in enterprises in which there is no representative trade union and by establishing effective and deterring penalties for employers who violate this collective right of employees.

Employees in Serbia would be able to count on better protection if the aforementioned rules were clearer and more reliable, and if other rules would adapt to the changes in the world of work and the developmental needs of society, to which labour legislation needs to be more sensitive.

---

93 Arnaud Martinon, *Essai sur la stabilité du contrat de travail à durée indéterminée* (2005), 30.

Nevertheless, such contributions of labour legislation to the development of Serbian society must not result in excessive employment insecurity or violation of the basic economic and social rights of employees, which are especially jeopardized due to the high unemployment rate and the fact that employers exert a much greater influence over employees than entitled by the law. All the more so due to the fact that social partnership in Serbia is underdeveloped and access to social justice is difficult, because, among other things, labour inspection is burdened with numerous problems, the most significant of which is its modest financial resources, as well as the low number and insufficient training of inspectors. A contributing factor is also the unclear structure of the inspectors' jurisdiction, which often results in cases being designated as outside of their jurisdiction. On the other hand, most of the labour disputes are solved before the court (general courts), in lawsuits that last around four years on average. The case law in the field of the protection of employees' rights in the event of transfers of undertakings is inappropriately developed and quite heterogeneous, while judges do not recognize the importance of the interpretative use of European labour law. Apart from this, the potential that the peaceful resolution of labour disputes can have on establishing and maintaining social peace is not being used nearly enough, which only increases the importance of improving the legal solutions in the field.

Bibliography

Čedanka Andrić, "Protection of Employees' Rights in the Processes of Companies Restructuring in Serbia: Views from the Trade Unions", in Ljubinka Kovačević, Mirjana Radović (eds.), *Restructuring of Companies and Protection of Employees' Rights: Views from the EU, Austria, Serbia and Macedonia — Collection of Extended Abstracts of Contributions Presented at the International Conference Held at the University of Belgrade Faculty of Law on March 2nd 2017* (University of Belgrade Faculty of Law, Belgrade, 2017), 66.

Roger Blanpain, *Belgium* (Wolters Kluwer, The Hague, 2012).

Roger Blanpain, *European Labour Law* (13th edition, Kluwer Law International, The Hague/London/New York, 2012).

Vlajko Brajić (ed.), *Radno pravo u praksi: Priručnik sudske prakse* (Službeni list SFRJ, Belgrade, 1974).

Commission Report on Council Directive 2001/23/EC of 12 March 2001 on the approximation of the laws of the Member States relating to the safeguarding of employees' rights in the event of transfers of undertakings, businesses or parts of undertakings or businesses [SEC(2007) 812], COM/2007/0334 fin.

Nicola Countouris and Wanjiru Njoya, "2001/23/EC: Transfer of Undertakings", in Monika Schlachter (ed.), *EU Labour Law: A Commentary* (Wolters Kluwer, The Hague, 2014), 425.

Marija Dragićević, "Odgovornost za dospela potraživanja iz radnog odnosa u slučaju promene poslodavca", in Olga Jović-Prlainović (ed.), *Nacionalno i međunarodno pravo – aktuelna pitanja i teme* (Pravni fakultet Univerziteta u Prištini sa privremenim sedištem u Kosovskoj Mitrovici, Kosovska Mitrovica, 2017), 335.

Borivoje Gajić, "Solidarna odgovornost i statusna promena privrednog društva" (2016) 3 BVKS, 153.

Ivana Grgurev, *Croatia* (Wolters Kluwer, The Hague, 2013).

Zbigniew Hajn and Leszek Mitrus, *Poland* (Wolters Kluwer, The Hague, 2016).

Bob Hepple, "European Rules on Dismissal Law" (1996-1997) CLLJ, 208.

A-C. Hartzén, N. Hős, F. Lecomte, C. Marzo, B. Mestre, H. Olbrich and S. Fuller, *The Right of the Employee to Refuse to be Transferred: A Comparative and Theoretical Analysis*, EUI Working Paper LAW No. 2008/20 (European University Institute, Florence, 2008), 28.

Zoran M. Ivošević and Milan Z. Ivošević, *Komentar Zakona o radu* (Službeni glasnik, Belgrade, 2006).

Senad Jašarević, "Harmonizacija prava i prakse u oblasti participacije zaposlenih – Srbija i EU" (2011) 3 ZRPFNS, 379.

Predrag Jovanović, "Putevi i stranputice industrijske demokratije u Srbiji", in Etelka Korpič Horvat and Darja Senčur Peček (eds), *Tendence v razvoju delovnega prava* (Inštitut za delovna razmerja in socijalno varnost pri Pravni fakulteti Univerze v Mariboru, Maribor, 2009), 18.

Jeff Kenner, *EU Employment Law: From Rome to Amsterdam and Beyond* (Hart Publishing, Oxford/Portland, Oregon, 2003).

Ljubinka Kovačević, *Pravna subordinacija u radnom odnosu i njene granice* (Pravni fakultet Univerziteta u Beogradu, Belgrade, 2013).

Sandra Laleta, *Prestanak ugovora o radu*, Ph.D. dissertation (University of Zagreb Faculty of Law, Zagreb, 2011).

Branko Lubarda, *Evropsko radno pravo* (CID, Podgorica, 2004).

Branko Lubarda, *Radno pravo. Rasprava o dostojanstvu na radu i socijanom dijalogu* (Pravni fakultet Univerziteta u Beogradu, Belgrade, 2012).

Arnaud Martinon, *Essai sur la stabilité du contrat de travail à durée indéterminée* (Dalloz, Paris, 2005).

John McMullen, "Re-structuring and TUPE" (2012) 3 ILJ, 358.

Brian Napier, "Dismissal – The New I.L.O. Standards" (1983) 1 ILJ, 25.

Ruth Nielsen, *European Labour Law* (DJØF Publishing, Copenhagen, 2000).

Jean Pélissier, "Les restructurations d'entreprises et leur effets sur l'emploi" (1990) 1 RIDC, 154.

Jean Pélissier, Alain Supiot and Antoine Jeammaud, *Droit du travail* (21e édition, Dalloz, Paris, 2002).

Jean Pélissier, Gilles Auzero and Emmanuel Dockès, *Droit du travail* (27e édition, Dalloz, Paris, 2013).

Mirjana Radović, "Odgovornost društva sticaoca za obaveze društva prenosioca kod statusnih promena podele i izdvajanja", in Vuk Radović (ed.), *Usklađivanje poslovnog prava Srbije sa pravom Evropske unije* (Pravni fakutet Univeriteta u Beogradu, Belgrade, 2017), 145.

Mirjana Radović, "Odgovornost sticaoca za obaveze prenosioca u slučaju prenosa preduzeća" (2017) 4-6 PIP, 95.

Lenia Samuel, *Droits sociaux fondamentaux: Jurisprudence de la Charte sociale européenne* (2e édition, Editions du Conseil de l'Europe, Strasbourg, 2002).

Guiseppe Santoro-Passarelli, "The Transfer of Undertaking: Striking a Balance Between Individual Workers' Rights and Business Needs" (2007) 3 IJCLLIR, 325.

Darja Senčur Peček, "Aktualna vprašanja spremembe delodalajca" (2010) 2-3 DID, 312.

Darja Senčur Peček, "Sprememba delodajalca", in Nataša Belopavlovič, Barbara Kresal, Katarina Kresal Šoltes and Darja Senčur Peček (eds.), *Zakon o delovnih razmerjih s komentarjem* (GV Založba, Ljubljana, 2016).

Nicola Smit, "A Chronicle of Issues Raised in the Course of Dismissals by the Transferor and/or Transferee in Circumstances Involving the Transfer of an Undertaking" (2005) ILJJ, 1882.

Stalno radno telo Socijalno-ekonomskog saveta za ekonomska pitanja, *Efekti privatizacije u Srbiji* (Socijalno ekonomski savet Republike Srbije – Solidar suisse/ Swiss Labour Assistance SLA – Kancelarija u Srbiji, Belgrade, 2011).

Tiziano Treu, *Italy* (Wolters Kluwer, The Hague, 2016).

Bradley Workman-Davies, "The Right of Employers to Dismiss Employees in the Context of Business Transfers – An Analysis of the Automatically Unfair Dismissal Provisions of the Labour Relations Act" (2007) ILJSA, 2137.

Regulations and case law

Council Directive 2001/23/EC of 12 March 2001 on the approximation of the laws of the Member States relating to the safeguarding of employees' rights in the event of transfers of undertakings, businesses or parts of undertakings or businesses (*Official Journal* L 82, 22.03.2001, 16-20).

Act on Privatization (OJRS, no. 38/01, 18/03, 45/05, 123/07, 123/07, 30/10, 93/12, 119/12, 51/14, 52/14).

Labour Act (OJRS, no. 24/05, 61/05, 54/09, 32/13, 75/14, 13/17, 113/17, 95/18).

Act on Scientific Research Activities (OJRS, no. 110/05, 50/06, 18/10, 112/15).

Act on Associations (OJRS, no. 51/09, 99/11).

Act on Bankruptcy (OJRS, no. 104/09, 99/11, 71/12, 83/14, 113/27).

Act on Endowments and Funds (OJRS, no. 88/10, 99/11).

Act on Sports (OJRS, no. 24/11, 99/11).

Act on Companies (OJRS, no. 36/11, 99/11, 5/15, 44/18, 95/18).

Act on Cooperatives (OJRS, no. 112/15).

Act on Public Companies (OJRS, no. 15/16).

Decision on Establishing the Program for Dealing with Redundancies in the Process of Privatization for 2015, 2016, 2017, 2018 and 2019, OJRS, no. 9/15, 84/15, 109/15, 16/16, 82/16, 5/17, 92/17, 29/18, 59/18, 3/19.

Decision of the Constitutional Court of the Republic of Serbia IU number 44/2008, of 18 December 2008 (OJRS, no. 9/09).

Opinion of the Ministry of Labour and Social Policy, no. 001-00-787/2010-02, of 29 October 2010.

Case 19/83 07.02.1985, *Knud Wendelboe and others v. L.J. Music ApS, in liquidation*, ECR 1985, 00457.

Case 237/84, 15.04.1986, *Commission of the European Communities v. Kingdom of Belgium*, ECR 1986, 1247.

Joined cases 144 and 145/87, 05.05.1988, *Harry Berg and Johannes Theodorus Maria Busschers v. Ivo Martin Besselsen*, ECR 1988, 02559.

Case C/319-94, 12.03.1998, *Jules Déthier Équipement SA v. Jules Dassy and Sovam SPRL*, ECR 1998, I-1061.

Case C-343/98, 14.09.2000, *Renato Collino and Luisella Chiappero v. Telecom Italia SpA*, *Reports of Cases*, 2000, I-06659.

List of abbreviations

BVKS	*Bilten Vrhovnog kasaciong suda*
CLLJ	*Comparative Labour Law Journal*
DID	*Delavci in delodajalci*
ECR	*European Court Reports*
IJCLLIR	*International Journal of Comparative Labour Law and Industrial Relations*
ILJ	*Industrial Law Journal*
ILJJ	*Industrial Law Journal Juta*
ILJSA	*Industrial Law Journal (South Africa)*
OJRS	*Official Journal of the Republic of Serbia*
PIP	*Pravo i privreda*
RD	*Recueil Dalloz*
RIDC	*Revue internationale de droit comparé*
ZRPFNS	*Zbornik radova Pravnog fakulteta u Novom Sadu*

Transfer of Undertakings and Protection of Employees' Individual Rights in the Republic of Macedonia

*Todor Kalamatiev**
*Aleksandar Ristovski**

Summary

A. Introduction

Work that is subject to each individual employment relationship (i.e. employment contract) is of a strict personal and legal nature (*intuitu personae*), which means that nobody else can perform the work on behalf of and on

---

* Professor at Ss "Cyril and Methodius" University in Skopje, "Iustinianus Primus" Faculty of Law.

* Assistant Professor at Ss "Cyril and Methodius" University in Skopje, "Iustinianus Primus" Faculty of Law.

the account of the employee. Hence, one of the most substantial elements of the employment relationship, without which the employment relationship would not exist, constitutes the element of "personal connection".[1] The *personal connection* means that work that is subject to the employment contract cannot be taken over, nor can it be handed over to another person, apart from the person who has established the employment relationship.[2] However, the *personal connection*, as a substantial element of the employment relationship, first and foremost refers to one of its parties, the *employee*.[3] This is so because the work that is the subject of the employment relationship, i.e., the employment relationship itself, can be temporarily or permanently continued with a party (on behalf of the employer) that is different than the one with which the employment relationship was established, i.e., the party who was the initial subject of the employment contract (situation of a change of employer).

The matter related to the change of employer and the consequences of this change for the employees, was subject to regulation in Macedonian legislation for the first time with the Law on Labour Relations in 2005 (Article 68).[4] The regulation of this matter is first and foremost an expression of the thorough changes in the Macedonian economy that are a consequence of the privatisation of undertakings with state ownership, the different types of restructuring of the companies in terms of increasing their competitiveness on the market and, finally, the harmonisation of Macedonian labour legislation with the EU "acquis communautaire". The harmonisation of the Macedonian labour legislation with the EU "acquis" repre-

1 Todor Kalamatiev and Aleksandar Ristovski, "The Concept of 'Employee': The Position in the Republic of Macedonia" in Bernd Waas and Guus Heerma van Voos (eds.), *Restatement of Labour Law in Europe*, Volume I (2017), 220.

2 Andrej Frimerman and Aleksandar Nikolič, *Samoupravni Radni Odnosi* (1980) 14.

3 In the legal doctrine of British labour law, the element of "personal connection" can be placed in the context of the opposite side of the employment contract, the employer. The employer can be a natural person or legal entity (corporate entity). If the employer has the status of a corporate entity, through the "personal connection", it could be treated as an "anthropomorphic" equivalent to the "human archetype", i.e. of the employer natural person. In that context, any change in the employer's side (as a subject of the employment contract) could lead to a change in the employment contract, rather than to its "automatic" transfer to the new employer. See: Mark Freedland and Nicola Kountouris, *The Legal Construction of Personal Work Relations*, (2011) 253.

4 See Тодор Каламатиев, Љубинка Ковачевиќ.Љ and Александар Ристовски, Заштита на правата на вработените во случај на промена на работодавачот во Република Македонија и Република Србија (компаративна анализа), *Деловно Право* (Година XVIII), 220.

sents the last, but not the least, important reason that changes were induced in the positive law of the Republic of Macedonia. Indeed, it is the basic reason because of which amendments and supplements were introduced to the Law in 2010[5] in the section referring to the protection of the employees' rights in the event of an employer change following the Directive 2001/23/EC on safeguarding of employees' rights in the event of transfer of undertakings, businesses, parts of undertakings or businesses (or so-called Transfer of Undertakings Directive or Acquired Rights Directive). Apart from the numerous critics and drawbacks, these amendments and supplements to the Law are still valid and envisage an important part of the rules for the protection of employees in the events of transfers of undertakings, i.e. changes of employer.

B. *Notion of "Transfer of Undertakings" and Scope of the Rules for the Safeguarding of Employees' Rights in the Event of a Change of the Employer*

Transfers of undertakings, i.e., the change of an employer, occurs in a situation when two essential assumptions are fulfilled: first, the existence of any of the legal reasons (basis) in order for the transfer to occur; and second, the determination of the subject of such a transfer and the maintenance of its identity after the transfer.[6] This means that the protection of the employees' rights in the event of a transfer of undertakings is dependent on the fulfilment of these two cumulative conditions.[7]

I. *Legal Reasons for Transfer of the Undertaking (Cases of Change of Employer)*

According to the Directive 2001/23/EC "the transfer of undertaking/part of the undertaking/business/part of business" can be the result of a legal transfer or merger.[8] Hence, the Directive 2001/23/EC and its provisions concerning the safeguarding of the employment of employees and the preser-

---

5 See Law on amendments and supplements to the Law on Labour Relations, "Official Gazette of the Republic of Macedonia No. 124, from 20.03.2010".

6 Fernando Valdés Dal-Ré, "Transfers of Undertakings: An Experience of Clashes and Harmonies between Community Law and National Legal Systems", in Silvana Sciarra (ed.), *Labour Law in the Courts, National Judges and European Court of Justice* (2001) 193.

7 See Љубинка Ковачевић, *Ваљани разлози за отказ уговора о раду* (2016), 481.

8 Council Directive 2001/23/EC, paragraph 1 (a).

vation of their acquired rights will be applied in all cases that will result in an agreed change of the employer (legal entity or natural person) who is responsible for performing the business activities and, as a consequence, will take over the responsibilities of the "employer" regarding the employees in the undertaking that is subject to the transfer. This means that every legal act on the basis of which there is a transfer of the function of the employer may be encompassed by the directive and its scope of regulation. The nature of the legal transaction, i.e., the case on the basis of which one employer is substituted by another, has no meaning in the determination of the existence of the "transfer".[9]

Being willing to "harmonise" with Directive 2001/23/EC, the Law on Labour Relations of the Republic of Macedonia (Закон за работните односи)[10] establishes the legal reasons for transfers of undertakings that, first and foremost, do not correspond with the legal terminology that is subject to regulation of the *Law on Trade Companies* (Закон за трговските друштва),[11] and then with other regulations in the field of broader contract law. The Law on Labour Relations envisions the "*status changes*"[12] as "cases" on the basis of which a change of employer may occur on one side, as well as the "*legal transfers*" or "*mergers*"[13] on the other. From the point of view of the Macedonian legal system, it seems that the notion of "legal transfer" is too general and can include different ways of transfer of undertakings, i.e. different cases of a change of an employer, while the notion "merger" is one of the possible types of status changes that are present in Macedonian company law. In pursuit of greater clarity in the legal reasons for transfers of undertakings and their application in the Macedonian legal system, we provide the following "framework" legal reasons (basis): status changes and legal acts.

---

9 Sylvaine Laulom, "The European Court of Justice in the Dialogue on Transfers of Undertakings: A Fallible Interlocutor?" in Silvana Sciarra (ed.), *Labour Law in the Courts, National Judges and European Court of Justice* (2001) 150.

10 Law on Labour Relations (Закон за работните односи), "Official Gazette of the Republic of Macedonia No. 62/05".

11 Law on Trade Companies (Закон за трговските друштва), "Official Gazette of the Republic of Macedonia No. 28/04".

12 See Закон за работните односи, Чл. 68, став 1.

13 See Закон за работните однос,Чл. 68-а.

1. *Status Changes of Companies (Changes in the Organisation and Management of the Business of the Employer)*

In the Republic of Macedonia, status changes are subject to regulation by the Law on Trade Companies. This law identifies three main forms of status changes: accessions, mergers and divisions.[14] Status changes of companies are the first major legal reason that can lead to a change of the employer (transfer of undertakings). In all of the status changes, a transfer of the assets and liabilities of the company inflicted by the status change takes place, but, unlike in some cases of accessions or mergers where a universal transfer of all assets and liabilities takes place, others (certain forms of divisions) can feature a particular transfer of part of the assets and liabilities of the company.

The Law on Trade Companies is a material law that regulates the possible types of status changes, while the Law on Labour Relations constitutes a material law that regulates the legal consequences for the employees deriving from the status changes which result in a change of the employer. In this vein, the Law on Labour Relations stipulates that *all the rights, obligations and responsibilities of the employment contract and employment relationship* are transferred to the new employer in all events when the status changes occur.[15] In the major part of the events of status changes that lead to transfers of undertakings (for example accessions, mergers, divisions of companies via separation), the holder of the undertaking ceases to exist (without undergoing a liquidation procedure) and is replaced by another holder.

This kind of universal succession of assets and liabilities of the companies is not present only in the case of legal entities (i.e., trade companies), but also with natural persons (i.e. sole proprietors, craftsmen and other self-employed persons) as a consequence of their death. If, after the death of the employer natural person, his company/business is transferred to his legal successors, then these successors acquire the function of the "employer" in relation to the employees. According to the Law on Labour Relations, *the employment contract shall cease to be valid upon death of the employer natural person*.[16] The Law on Labour Relations, on one hand, clearly states "death" of the employer natural person as a legal ground for *ex lege* termination of the employment relationship, but, on the other hand, does

---

14 Закон за трговските друштва, Чл. 3, став 1, точка 47.

15 Закон за работните односи, Чл. 68, став 1.

16 See Закон за работните односи, Чл. 62, став 1, точка 2.

not regulate the "inheritance of the undertaking" as a possible basis for transferring the employment contracts of the employees to the legal successors of the employer after his death. This legal state imposes dilemmas regarding the "continuity" or "discontinuity" (termination) of the employment relationship of the employees whose employer natural person died, even though the company, i.e., the business he owned, "continued to live" through his legal successors.

2. *Legal Acts (Changes in the Undertaking's Ownership)*

Legal acts (legal transactions) are the second major legal reason that can lead to a change of the employer (transfer of the undertaking). The change of the employer can occur as a consequence of several different legal acts, such as: *sale of the undertaking, giving the undertaking as a gift, acquiring shares that are stock in the company, venture, lease, concession*, etc.[17]

The Law on Labour Relations regulates only one of the possible cases of a change of employer that is a consequence of a "legal transaction": the lease, i.e., rent. In that regard, the Law stipulates that

> "*if the employer on the basis of a legal transaction (lease, rent), temporarily transfers the overall or part of the business to another employer, after the termination of the validity of the legal transaction, the employees shall again be transferred to the previous employer or to the new employer transferee of the business*".[18]

In this case, the Law on Labour Relations refers to a temporary transfer of the business or a part of the business from the original employer to another employer on the basis of a *lease contract*. With the lease, the undertaking/part of the undertaking, business/part of the business subject to the lease is ceded to another employer (transferee) for use for a determined period of time. The new employer (transferee) continues to perform the same business activity that was performed by his predecessor.[19] Analysing the applicable provision of the Law on Labour Relations that regulates the legal destiny of the employment contracts of the employees after the expiration of

17 Domagoj Franjo Frntič, Iris Govič Pentič, Darije Hanzelak, Darko Milkovič, Nataša Novakovič and Krešimir Rožman, *Detaljni Komentar Zakona o Radu* (2017) 790.

18 Закон за работните односи, чл.68, став 5.

19 See Васил Мръчков, КрасимираСредкова and Атанас Василев, *Коментар на Кодекса на труда*, (12 издание, 2016), 379.

the lease of the business or a part of the business, it seems that the Law gives the possibility of choice, whether or not the employment relationship of the employees, after the termination of the lease, will be *again returned to the old employer* or *they will continue to exist at the new employer.* This legal solution is unclear and opens several dilemmas. First, the following question arises: what if the old and new employer, in the lease contract, did not agree about the legal destiny of the employment contracts of the employees included in the transfer? Second, it must be taken into consideration that the employment contracts of the employees are a "constitutive part" of the business itself or of the part of the business of the employer, which is subject to transfer via the lease contract. It means that, by transferring the business or part of the business, the employment contracts of the employees are also transferred so, after the lease has expired, the business will be returned to the previous employer, and, therefore, it would be justified to expect that the employment contracts of the employees that were transferred to the leasee will also be returned to their original employer. In practice, it can happen that the *number of employment contracts* that were in force in the moment after the expiration of the lease contract and the return of the undertaking/part of the undertaking, business/part of the business belonging to the old employer, is not the same as the *number of employment contracts* that existed in the moment when the transfer was carried out. The proportion of the number of employment contracts before and after the lease can be determined in the lease contract concluded between the lessor and the leasee. In our view, the interpretation on the basis of which the old employer (transferor) would not be obliged to take over the employment contracts of the "new" employees that established a "new" employment relationship with the new employer (transferee) during the lease of the undertaking, would be more proper. The obligation of the old employer for taking back, i.e., returning to himself, would refer only to those employees whose employment contracts were included in the transfer of the undertaking/part of the undertaking or business/part of the business.

II. Determination of the Subject of Transfer and Maintenance of its Identity

If a comparison is made between the "subject of transfer" regulated with the Directive 2001/23/EC (which is the *undertaking/part of the undertaking, business/part of the business*)[20] and the notion "subject of transfer" according to the Law on Labour Relations (which is *a trade company or parts of a trade company*),[21] we will face an obvious terminological and crucial non-compliance between these two acts. The trade company is and can only be a subject to law, and not an object that is to be put in a legal circulation and to be subject of transfer.[22] Such an object (subject) could only be the undertaking, defined as a collection of rights, assets and factual relations that have a property value and that belong to the trade business of the merchant, which is an entire and independent legal entity that can be put in circulation.[23] In short, the undertaking is a unity of property and people, a connection of capital and labour, under a sole management directed towards achieving the economic objectives that have been set by the owner. The part of the undertaking (organisational unit, the plant, etc.) contains all the elements that the undertaking also contains, but only in terms of that particular part. It is an organisational structure within the undertaking that can perform a certain economic activity (for example: a shop, atelier, restaurant, hotel, etc.).

The transfer of the employment contracts of the employees is dialectically related to the fulfilment of another cumulative condition, the condition of the "transferred undertaking to retain its identity" (i.e., economic wholeness). In this regard, Directive 2001/23/EC stipulates that a transfer of undertaking/part of an undertaking/business/part of a business is considered to be a transfer of an "*economic entity which retains its identity, meaning an organised grouping of resources which has the objective of pursuing an economic activity, whether or not that activity is central or ancillary*".[24] The transferred undertaking will retain its identity if the new employer continues or resumes carrying out the business that was previously performed by the former employer.[25] The existence of other circumstances should be taken into consideration too, without prejudice as to their "relative weight" and impact on the qualification of one transfer as "a transfer of undertaking

---

20 See Council Directive 2001/23/EC, Article 1, paragraph 1.

21 See Закон за работните односи, чл.68-а.

22 See Тито Беличанец и Даница Миладинова, Заштита на правата на работниците во случај на статусна промена или пренесување на претпријатие, бизнис или дел од бизнис од едно во друго трговско друштво, *Деловно Право*, (Година XII), 78-79.

23 Закон за трговските друштва, Чл. 3, став 1, точка 40.

24 See Council Directive 2001/23/EC, paragraph 1 (b).

25 See Roger Blanpain, *European Labour Law* (2012), 759.

that retained its identity".[26] In any case, the basic prerequisite for having continuity in employment is to have continuity in the performance of the business activities that fall in the "hands" of the new, changed employer.[27]

Macedonian labour legislation follows the model of Directive 2001/23/EC and is at least formally harmonised with the legal assumption of the directive that the transfer of employment contracts of the employees as a result of the transfer of the undertaking depends *inter alia* on the retaining of the identity of the transferred undertaking. The Law on Labour Relations stipulates that the transfer of the trade company or part of the trade company means a transfer of an economic entity "*which retains its identity, meaning an organised grouping of resources which has the objective of pursuing an economic activity, whether or not that activity is central or ancillary*".[28]

A crucial question in terms of the transfer of undertakings and maintenance of their identity is solving the dilemmas coming from the ever expanding business practice of "contracting out" of services (or outsourcing) in EU Member States.[29] From the point of view of EU labour law, the main problem of this business practice is the application or non-application of the regulations governing transfer of undertakings and their consequences for employees in the event of "transfer of service activities which may take place without any transfer of tangible or intangible assets from the transfer-

26 Such circumstances may include: the type of undertaking or business; the fact whether or not the tangible assets of the business (such as buildings or movable property) were transferred; the value of the tangible assets at the time of the transfer; whether or not the majority of the employees were taken over by the new employer; whether or not the customers were transferred and the degree of similarity between the activities carried on before or after the transfer and the period, if any, for which those activities were suspended (See: Case 24/85, 18.03.1986, Jozef Maria Antonius Spijkers v. Gebroeders Benedik Abattoir CV et Alfred Benedik en Zonen BV, ECR 1119).

27 Gwyneth Pitt, *Employment Law* (1997) 242.

28 See Закон за работните односи, Чл. 68-а, став 2.

29 At the time when the Directive 2001/23/EC was adopted, the business practice of a "transfer of the performance of certain service-providing activities to external contractors" (for example, cleaning, catering, security, etc.) or so called "contracting out" was not present to a large extent in the business and production activities of European companies. However, at the end of the 1980s, it started to take a more significant place in the strategies of "vertical disintegration" of companies as a consequence of their interest in reducing the costs and increasing hiring and firing flexibility.

or to the transferee".[30] Evidently, this type of "outsourcing" refers to the contracting out of labour-intensive service activities (such as cleaning, catering, security and similar activities). In this regard, in the "*Schmidt*" case, the ECJ found that a key criterion, on the basis of which it was established that there is a "transfer of the undertaking which retained its identity", was that the activity (cleaning and maintenance) subject to the transfer retained its "essential identity", while the employer successor, taking over the activity, continued to perform the same or similar activities as those performed by his predecessor. Two conditions have bearing here. First, the transfer includes an ancillary (lateral) activity of the employer transferor which is not necessarily related to the facilities in which his central activity is performed. Second, the transfer is not accompanied by transfer of tangible assets nor to a larger number of employees. In this specific case, the transfer of the employment contract of the affected employee and the continuity of the employment are preserved.[31] Hence, the basic criterion for justifying the transfer in this particular case as a "transfer of an undertaking" is that the activity "cleaning and maintenance" existed and was carried out *before* and *after* the realisation of the transfer.[32]

The second cardinal case in which the ECJ reviewed its stance taken in the "*Schmidt*" case to the greater extent is the "*Süzen*" case. In the "*Süzen*" case, the ECJ determined that Directive 2001/23/EC *shall not be applied* in the event when one employer who had entrusted the cleaning of his premises to another employer terminated the contract with that employer and concluded a new contract with a third employer for performing similar work, without any concomitant transfer of *tangible or intangible assets* or *transfer of the majority of the employees in terms of their numbers and skills*.[33] The criterion of "taking over the majority of the employees" not only refers to the number of employees taken over by the new employer, but also to the skills they possess. Hence, it would be sufficient to take over two employees from an undertaking with a total workforce subject to transfer of ten employees, if the employees who have been taken over indeed have suitable skills, the application of which is essential for performing the transferred activity. Taking over these employees would lead to an automat-

---

30 See Sylvaine Laulom, "The European Court of Justice in the Dialogue on Transfers of Undertakings: A Fallible Interlocutor?" in Silvana Sciarra (ed.), *Labour Law in the Courts, National Judges and European Court of Justice* (2001) 153.

31 See Case C-392/92, 14.04.1994, *Christel Schmidt*.

32 Malcolm Sargeant and David Lewis, *Employment Law* (2010) 315.

33 See Case C-13/95, 11.03.1997, *Ayse Süzen*, ECR I-1259.

ic transfer of the employment contracts to the remaining employees employed in the undertaking/business that is subject to the transfer.[34]

In short, a primary criterion for the application of the transfer of undertakings regulations is the existence of a transfer of tangible or intangible assets (property) from the employer transferor to the employer transferee. If in the specific case, no such transfer (as in the cases of transferring labour-intensive activities) takes place, the employment contracts of the employees will be nevertheless transferred to the new employer if he takes over a "substantial" part of the workforce of his predecessor.[35] This will particularly apply to those economic sectors that encompass economic activities which are not composed of specific operating resources (for example, catering, maintenance and cleaning, security), and the takeover of the workforce will be a sufficient criterion that will lead to a transfer. In other words, in labour-intensive sectors, the takeover of the employees is a decisive criterion for the existence of a transfer.[36]

The business practice of "contracting out" and its legal consequences in relation to employees is not an "open subject for discussion" only on the level of the European Communities. They are unsolvable enigmas in the Macedonian legal system, even though at first sight, the Law on Labour Relations seems to prescribe certain directions in favour of them being solved. To this end, the Law stipulates that in the event of the

> "*transfer of activities of a trade company or parts of a trade company or in case of transfer of tasks or part of them from the employer transferor to another employer transferee, the rights and obligations deriving from employment shall be completely transferred to the employer transferee to whom the transfer is made. The transfer of the rights and obligations deriving from the employment relationship takes place regardless of the legal reason and regardless of the fact whether the ownership rights are transferred to the transferee or not. The employer transferee, as an employer, is authorized to continue to perform the tasks or activities of the previous employer or to perform similar tasks and activities. The tasks and activities related to production or services provision or similar activities offered by the legal entity or natural*

34 Antonio Lo Faro, "Judicial Developments of EC Social Policy and Intra-Community Institutional Dialogues: How to Define a 'Legal Transfer'" in Silvana Sciarra (ed.), *Labour Law in the Courts, National Judges and European Court of Justice* (2001), 224.

35 Ibidem, 223.

36 See Sylvaine Laulom, "The European Court of Justice in the Dialogue on Transfers of Undertakings: A Fallible Interlocutor?" in Silvana Sciarra (ed.), *Labour Law in the Courts, National Judges and European Court of Justice* (2001) 168.

person on their behalf and on their responsibility in the facilities or premises determined for their performance shall be considered as tasks or activities of the employer".[37]

With this provision, the Law on Labour Relations (purposefully or de facto) makes a clear distinction between the notion "*undertaking/part of the undertaking/business/part of the business*" that refers to the performance of the central or ancillary activity of the employer and the notion "*activity/ task*" that refers to the performance of certain stable and regular production or service-providing activities that are not central nor ancillary activities of the employer and that can be "outsourced". However, on the other hand, the consequences from the transfer of the "activity/task" in relation to the employees are identical to the consequences from the transfer of the "undertaking/part of the undertaking/business/part of the business". Both the first and second cases cause (or are supposed to cause) transfer of the employment contracts of the employees and safeguarding of their acquired rights. However, in practice, the legal consequences in relation to the employees that occur after the transfer of the activity/task has been realised are diametrically opposed to those stipulated in the Law on Labour Relations. Usually, in the event that the employer decides to "outsource" a certain activity or task to an external contractor (regardless whether or not the activity is capital-intensive or labour-intensive), the employment contracts of the employees who have been previously employed by the employer that organised the performance of the activity or task in question are *terminated*, or are *taken over by the new employer, but under different (deteriorated) conditions* than the conditions the employees previously had. *In the first case*, the employment contracts are terminated with a dismissal notice given by the employer due to business reasons; as a consequence of this dismissal, the employees acquire the right to a severance pay.[38] *In the second case*, the employees are taken over by another employer without vacancy announcements with whom they conclude a (new) employment contract for performing tasks suitable to their professional training and qualification.[39]

37 See Закон за работните односи, Чл. 68-а, став 4.

38 See Закон за работните односи, Чл. 97.

39 See Закон за работните односи, Чл. 96, став 1, точка 1.

C. *Safeguarding of Employment and Preservation of the Conditions of the Employment Relationship*

The principle of safeguarding of the employment relationships of employees and the preservation of their terms and conditions of employment in the event of a change of the employer is inspired by the idea of "legal succession" that has been known to civil and commercial law for centuries; later, this idea was also transmitted to labour law.[40] The basic rule inspired by Directive 2001/23/EC is that the *transferor's rights and obligations arising from a contract of employment or from an employment relationship existing on the date of a transfer shall, by reason of such transfer, be transferred to the transferee.*[41] This rule does not have an identical transposition within Macedonian labour legislation, but a conclusion can be drawn from several provisions of the Law on Labour Relations that the new employer (transferee) takes over all the rights and obligations deriving from the transferred employment contracts in an unchanged form and scope.[42] It is considered that the contracting parties (employees employed at the previous employer and the new employer) should not conclude new employment contracts, because those are not "new" contracts, but it is a transfer of their "old" contracts of employment which are automatically transferred to the new successor employer. The rights and obligations of the employees before and after the transfer of their employment contracts should be viewed as a whole. In this sense, the rights arising from the continuity of the employment relationship (i.e., the years of service) of the employees with both employers (the previous employer and its successor), such as the rights to severance pay and period of notice, are of particular importance. Additionally, the principle of "safeguarding the employment of the employees and the preservation of their employment conditions" entails all other rights that the employee had with the previous employer, including the rights to identical salary, salary structure and other material compensations that derive from the employment relationship.[43]

A criticism that can be directed towards the Macedonian legislature in the regulation of this part of the legal provisions regarding the transfer of undertakings is that the Law on Labour Relations did not determine the exact "*moment*" for the transfer of the employment contracts of the em-

40 See Васил Мръчков, *Трудово право*, (9 издание, 2015), 311.

41 See Council Directive 2001/23/EC, Article 3, para 1.

42 See Закон за работните односи, Чл 68, став 1; Чл. 68, став 2.

43 See Roger Blanpain, *European Labour Law* (2012) 783.

ployees. It only provides that *all the rights, obligations and responsibilities under the employment contract and the employment relationship shall be transferred to the new employer…*[44] From the point of view of Macedonian law, as a date of the transfer of the undertaking can be considered the date when the legal consequences of such a transfer occurred in accordance with the regulations that govern the legal reason on the basis of which the transfer was carried out (for example, *in the event of status changes the date of the transfer can be considered the date of the publication of the entry of the status change in the trade registry*).[45]

I. Consent of the Employee for the Transfer of the Employment Contract

The key question in the event of a transfer of an undertaking, i.e., the change of the employer, is the following: *whether the replacement of one employer with another causes an automatic (ex lege) transfer of the employment contracts of the employees, or the employees have the free disposition to "block" the transfer of their employment contracts to the new employer?* Directive 2001/23/EC does not give an explicit solution to this dilemma, so "part" of the answer to this question can be looked for in the approach of the ECJ. Compared to the decisions of some older cases (for example, the "Daddy's Dance Hall" case[46] or the "Berg" case)[47] in which the ECJ explicitly accepted the rule for the automatic transfer of employment contracts regardless of the will of the employees, in the "Katsikas" case[48] the Court alleviated its stance in favour of the discretion right of the employees to "object" to the transfer of their employment contracts. In this case, the European Court of Justice states that the rules for transfer

44 See Закон за работните односи, Чл. 68, став 1.

45 See Милан Недков and Тито Беличанец, *Право на Друштвата* (2008), 374.

46 In this case, the ECJ had the stance that "*the transfer of the employment contracts does not depend on the willingness of the contracting parties since it is subject to the interest of the public policy*". See: Case 324/86, 10.02.1988, Daddy's Dance Hall A/S ECR 739.

47 In this case, the ECJ ascertained that "*the change of employer brings an automatic transfer of the obligations of the employer, from the transferor to the transferee*". See: Joined Cases 144 and 145/87, 5.05.1988, Harry Berg and Johannes Theodorus Maria Busschers v. Ivo Martin Besselsen, ECR 2559.

48 See Joined Cases C-132/91, C-138/91 and C-139/91, Grigorios Katsikas, IRLR 179.

> "*must not oblige the employee to continue the employment relationship with the transferee*"[49] ... "*because such an obligation would jeopardize the fundamental rights of the employee, who must be free to choose his employer and cannot be obliged to work for an employer whom he has not freely chosen*".[50]

Apart from this stance (which to a greater extent is expected and acceptable), the court does not solve the essential dilemma as to "whether the employment contract or the employment relationship of the employee who has voluntarily refused the transfer of his employment contract to the transferee will continue to be applied with the original employer (transferor) or not". If it is considered that the employment contract "remains" with the transferor, can the employer terminate the contract or make a substantial change in the employment conditions of the employee without any founded reasons and as a "retaliation" for the objection of the employee to continue the employment relationship with the new employer? Instead of a solution to these dilemmas, the court left it up to the Member States to individually decide upon the "legal destiny" of the employment contracts concluded with the transferor. In reality, this situation could lead to three potential outcomes. The first (most desirable) outcome: when, despite the objection of the employee to the automatic transfer, his employment contract continues to exist with the original employer; the second (least desirable) outcome: when the objection of the employee would be seen as legitimate grounds for dismissal by the original employer and the third (compromised) outcome: when the objection of the employee to accepting the transfer could be treated as a termination of the employment contract on the employee's initiative.[51]

The Macedonian labour law system guarantees the principles of "voluntarity" and "consensuality" in employment relationships.[52] In this regard, in the event of a transfer, the refusal of employees to continue the employment relationship with a new employer is complementary with the principle of freedom of work and employment guaranteed by the Macedonian Constitution.[53] However, the Law on Labour Relations does not stipulate a single concrete provision with which the dilemmas arising from the "auto-

49 Case *Katsikas* v. *Konstantinidis*, paragraph (31).

50 Case *Katsikas* v. *Konstantinidis*, paragraph (32).

51 See Sylvaine Laulom, "The European Court of Justice in the Dialogue on Transfers of Undertakings: A Fallible Interlocutor?" in Silvana Sciarra (ed.), *Labour Law in the Courts, National Judges and European Court of Justice* (2001), 173.

52 Гзиме Старова, *Трудово Право*, (2005), 342.

53 Constitution of the Republic of Macedonia (Official Gazette of the Republic of Macedonia No. 52/92).

matic" (*ex lege*) transfer of the employment contract of the employees would be solved. It neither sets forth the obligation of the transferor to give *written notice* to the employees entailed with the "transfer" for the forthcoming transfer of their employment contracts to the transferee, nor does it prescribe a *term* within which all these employees would be able to give their consent for the transfer. In such circumstances, it is fully unclear what the outcome will be if the employees "explicitly" or "tacitly" refuse the transfer of their employment contracts to the new employer. The only provision of the Law on Labour Relations that implies a possible solution of the existing dilemmas is the provision with which the employee is guaranteed certain rights and benefits, even though he is the one terminating the employment contract and not the employer (*third outcome*). In that vein, the Law on Labour Relations stipulates *that if due to a change of the employer the rights under the employment contract deteriorate because of objective reasons and the employee therefore terminates the employment contract, the employee shall have the same rights (including the rights of a notice period and severance pay) as if the employment contract has been terminated for business reasons.*[54] However, we think that in the case of such an event, the employee should have proven that the "objection" to the transfer of the employment contract is motivated by the fact of a certain "deterioration of his rights" (for example, fundamental reduction of the amount of the salary that would be received from the new employer).

II. Prohibition of Dismissals

In most cases, transfers of undertakings are followed by dismissals of employees entailed in such transfers.[55] Hence, the provisions that govern the safeguarding of the employment of employees in the event of transfers inevitably envisage and regulate this situation. The legal framework with which the transfers are regulated refers to both the "prohibited" and "allowed" cases of termination of the employment contracts of the employees in question. In this regard, Directive 2001/23/EC "*prohibits*" the dismissals of employees, the basic reason for which is the transfer of the undertaking itself, but "*allows*" the dismissals due to economic, technical or organisa-

---

54 See: Закон за работните односи, Чл. 68, став 3.

55 See: Sylvaine Laulom, "The European Court of Justice in the Dialogue on Transfers of Undertakings: A Fallible Interlocutor?" in Silvana Sciarra (ed.), *Labour Law in the Courts, National Judges and European Court of Justice* (2001) 174.

tional reasons entailing changes in the workforce.[56] The prohibition of dismissal of the employees exists in all the events in which a "causal" link can be shown between the dismissal and the transfer of the undertaking.[57] This prohibition is binding for both the transferor (referring to the dismissals before the transfer date) and the transferee (referring to the dismissals after the date of the transfer of the undertaking). This means that if the employee was dismissed because of the "fact" that the undertaking has been transferred, this dismissal would be deemed illegal, regardless of whether or not the dismissal was given to the employee by the employer predecessor or the employer successor.[58] In reality, there is a very "thin" demarcation line between the prohibited (inadmissible) and the permitted (admissible) reasons for termination of the employment contracts of the employees in the event of transfer of undertakings. This is so, because when the transfer encompasses an undertaking which is experiencing economic difficulties, it can often be pre-conditioned by pre-rationalisation of the workforce in order for the transfer to take effect. In practice, this situation can lead to an abuse of the employment security of the employees because the old or the new employer (depending on the fact that one of them dismissed the employees) "formally" presents an "apparently" valid reason for dismissal (such as an economic, technical or organisational reason), but the "real" reason behind the dismissal of the employees is the restructuring of the company, i.e., the transfer of undertakings itself. When determining the real reasons for dismissal of the employees, the courts should take into consideration the objective circumstances that led to the dismissal. In this regard, they should solve the following dilemmas: "*whether in the concrete case, the employment contracts of the employees are terminated on a date that immediately precedes the date after the transfer of the undertaking has been made*" (in theory, it is thought that the further removed in time the dismissal is from the transfer, the less likely it is that the causal link will be established)[59] or "*whether after the transfer has been effectuated, the transferee employed the same persons whose employment contracts were terminated by the transferor*" is of great importance. If the answers to these questions are affirmative, there is a great probability that the transferor or the transferee ille-

56 See: Council Directive 2001/23, Article 4, paragraph 1.

57 See Gwyneth Pitt, *Employment Law*, (1997) 249.

58 See Domagoj Franjo Frntič, Iris Gović Pentič, Darije Hanzelak, Darko Milkovič, Nataša Novakovič and Krešimir Rožman, *Detaljni Komentar Zakona o Radu* (2017) 794.

59 See Gwyneth Pitt, *Employment Law* (1997) 249.

gally and unlawfully terminated the employment contracts of the employees entailed in the transfer of undertaking.

Macedonian labour legislation regulates the issue of "termination of the employment contracts in the event of transfer of undertakings" following the model of Directive 2001/23/EC. In this regard, the Law on Labour Relations stipulates that the *transfer of the trade company or parts of the trade company shall not by itself constitute a ground for dismissal of employees, except the dismissals from economic, technological or organizational reasons that entail staff changes*.[60] Analogous to European labour legislation, Macedonian labour legislation "prohibits" dismissals conducted with the sole reason being the transfer of the undertaking, but "allows" the dismissals based on business grounds on the initiative of the employer (predecessor or successor). Employees have the right to protection in the event of dismissals or in the case of deterioration of their acquired rights due to reasons which are connected to the transfer of undertakings, while the employers are responsible to indemnify for infringing the rights of the employees in such cases. This issue is more thoroughly regulated in Directive 2001/23/EC, which stipulates that *after the date of transfer, the transferor and the transferee shall be jointly and severally liable in respect of obligations which arose before the date of transfer from a contract of employment or an employment relationship existing on the date of the transfer*.[61] This means that if the employer predecessor illegally terminated the employment contracts of the employees due to reasons related to the transfer of the undertaking to the employer successor, the new employer is jointly and severally liable with his predecessor regarding the obligations that occurred until the date of the transfer of undertakings. Or, if the employer predecessor, on the date of the transfer, owed salary or another material compensation to the employees entailed with the transfer, the two employers (successor and predecessor) shall be jointly and severally liable for their indemnification. This means that the employees have a free disposition to decide which of the potential employers they will request indemnification from (from the employer predecessor, from the employer successor or from both).[62] Macedonian labour legislation does not regulate this issue completely and properly. In one rather confusing provision, the Law on Labour Relations states that the

60 Закон за работните односи, Чл. 68-д. став 4.

61 See: Council Directive 2001/23/EC, Article 3, paragraph 1.

62 See Domagoj Franjo Frntič, Iris Govič Pentič, Darije Hanzelak, Darko Milkovič, Nataša Novakovič and Krešimir Rožman, *Detaljni Komentar Zakona o Radu* (2017) 794.

> *"previous and the new employer shall be jointly and severally liable to indemnify the employee only if the employment contract is terminated on the initiative of the employee if, due to a change of the employer, the rights under the employment contract deteriorate because of objective reasons and the termination is treated as a dismissal on the initiative of the employer due to business reasons".*[63]

Apart from the general prohibition against dismissing employees due to a transfer, in practice there are examples of abuse of this prohibition. First and foremost, it concerns cases in which one company ceases to exist (by *closure of the undertaking*), but, at the same time (or in a very short period of time) it founds another company (*newly established company*) that continues to perform the same or similar business activities. The closure of the undertaking causes termination of the employment relationship of the employees (whose employment contracts most often formally and legally are terminated on the basis of "*consensual termination*", which requires a consent of the employees concerned), while the newly established company becomes a new employer of the same employees who *sign new employment contracts, but this time with less favorable conditions*. If the employees give their consent to the "consensual termination of their employment contracts", it seems that they would be in a "stalemate" position, while the transfer of their employment contracts with all the acquired rights would be tantamount to a "*mission impossible*". In this case, the following dilemma imposes the question as to "whether and how the rights of the employees may be protected from this type of obvious abuse of their continuity in the employment and their acquired rights"? In our view, *de lege ferenda*, safeguarding of employees' rights would be enabled only if the legislator (in future changes and amendments to the labour legislation) provides for a new provision through which the "malevolent" avoidance of the employers to fulfil their obligations regarding the employees in the event of a change of the employer would be explicitly sanctioned.[64] A provision with such contents would enable the employee (who, after the consensual termina-

---

63 Закон за работните односи, Чл. 68, став 4.

64 For example, in the labour legislation of the Republic of Croatia, there is a provision with which the "abuse" of employees' rights in the event of a transfer of undertakings is regulated in the following manner: *the person who, with the transfer of an undertaking, part of undertaking, business or part of business or in any other way, malevolently, avoids to fulfill his/her obligations regarding the employee, upon the request of the employee, the competent court will oblige this person to fulfill the obligations even in the event when the employment contract is not concluded with him/her.* (Labor Act, Official Gazette No. 93/2014, Article 129).

tion of the employment relationship with the employer predecessor has concluded a new employment contract with the employer successor on less favorable terms) to file a lawsuit for exercising the rights from the employment contract against the "new" employer who has not "formally" taken over the undertaking and, as a consequence, has "malevolently" avoided the fulfillment of his obligations towards the employee, guaranteeing the acquired rights that the employee had with the previous employer.[65]

D. Conclusion

The basic aims of the legal regime for regulating the consequences of changes of employer (i.e., transfer of the undertakings) in relation to employees, both in terms of EU labour law and in terms of Macedonian labour legislation, are: safeguarding of the security and stability of the employment relationships of the employees; prohibition of dismissals due to the fact that there is a change of the employer and preservation of the acquired employment conditions and rights that had existed before the change of the employer has taken place.

Considering the approach of the Macedonian legislature in the regulation of this legal matter, in our opinion, the current legal framework for safeguarding employees' rights in the event of transfers of undertakings is partially harmonised with Directive 2001/23/EC.

Starting from the obvious difference in the meaning of the terms "undertaking/part of an undertaking" and "trade company/part of a trade company", we come to a conclusion that the Law on Labour Relations has incorrectly and improperly been using the term "transfer of a trade company/part of a trade company", reflecting the horizontal non-compliance with other special laws (primarily with the Law on Trade Companies), as well as vertical non-compliance (primarily with Directive 2001/23/EC).

Furthermore, the Law on Labour Relations establishes a "partial" regulation of the legal reasons for transfers of undertakings. While the law on the one hand explicitly provides for the "status changes" as a possible "framework" legal reason that may lead to a change of employer, on the other hand, it envisages the "lease, i.e. rent of the business" as a single case for transfer which could be subsumed under the more general category of

65 See Domagoj Franjo Frntič, Iris Govič Pentič, Darije Hanzelak, Darko Milkovič, Nataša Novakovič and Krešimir Rožman, *Detaljni Komentar Zakona o Radu* (2017) 799.

"legal acts" (contractual transactions) as the other "framework" legal reason on the basis of which the transfer of the undertaking may occur.

Within the modern business environment, the issue of the consequences for the employees in the event of "contracting out" (outsourcing) of a certain activity or task by the employer is also a very significant issue. Despite the "encouraging" provisions in the Law on Labour Relations that can be interpreted in favour of the employees who are entailed in the transfer of the activity or the task, in practice, the employees are left without or with minimal protection.

Finally, in the event of a transfer, the questions about the employees' protection from dismissals and the preservation of the employees' acquired rights are of exceptional importance. In this field, the Law on Labour Relations is harmonised with Directive 2001/23/EC, but, in reality, transfers of undertakings are usually followed by dismissals of employees and/or systematic decrease of their employment conditions arising from transferred employment contracts.

In the absence of an adequate national court practice through which it will be possible to examine and assess the court's position on all "problematic" aspects of the legal provisions governing transfers of undertakings, we consider that this paper can serve as a useful guide for the correct interpretation of the legal framework for the safeguarding of employees' individual rights in the event of a transfer of undertakings in the Republic of Macedonia.

Bibliography

Andrej Frimerman and Aleksandar Nikolič, *Samoupravni Radni Odnosi*, (Centar za radničko samoupravljanje, Beograd, 1980).

Antonio Lo Faro, "Judicial Developments of EC Social Policy and Intra-Communuty Institutional Dialogues: How to Define a 'Legal Transfer'" in Silvana Sciarra (ed.), *Labour Law in the Courts, National Judges and European Court of Justice* (2001).

Васил Мръчков, *Трудово право*, (*Сиби*, 9 издание, 2015).

Васил Мръчков, Красимира Средкова and Атанас Василев, *Коментар на Кодекса на труда*, (Сиби, 12 издание, 2016).

Domagoj Franjo Frntič, Iris Govič Pentič, Darije Hanzelak, Darko Milkovič, Nataša Novakovič and Krešimir Rožman, *Detaljni Komentar Zakona o Radu*, (Biblioteka Radno Pravo, 2017).

Fernando Valdés Dal-Ré, "Transfers of Undertakings: An Experience of Clashes and Harmonies between Community Law and National Legal Systems" in Silvana Sciarra (ed.), *Labour Law in the Courts, National Judges and European Court of Justice*, (Hart Publishing, 2001).

Gwyneth Pitt, *Employment Law*, (Third Edition, 1997).

Гзиме Старова, *Трудово Право*, (Просветно Дело А.Д Скопје, 2008).

Љубинка Ковачевић, *Ваљани разлози за отказ уговора о раду*, (Универзитет у Београду, Правни Факултет, 2016).

Mark Freedland and Nicola Kountouris, *The Legal Construction of Personal Work Relations*, (Oxford University Press, 2011).

Милан Недков и ТитоБеличанец, Право на Друштвата, (USAID, 2008, Скопје);

Roger Blanpain, *European Labour Law (Thirteenth Revised Version*, 2012).

Sylvaine Laulom, "The European Court of Justice in the Dialogue on Transfers of Undertakings: A Fallible Interlocutor?" in Silvana Sciarra (ed.), *Labour Law in the Courts, National Judges and European Court of Justice* (Hart Publishing, 2001).

Тито Беличанец and Даница Миладинова, Заштита на правата на работниците во случај на статусна промена или пренесување на претпријатие, бизнис или дел од бизнис од едно во друго трговско друштво, *Деловно Право*, (Година XII, Бр.25, Скопје, 2011).

Todor Kalamatiev and Aleksandar Ristovski, "The Concept of 'Employee': The Position in the Republic of Macedonia" in Bernd Waas and Guus Heerma van Voss (eds.), *Restatement of Labour Law in Europe*, (Volume I, Hart Publishing, 2017).

Тодор Каламатиев, Љубинка Ковачевић and Александар Ристовски, Заштита на правата на вработените во случај на промена на работодавачот во Република Македонија и Република Србија (компаративна анализа), (*Деловно Право*, Година XVIII, бр.37, Скопје).

Legislation

Council Directive 2001/23/EC on the approximation of the laws of the Member States relating to the safeguarding of employees' rights in the event of transfers of undertakings, businesses or parts of undertakings or businesses (Official Journal L 082, 22/03/2001 P. 0016-0020).

Constitution of the Republic of Macedonia (Official Gazette of the Republic of Macedonia No. 52/92).

Law on Labour Relations (Закон за работните односи) (Official Gazette of the Republic of Macedonia No. 62/05).

Law on Trade Companies (Закон за трговските друштва) (Official Gazette of the Republic of Macedonia No. 28/04).